Key Issues

RELIGIOUS SCEPTICISM
Contemporary Responses to Gibbon

Key Issues

RELIGIOUS SCEPTICISM

Contemporary Responses to Gibbon

Edited and Introduced by
DAVID WOMERSLEY
Jesus College, Oxford

Series Editor
ANDREW PYLE
University of Bristol

THOEMMES PRESS

© Thoemmes Press 1997
Introduction © David Womersley, 1997

Published in 1997 by
Thoemmes Press
11 Great George Street
Bristol BS1 5RR, England

US office: Distribution and Marketing
22883 Quicksilver Drive
Dulles, Virginia 20166, USA

ISBN
Paper : 1 85506 510 X
Cloth : 1 85506 509 6

Religious Scepticism
Key Issues No. 15

British Library Cataloguing-in-Publication Data
A catalogue record of this title is available
from the British Library

All rights reserved. No part of this publication may be reproduced, stored in a retrieval system, or transmitted in any way or by any means, electronic, mechanical, photocopying, recording or otherwise, without the written permission of the publisher.

Printed in Great Britain by Antony Rowe Ltd., Chippenham

Contents

INTRODUCTION
by David Womersley vii

REMARKS ON THE TWO LAST CHAPTERS OF
MR. GIBBON'S HISTORY (1776)
[by James Chelsum] 1

AN APOLOGY FOR CHRISTIANITY, IN A SERIES
OF LETTERS ADDRESSED TO EDWARD
GIBBON, ESQ. (1776)
by Richard Watson 44

A REPLY TO THE REASONINGS OF
MR. GIBBON (1778) pp. 1–236
by Smyth Loftus 116

AN EXAMINATION OF THE FIFTEENTH AND
SIXTEENTH CHAPTERS OF MR. GIBBON'S
HISTORY (1778), pp. i–iv, 1–25, 156–8, 274–84
by Henry Edwards Davis 185

GIBBON'S ACCOUNT OF CHRISTIANITY
CONSIDERED (1781), Sections I and VIII of Part 1,
and Conclusion
by Joseph Milner 215

AN HISTORY OF THE CORRUPTIONS
OF CHRISTIANITY, 2 vols. (1782), vol. 2, pp. 440–66
by Joseph Priestley 235

BAMPTON LECTURES, Sermon III (1784)
pp. 136–45 and appendix
by Joseph White 250

ABBREVIATIONS

The following abbreviations are used in the footnotes to the introduction:

A	*The Autobiographies of Edward Gibbon*, ed. J. Murray (1896).

DF	Edward Gibbon, *The History of the Decline and Fall of the Roman Empire*, ed. D. J. Womersley, 3 vols. (1994).

EE	*The English Essays of Edward Gibbon*, ed. P. B. Craddock (Oxford, 1972).

L	*The Letters of Edward Gibbon*, ed. J. E. Norton, 3 vols. (1956).

MW	Edward Gibbon, *Miscellaneous Works*, ed. Lord Sheffield, 5 vols. (1814).

Norton	J. E. Norton, *A Bibliography of the Works of Edward Gibbon* (Oxford, 1940).

INTRODUCTION

The scholarly consensus about the confrontation in the last quarter of the eighteenth century between the historian Edward Gibbon and the spokesmen for an Anglican orthodoxy indignant at his treatment of Christianity in *The Decline and Fall of the Roman Empire* vividly illustrates the distortions which arise when the enduring account of an episode is written by a participant. This selection from the most important of the early attacks on Gibbon allows the reader to sample the writings of those whom scholars since Gibbon's day have tended to dismiss as impertinent insects crawling in ignorance over the surface of a great monument of erudition and enlightenment. It is the purpose of this introduction to describe and analyse the process which, beginning with Gibbon's own masterly misrepresentations of the controversy, bequeathed to us the skewed but durable narrative which scholars are only now beginning seriously to question and dismantle.[1]

---

[1] Notable amongst those who have been content to accept Gibbon's version of the controversy, mediated by later commentators such as Dean Milman, are Hugh Trevor-Roper ('Preface' to 1961 reprint of Gibbon's *Vindication*, especially p. vii); Patricia Craddock (*Edward Gibbon, Luminous Historian 1772–1794* (Baltimore: The Johns Hopkins University Press, 1989), pp. 121–31), and Roy Porter (*Edward Gibbon: Making History* (1988), p. 3). Amongst an earlier generation of scholars, J. E. Norton voiced reservations about the received version of the controversy, but nevertheless judged Gibbon's opponents to be 'almost all entirely unreadable' (Norton, pp. 78–93); while S. T. McCloy's study of 1933, *Gibbon's Antagonism to Christianity*, although now in some respects dated, has the merit of arguing that 'Gibbon's opponents [were] men of greater interest and ability than has commonly been supposed' (p. 7). Two recent studies advance and complicate our knowledge dramatically: Nigel Aston, 'A "Disorderly Squadron?" A Fresh Look at Clerical Responses to *The Decline and Fall*' and Paul Turnbull, '"Une Marionnette Infidèle": The Fashioning of Edward Gibbon's Reputation as the English Voltaire', both in D. Womersley (ed.), *Gibbon: Bicentenary Essays* (Oxford: The Voltaire

Gibbon composed two accounts of his clash with 'the Clergy' over his handling of Christianity: the first, in the *Vindication* of 1779, the second in draft 'E' of the *Memoirs*, completed on 2 March 1791. The image he created of himself was in each case different. In the *Vindication*, Gibbon was a Lear of the world of historiography, more sinned against than sinning:

> When I delivered to the world the First Volume of an important History, in which I had been obliged to connect the progress of Christianity with the civil state and revolutions of the Roman Empire, I could not be ignorant that the result of my inquiries might offend the interest of some and the opinions of others. If the whole work was favourably received by the Public, I had the more reason to expect that this obnoxious part would provoke the zeal of those who consider themselves as the Watchmen of the Holy City. These expectations were not disappointed....[2]

'I could not be ignorant': Gibbon admitted here what he would later deny, namely that he had knowingly run the risk of offending those he contemptuously dubbed 'the Watchmen of the Holy City'. In the *Vindication* he professed to be unperturbed by the 'ordinary, and indeed obsolete charges of impious principles'.[3] He had been stung to reply only because Henry Davis had attempted 'the ruin of my moral and literary character'.[4]

Composing his *Memoirs* twelve years later, however, Gibbon retouched this self-portrait. The outcry of the orthodox was now entirely unforeseen by their innocent quarry:

Foundation, forthcoming). It is with pleasure that I acknowledge my indebtedness to these most important essays.

[2] *EE*, p. 232. Cf. East Apthorp, *Letters on the Prevalence of Christianity* (1778), p. vi: 'the Jewish and Christian revelations were *providentially* connected with the great revolutions in civil history' in order that their proofs should be written into the historical record without 'doubt, mistake, or ambiguity' (my emphasis).

[3] *EE*, p. 233.

[4] *EE*, p. 234.

I had likewise flattered myself that an age of light and liberty would receive, without scandal, an enquiry into the *human* causes of the progress and establishment of Christianity.

In addition, the pose of necessity struck in the *Vindication* ('I had been obliged to connect...') was in the *Memoirs* moderated into an admission that the subject might have received a more emollient treatment:

> Had I believed that the majority of English readers were so fondly attached even to the name and shadow of Christianity, had I foreseen that the pious, the timid, and the prudent would feel, or affect to feel, with such exquisite sensibility, I might perhaps have softened the two invidious Chapters, which would create many enemies and conciliate few friends.[5]

Gone, too, was the proud and unshaken defiance of the *Vindication*. In the *Memoirs*, Gibbon explained the sequence of his emotions differently:

> Let me frankly own that I was startled at the first vollies of this Ecclesiastical ordnance; but as soon as I found that this empty noise was mischievous only in the intention, my fear was converted to indignation, and every feeling of indignation or curiosity has long since subsided in pure and placid indifference.[6]

It is difficult to see how the heroic figure of the *Vindication* and the inadvertent figure of the *Memoirs* can both be true; indeed, as we shall see, the evidence of Gibbon's revisions reveals them both to be in some measure false. The *Vindication* is misleading in its suggestion that Gibbon stoically endured the assaults of his detractors until his character as a gentleman was challenged: the revisions to the second and third editions show him anticipating, eluding and finally rebutting his adversaries on points of religious history.

---

[5] *A*, p. 316.

[6] *A*, p. 319. Cf. also: 'The freedom of my writings has, indeed, provoked an implacable tribe; but as I was safe from the stings, I was soon accustomed to the buzzing of the hornets...' (*A*, p. 346).

x   *Introduction*

For their part, the *Memoirs* are less than candid in their suggestion that the unaware historian was overtaken by a controversy the possibility of which had not occurred to him: the revisions to the second edition, made before any attack had been published, show that Gibbon possessed a very accurate sense of which areas of his history would be offensive, and why.

In order to see past these deceptive authorial accounts of the controversy, we must retrieve, by means of, in the first place surviving manuscripts, and secondly the information to be inferred from the revisions to the first volume, that suppressed and secret history which will reveal Gibbon's actual response to his clerical opponents. We can then proceed to consider those opponents in their own terms, freed from the condescension of both posterity and their celebrated antagonist.

The Sheffield papers at Yale contain two drafts of a note which Gibbon's friend and literary executor, Lord Sheffield, considered inserting in the two-volume 1796 edition of Gibbon's *Miscellaneous Works*. As we have seen, in draft 'E' of his *Memoirs* Gibbon had asserted that 'had I believed that the majority of English readers were so fondly attached even to the name and shadow of Christianity, ... I might perhaps have softened the two invidious Chapters, which would create many enemies and conciliate few friends'. Sheffield was initially minded to offer the following in corroboration of the historian's self-exculpation:

> I mention the following Anecdote to shew that Mr Gibbon was not, in the first instance, aware how offensive his Irony, and manner of mentioning the Christian Religion, must be; and that he did not mean to outrage Society in the Degree that has been supposed – Some time after the Attack on the 15th and 16 [sic] Chapters had commenced, he said to me that he had flattered himself his History (the first Vol) would be rated somewhat above mediocrity, that he was not less surprized to find it valued so highly as it was, by one set of men, than that it should be so much ^reprobated^ ~~abused~~ by another and then asked whether I thought it advisable to withdraw the offensive passages from the second Edition then at the Press – I He was answered that the mischief was

Introduction xi

done, and he was asked how he could suppose it possible to withdraw them: did he not know that such an Attempt would only raise the demand for the first Edition. Possibly he only wished to know my Opinion, but before the publication of the Work, and while it was in hand, he said to me that there would be much difficulty and Delicacy in respect to that part which gives the History of the Christian Religion. When the mischief and wantonness of disregard to established Opinions was mentioned, he exceeded in expression all that was said. He was so habituated to the infinitely more extravagant writings of Voltaire and others, and to the extreme levity of conversation, among the generality of those with whome he had lived, that he thought himself comparatively decent; and has often expressed great surprise that it | ^ He had given so much Offence ^ should be so reprobated. He had always shewn more civility than is common to Age and situation, and, particularly in mixed Company, avoided saying any thing that could shock or offend; but many were now disposed to pronounce him not only a Deist, but an Atheist, (which he was not) and he has since often jocosely remarked, the bad effect of *taking away a persons Character*, as to Religion, as well as in other respects, and that it could answer no worldly purpose to him, longer to put himself under restraint of any kind.[7]

The second edition of the first volume of *The Decline and Fall* was published on 3 June 1776, and had been at least decided upon, if not actually begun, by the end of March.[8] So we can date this conversation between Gibbon and Sheffield to the spring of 1776, perhaps to the meeting of the two men in London in late April or early May.[9] The precise date is of

---

[7] Beinecke Library, Yale University: MS Vault, Sect. 10, Drawer 3, Sect. B, item 11i. Words and phrases entered above the line are flanked by ^; | indicates a page break. The note seems to have been omitted on the advice of William Hayley. The quoted draft bears the following endorsement in Hayley's hand, written vertically on the verso of the second sheet: 'suppress the whole Note – the Ground does not admit of any very solid & satisfactory defence – a slight palliation will only provoke more Severity against the delinquent –'

[8] Norton, p. 42; *L*, vol. 2, p. 100.

[9] 'I rejoyce to hear of your approaching arrival...': Gibbon to Sheffield, 27

interest, because by this time the attack on Gibbon's supposed irreligion was, despite Sheffield's statement to the contrary, *not* yet properly begun. James Chelsum was the first to the assault with his *Remarks on the Two Last Chapters of Mr. Gibbon's History*, published on 17 October 1776, long after the publication of the second edition of Gibbon's first volume.[10]

However, Gibbon had suspected for some time that he would be attacked. Even before *The Decline and Fall* was published, he had known that his subject matter possessed the potential to offend, and had sought the opinions of others on the question of whether or not his history would be considered scandalous by the religious establishment. George Lewis Scott, the mathematician and sometime tutor to the future George III, had been acquainted with Gibbon since the 1760s. In 1762 he had advised the young Gibbon on a course of reading in mathematics; and in 1767 Gibbon had asked Scott to write an article on the state of mathematical learning in Britain for the *Mémoires Littéraires de la Grande Bretagne*, the journal he had begun with his friend Deyverdun. In late 1775, Gibbon sent the sheets of at least some of *The Decline and Fall* to Scott, who in December replied as follows:

> I am obliged to you for the liberty of perusing part of your work. What I have read has given me a good deal of pleasure. I have found but few slips of the press, and have marked with a led pencil, & afterwards with Red Chalk. *Millenium*, should, I think, be spelt with two LL's, being derived from *Mille*.
>
> The stile of the work is clear & every way agreeable & I dare say you will be thought to have written with all due moderation & decency with respect to received, (at least once received) opinions. The notes and quotations will add a little to the value of your work. The authority of French writers, so familiar to you; have not infected you, however, with the faults of superficial and careless

---

April 1776 (*L*, vol. 2, p. 103). Sheffield and his family had also been in London in March (*L*, vol. 2, p. 100), but it is unlikely that the second edition was then 'at the Press'.

[10] *L*, vol. 2, p. 117, note 4.

quotation.[11]

It is clear, then, that Sheffield's statement that Gibbon was unaware of the possibility that his freedom of manner when writing of Christianity might cause offence is misleading. So aware was he of this possibility that, as the second paragraph of Scott's letter shows, he sought reassurance on just this point while the work was still in press, and therefore while no hostile response to it could possibly exist.

Nor is it really credible that Gibbon could have been genuinely ignorant that, in the very act of writing of the decline of the Roman empire, he was traversing historical ground of the utmost religious delicacy. Hume's letter of congratulation to Gibbon on the publication of volume one shows how interconnected in the philosophical mind were the subjects of imperial decline and the growth of Christianity:

> When I heard of your undertaking (which was some time ago) I own, that I was a little curious to see how you would extricate yourself from the subject of your two last chapters. I think you have observed a very prudent temperament; but it was impossible to treat the subject so as not to give grounds of suspicion against you, and you may expect that a clamour will arise.[12]

For enlightened minds such as those of Hume and Scott (who seems to have imbibed both Jacobitism and irreligion from Bolingbroke), *The Decline and Fall* was unexceptionable. However, as Gibbon was quickly to discover, his history was not so well adapted to all tastes and dispositions.

The first edition of the first volume of *The Decline and Fall* was published on 17 February 1776.[13] Writing to his

---

[11] British Library Add. MS 34886, f.50. Sheffield published a lightly edited version of this letter in the *Miscellaneous Works* (vol. 2, pp. 141–2).

[12] *A*, p. 312. John Whitaker alleged that Gibbon had shown him a copy of the first volume minus chapters fifteen and sixteen, thereby eliciting from him a more favourable opinion than he would otherwise have given. However, the letters from Whitaker to Gibbon first published in 1815 as part of the third, supplemental, volume of the *Miscellaneous Works*, sufficiently discountenance this allegation (*MW*, vol. 2, pp. 146–52; Craddock, *Luminous Historian*, pp. 375–6, note 2).

[13] Norton, p. 37.

xiv *Introduction*

stepmother on 26 March, Gibbon conveyed two important pieces of information:

> My book has been very well received...by every set of people except perhaps by the Clergy who seem (I know not why) to shew their teeth on the occasion. A thousand Copies are sold, and we are preparing a second Edition, which in so short a time is, for a book of that price a very uncommon event.[14]

This is the first indication that Gibbon knew for a fact he had provoked 'the Clergy', although for the time being he knew neither who would enter the lists against him, nor what they would write.[15] In the same breath, he reported that the second edition was in preparation. It is of the first importance to appreciate that the revisions Gibbon made for the second edition were planned and executed in this period of uncertainty. On 24 May, once again to his stepmother, he returned to the subject of the second edition:

> My mornings have been very much taken up with preparing and correcting (though in a minute and almost imperceptible way) my new Edition which will be out the first of June.[16]

April and May 1776 were thus the months given over to revision. The second edition appeared, as we have seen, on 3 June. The revisions it embodied, though minute, were far from imperceptible.[17] They demonstrate, moreover, that,

---

[14] *L*, vol. 2, p. 100.

[15] Even as late as June 1776 Gibbon was unsure about the identities of those who were to oppose him. On 6 June he wrote to Holroyd that 'I now understand from pretty good authority that Dr Porteous the friend and chaplain of St Secker is actually sharpening his goosequill against the two last Chapters' (*L*, vol. 2, p. 111). Porteous never published an attack on Gibbon, although Travis's *Letters* were dedicated to Porteous, and it may be that the hand of the Bishop of Chester guided the pen of his Archdeacon.

[16] *L*, vol. 2, p. 110.

[17] Gibbon's revisions to the second, third and fourth editions of *The Decline and Fall* produced several thousand variants. Many of these are very small, and in general Gibbon restricted his revisions so that in virtually all cases

Introduction xv

despite his protestation to the contrary, Gibbon had a very good idea of where and how he had offended the orthodox. In the second edition, the revisions for which had been made while Gibbon was apprehensive of attack, we find that the revisions cluster in just those areas of the history – often, in the very passages – which were to be the site of polemical struggle. Their tendency is uniform: in the second edition of volume one, we find Gibbon throughout muting or removing words and phrases of a recognizably deistical character. In anticipation of the attack about to be launched against him, he minimizes the target he presents to the spokesmen for outraged religious orthodoxy.

A good example of such self-protective revision arises during Gibbon's discussion of the doctrine of the immortality of the soul in chapter fifteen. He remarks that this doctrine was more prevalent among barbarians than amongst the pagans of Greece and Rome, and that 'since we cannot attribute such a difference to the superior knowledge of the barbarians, we must ascribe it to the influence of an established priesthood, which employed the motives of virtue as the instrument of ambition'. To this, in the first edition, he had appended a note:

The Druids borrowed sums of money on bonds made payable to the creditor in the other world. The success of such a trade is one of the strongest instances of sacerdotal art and popular credulity.[18]

the pagination, and very often even the lineation, of the text could be preserved. This was clearly convenient for the compositor setting up the new edition; it may be that Strahan and Cadell requested Gibbon so to restrict his revisions. For a selection of these variants, see Appendix I to volume one of the Penguin edition of *The Decline and Fall* (vol. 1, pp. 1084–1105). For a full account of the tendency of Gibbon's revisions to chapters fifteen and sixteen in the first three editions of his first volume, see D. Womersley, 'Gibbon and the "Watchmen of the Holy City": Revision and Religion in *The Decline and Fall*', in R. McKitterick and R. Quinault (eds.), *Gibbon and Empire* (Cambridge, 1997), pp. 190–216.

[18] *DF*, vol. 1, pp. 465 and 1100. This detail was noted, and dismissed as 'but a silly story', by Henry Taylor in *Thoughts on the Nature of the Grand Apostacy* (1781), p. 43.

The text, with its allusion to an established priesthood using virtue as the instrument of ambition, was already tinctured with deism. The footnote, however, strengthened that colouring into a virtual statement of allegiance. 'Sacerdotal art' and 'popular credulity' were phrases drawn from the idiom of writers such as Blount, Toland and Tindal, and their use amounted to a declaration of hostility towards the power exerted by priests in civil society. In the second edition, however, the footnote was completely rewritten:

> If we confine ourselves to the Gauls, we may observe, that they entrusted, not only their lives, but even their money, to the security of another world. Vetus ille mos Gallorum occurrit (says Valerius Maximus, l. ii. c. 6. p. 10.), quos memoria proditur est, pecunias mutuas, quæ his apud inferos redderentur, dare solitos. The same custom is more darkly insinuated by Mela, l. iii. c. 2. It is almost needless to add, that the profits of trade hold a just proportion to the credit of the merchant, and that the Druids derived from their holy profession a character of responsibility, which could scarcely be claimed by any other order of men.[19]

The inclusion of references and quotation immediately tilted the balance of the note away from polemic and towards historical scholarship, while the greater elaborateness of the syntax, and the superior politeness of the language, in which Gibbon first related the institution of these loans, and then commented on them, served to occlude his allegiances. Whereas in the first edition a hint of deism in the text was corroborated and amplified in the note, in the second edition the note moved away from the language and polemical style of the deists, thereby neutralizing the irreligious flavour of the text. The note in the second edition is, of course, 'ironic', and it would be no difficult task to unpick, for instance, the hostile implications of the comparison between the priest and the merchant. But here, as occasionally elsewhere, Gibbon's irony arose as the defensive complication of a deistical impulse which had been at first more nakedly expressed.

However, the tone of Gibbon's comments on his opponents

---

[19] *DF*, vol. 1, p. 465, note 56.

underwent a marked change once the attacks appeared in print, and the true gravity of the threat they posed could be assessed. During the period of suspense, in which he revised for the second edition, Gibbon wrote of the coming replies with flaunted playfulness and ostentatious unconcern:

> At present *nought* but expectation. The attack on me is begun, an anonymous eighteen penny pamphlet, which will get the author more Glory *in the next World* than in this. The Heavy troops, Watson and another are on their march.
>
> With regard to another great object of hostilities [that is to say, in addition to the war with the American colonies], *myself*, the attack has been already begun by an anonymous Pamphleteer but the heavy artillery of Dr Watson and another adversary are not yet brought into the field.[20]

Once Gibbon had read the attacks and judged their quality, his tone was inflected into hard accents. When he alluded to his opponents in a series of letters written in November 1776, after he had read the offerings of Chelsum and Watson, he did so with a contempt unadorned by imagination or metaphor:

> An anonymous pamphlet and Dr Watson out against me: both (in my opinion) feeble; the former very illiberal, the latter uncommonly genteel.
>
> By this time Mylady may see that I have not much reason to fear my antagonists.
>
> Two answers (which you have perhaps seen) one from Mr Chelsham [*sic*] of Oxford the other from Dr Watson of Cambridge, are already born and I believe the former is choleric, the latter civil, and both too dull to deserve your notice; three or four more are expected; but I believe none of them will divert me from the prosecution of the second Volume....[21]

When the play of fancy is succeeded by simple and unemotional disregard, it is tempting to read the earlier embell-

---

[20] *L*, vol. 2, pp. 117, 118.

[21] *L*, vol. 2, pp. 120, 121, 129.

ishment as a sign of agitation, and the posture of *insouciance* as the guise of anxiety. This is certainly what the revisions made for the third edition suggest, for they are of a tendency quite opposite to that of the revisions made in the second edition. Whereas before Gibbon had deferred to religious sensibilities, we now find him sharpening, rather than blunting, the deistical edge of his writing.

The different moods in which Gibbon emended for the second and third editions, and the different purposes those two phases of revisal served, are caught in the variants for a single footnote to chapter sixteen. Gibbon was in no doubt that the notorious passage in Josephus which referred to Jesus was a later interpolation. In the first edition, he expressed his disbelief as follows:

> The passage concerning Jesus Christ, which was inserted into the text of Josephus, between the time of Origen and that of Eusebius, may furnish an example of no vulgar forgery. The accomplishment of the prophecies, the virtues, miracles, and resurrection of Jesus, are fairly related. Josephus acknowledges that he was the Messiah, and hesitates whether he should call him a man.

In the second edition, 'distinctly' was substituted for 'fairly'.[22] A personal judgement was deleted, and its place was taken by a more objective, and to that extent more impersonal, term. It is a revision entirely of a piece with that withdrawal from positions of exposure, which we have identified as the dominant characteristic of the second edition. As had been the case elsewhere, Gibbon here proved to have a shrewd eye for what his enemies would be unable to digest. Francis Eyre (reading Gibbon in the second edition) devoted fourteen pages of his *Remarks on the History of the Decline and Fall* to an elaborate defence of the authenticity of this passage of Josephus, designed to show 'how weak is the sophistry of the incredulous'.[23] William Salisbury, whose *A History of the Establishment of Christianity* was published in 1776 and to

---

[22] *DF*, vol. 1, p. 529, note 36 and p. 1103.

[23] Francis Eyre, *A Few Remarks on the History of the Decline and Fall* (1778), pp. 48–61; quotation from p. 61.

Introduction xix

whom Gibbon may therefore be responding in a revision made in this passage for the third edition, also championed the integrity of Josephus's text at length.[24] In that third edition Gibbon allowed the correction of 'fairly' to 'distinctly' to stand, but expanded the note to almost twice its size by adding more authorities in support of his position:

> If any doubt can still remain concerning this celebrated passage, the reader may examine the pointed objections of Le Fevre (Havercamp. Joseph. tom. ii. p. 267-273.), the laboured answers of Daubuz (p. 187-232.), and the masterly reply (Bibliotheque Ancienne et Moderne, tom. vii. p. 237-288.) of an anonymous critic, whom I believe to have been the learned Abbè de Longuerue.[25]

The tone of this addition is one of impatient contempt ('if any doubt can *still* remain'); and the parade of authorities is a rhetorically crushing blow which seems to admit of no reply. The defiance of criticism which Gibbon showed in this revision was the ruling passion of the corrections he made for the third edition.[26]

---

[24] William Salisbury, *A History of the Establishment of Christianity* (1776), pp. 217-29. There was apparently no copy of Salisbury's work in Gibbon's library.

[25] *DF*, vol. 1, p. 529, note 36. Gibbon hardly ever revised on a second occasion a passage he had previously revised, or undid an earlier revision.

[26] The third edition allowed Gibbon in one respect greater scope for revisal. The surprisingly acceptable appearance made by putting the notes at the foot of the page, as had been done in the pirated Dublin edition, reconciled Gibbon to the same reorganization of the official editions (*L*, vol. 2, p. 116). In his *Memoirs*, he said that he had often regretted his compliance (*A*, p. 339, note 64). But the complete repagination of the volume clearly meant that the work of the compositor would now, and now only, be not greatly increased by the introduction of new material. Gibbon nevertheless restricted his revisals of the text so as to permit the retention of most of the lineation of the first two editions, thereby relieving the compositor of one consideration. However, he did take advantage of the opportunity to introduce new footnotes; inserted at the moment of transition from endnotes to footnotes, they were invisible to the merely scanning eye. In his letters Gibbon seems always to have under-represented the extent of his revisions. In the *Memoirs*, as part of the fascinating myth of composition he there constructed, he contrived to suggest that, in careless facility, he eschewed revision altogether (*A*, pp. 333-4), while at other moments laying claim to laborious rewriting (*A*, p. 308 (chapters 15 and 16) and pp.

xx Introduction

It is clear, then, that Gibbon foresaw that his history might provoke an attack from the orthodox, and was in addition sufficiently respectful of the damage such an attack might inflict that he sought to guard against it before publication; moreover, he at least initially deferred to his assailants, as the revisions to the second edition of volume one show. If, on inspection and as the revisions for the third edition suggest, his adversaries were not as formidable as he had originally feared they might be, this does not mean that they were as ridiculously contemptible as later writers have assumed: a writer may be unequally matched with Gibbon, and yet cut no mean figure. Dean Milman's vivid, metaphorical, encapsulation of the controversy has been richly and enduringly misleading:

> It is remarkable that...the more distinguished theological writers of the country stood aloof, while the first ranks were filled by rash and feeble volunteers. Gibbon, with a single discharge from his ponderous artillery of learning and sarcasm, laid prostrate the whole disorderly squadron.[27]

Milman was wrong to imply that this was a controversy in one act, decisively concluded in 1779 with the publication of Gibbon's *Vindication*. In fact, the attacks on Gibbon, judged in terms of number of publications, peaked in 1789; and it is becoming increasingly clear that the controversy over Gibbon's alleged irreligion became freshly intense during the period of the French Revolution.[28] Moreover, Milman was further mistaken when he characterized Gibbon's adversaries as 'rash and feeble'. They proved no match for Gibbon as

---

315–16 (the age of Constantine)).

[27] *The Quarterly Review*, vol. 50 (1834), p. 293.

[28] See Norton p. 88 for a table showing the number of attacks on Gibbon arranged by year. For an account of the revived campaign against Gibbon in the wake of the French Revolution, see Paul Turnbull, '"Une Marionnette Infidèle": the Fashioning of Edward Gibbon's Reputation as the English Voltaire'. For an analysis of how and why this exerted a continuing influence over Gibbon's writings in the last six years of his life see D. Womersley, 'Gibbon's *Memoirs*: Autobiography in Time of Revolution', in D. Womersley (ed.), *Gibbon: Bicentenary Essays* (Oxford: The Voltaire Foundation, forthcoming).

polemicists, and could not rival his depth of scholarship: yet these are tests which few can pass. Having established that Gibbon viewed his adversaries with more wariness than he was prepared to acknowledge in either the *Vindication* or his *Memoirs*, we may now turn to consider the calibre of those who entered the field against him.

In the *Vindication*, Gibbon dwelt upon the folly and youth of Henry Davis (whom John Whitaker, viewing his age more sympathetically, would laud as 'that extraordinary young man, that early victim to studiousness').[29] In choosing so to direct his fire, Gibbon made the attack upon him seem the work of rash immaturity. In fact, he had been attacked by writers from all shades of the theological spectrum, and from all ranks of the Church up to that of bishop. On one wing, we find George Horne, the High Church President of Magdalen College, Oxford and sometime Hutchinsonian; on the other, Richard Watson, the pre-eminent latitudinarian of late eighteenth-century Cambridge, and later Bishop of Llandaff. Grouped around these champions of the Church were parish priests such as Smyth Loftus, William Salisbury and East Apthorp, and confederates such as the Methodist Joseph Milner. Nor were the academic credentials of Gibbon's adversaries trivial: James Chelsum was a student of Christ Church, Thomas Randolph was the Lady Margaret Professor of Divinity, Joseph White the Laudian Professor of Arabic, William Disney the Cambridge Professor of Hebrew.

These men were the spokesmen for a religious orthodoxy which, no matter how assailed and mocked, had in fact always been one of the pillars of Hanoverian England, and which indeed had been newly resurgent since the accession of George III.[30] Their broad lines of attack on this latest outbreak of infidelity were two. In the first place, they set out to impugn Gibbon's scholarship, by showing either that he

[29] John Whitaker, *Gibbon's History of the Decline and Fall of the Roman Empire, in vols iv, v, and vi, quarto, Reviewed* (1791), p. 12.

[30] For the structural importance of the Church in Hanoverian England, see J. C. D. Clark, *English Society 1688–1832* (Cambridge, 1985). For the revival of High Church attitudes in the latter part of the eighteenth century, see Peter B. Nockles, *The Oxford Movement in Context: Anglican High Churchmanship 1760–1857* (Cambridge, 1994). Hume's letter of congrat-

had not examined at first hand the authors from whom he quoted, or that he had perverted and misrepresented their significance. It has been generally concluded that in this the defenders of the Church were unsuccessful, and that Gibbon's scholarship emerged from the fray triumphantly vindicated. Such, however, was not the judgement of all at the time, and the modern reader who approaches the attacks on *The Decline and Fall* dispassionately is likely to conclude that a number of their thrusts hit home. Just as Bentley's misguided, but independent-minded, commentary on Milton's language has the merit of drawing our attention to verbal details which those determined to venerate Milton had passed over, so the bitter fruits of the impressive if myopic intensity with which these clerics read Gibbon are not useless to his modern student. At the very least, they remind us that the case for Gibbon's greatness as an historian rests more securely on the vigour of his historical imagination, than on the solidity of his scholarship.

Their second main line of attack was to argue that Gibbon was doing nothing new in so attacking Christianity. They deplored *The Decline and Fall* either as (with Richard Watson) a typical production of those modern sceptics who were but 'miserable copiers of their brethren of antiquity', or as (with Smyth Loftus) a late eighteenth-century reprise of an earlier generation of deists, whose personnel included Blount, Toland, Collins and Bolingbroke.[31] Later writers have been quicker to dismiss this charge than to examine the evidence for it, perhaps feeling that to concede any accuracy to the observations of Gibbon's adversaries might involve joining them in their extravagantly hostile conclusions. Readers of this anthology can make up their own minds. If – as I suspect they will – they conclude that these allegations have a kernel of truth, they will be driven to reflect afresh on the paradox

---

ulation to Gibbon on the publication of volume one had noted this resurgence: 'among many other marks of decline, the prevalence of superstition in England prognosticates the fall of Philosophy, and decay of taste...' (A, p. 312).

[31] Richard Watson, *An Apology for Christianity* (Cambridge, 1776), p. 37; see below, p. 53. Smyth Loftus, *A Reply to the Reasonings of Mr. Gibbons* [sic] (1777), p. 31; see below, pp 124–5.

of a work which on publication was hailed by many as one of the finest products of the age, but which nevertheless affronted some of its most central beliefs.[32]

---

[32] In the words of Henry Kett: 'Any endeavour to loosen the ties of religious duty, is an affront to the pious principles of education implanted in every cultivated mind; and an act of hostility against the general interests of society', *A Representation of the Conduct and Opinions of the Primitive Christians...* (Oxford, 1791), p. 156.

REMARKS ON THE TWO LAST CHAPTERS OF MR. GIBBON'S HISTORY, OF THE DECLINE AND FALL OF THE ROMAN EMPIRE, IN A LETTER TO A FRIEND
[James Chelsum]

Dear Sir,
You have been pleased to desire my thoughts on a late distinguished publication. I have considered the work, with some degree of attention, and especially that part of it, to which your questions principally relate. Such remarks as have occurred to me, are wholly at your service.

Every true friend to christianity, cannot but feel himself interested in the concluding chapters of Mr. Gibbon's History. It is much to be lamented, that "the melancholy duty imposed upon the historian,"[1] should have appeared to him, so sacred, and indispensable. The validity of this plea may well be contested, should it be found, that one unhappy bias prevails throughout the whole course of his researches; that the Apologists of Christianity, are vilified on every occasion; the objections of its adversaries industriously brought forward, and the testimonies in favour of our religion, sometimes wholly concealed, at other times misrepresented.

The passages which I allude to, from the nature of the work itself, affect only, for the most part, the history of the first ages of christianity. But there are also, far too many oblique and ungenerous insinuations, which fail not to suggest their own proper inferences, and which affect materially, the general credit of christianity.

The enemy himself in the mean time, often lies hid behind the shield of some bolder warrior; and shoots his envenomed darts, under the protection of some avowed heretic, of the age. – It may be added, that the singular address of the historian,

---

[1] Ch. 15. p. 450. The first edition is all along referred to.

has served even to make the laboured arguments of modern writers, coincide with the description of a remote period of antiquity; and has introduced many well-known objections to christianity, which the refined scepticism of the present age, claims for its own.[2] I shall endeavour to oppose his oblique censures, by open argument; and shall enquire into the real weight of the objections, which he has thought fit to set before us, with the strictest candour.

It should be remarked carefully, that it is not the author's design, to account for the propagation of christianity from its earliest date, but during a particular period only.

The first, and most remarkable period of the history of its miraculous propagation, will not certainly, be found, to be concerned in his disquisitions, since it is not comprehended in his design. He will be found on examination, to have considered only, that later period, which commences after the times of the apostles, and which exhibits to us not the first planting, but the successive increase of christianity, after it had already taken root, and covered a very extensive tract of country.

If at any time he ascends higher, he deviates, strictly speaking, from his proper subject.

Our author has not indeed made any formal declaration, from what period he means to enquire into the progress of the establishment of christianity, because, probably it did not seem necessary. It must naturally be concluded, that he cannot have meant to enter into any earlier disquisition on the subject, than falls within the immediate compass of his history.

Respecting his general plan, he acquaints us, that it is his design, in his three first and introductory chapters, "to describe the prosperous condition of the empire, and afterwards from the death of Marcus Antoninus to deduce the most important circumstances of its decline and fall."[3] But the death of Marcus Antoninus, happened towards the close of the second century; and we must conclude therefore, even in justice to the

---

[2] We are obliged to attribute to the present age, the invention of many metaphysical subtleties, and perhaps of some arguments of another kind; but for the most part, even the licentiousness of modern infidelity, has been only able to revive old arguments, disguised under some new form. This is a truth, which must strike every one, versed in the history of infidelity, with the strongest conviction.

[3] Ch. 1.

historian, that his enquiry, as to its express and immediate design, cannot be meant to be carried any higher; and is not consequently, at all concerned about the propagation of Christianity, in the age of the Apostles.

But this age, contains the most striking period, of the history, of the propagation, of our religion. – A period, nevertheless so short, that taking its date, before the middle of the first century, it does not extend even to the close of it.

The last apostolic journey of St. Paul, ended in the year sixty eight. In the course of little more than thirty years after the death of Christ, his doctrine was spread, through a great part of the known world.

It was spread from the Euphrates to the Tiber, even in the most populous cities; and the foolishness of preaching overcame the wisdom of famous orators, and philosophers, as the steady piety of its votaries, overcame also the formidable opposition, of its most zealous enemies.

And the evidence of this period, it appears then we are still left in full possession of.

A period of such peculiar importance in the annals of christianity, that the judicious advocate of our faith, will ever, principally insist on it. He will however insist also, tho' in a less degree, on the succeeding singular growth of christianity, amidst the most cruel persecutions, and in spite of the most terrifying opposition. He will not decline, to give an answer, to many even of the most favourite objections, that are sometimes urged, as to the character and conduct of the first Christians; nor refuse to meet the enemy of his faith, though he has artfully made a diversion, into a country, which he is less properly called on, to defend.

With regard however to the character of the first Christians, the matter may perhaps, fairly be stated thus.

It is a debt, that we owe certainly to their memories, that we owe to christianity in general, to keep them untainted, as far as may be, by the breath of slander; and we need not fear on the whole to affirm, that their lives did honour to their profession. But if on the other hand, the sentiments of individuals should sometimes be found uncharitable and unbecoming; if even their lives should have been disgraceful to their faith, we are in no sort, concerned to defend their cause, as the cause of christianity itself. We may lament that so pure a religion should so soon have contracted a mixture of corruption, even during her first residence on earth, but we may find comfort in the reflexion, that every material evidence, by which it is supported, still remains in full force; and that the authentic records of her doctrines, may still teach us what fruits they ought to have brought forth in others, and should yet produce in us.

I shall now beg leave to turn your attention, to some of our author's disquisitions, as they present themselves in order. It is by no means my design to follow him through all his researches. My remarks will be confined rather to particular passages; and it will be more especially my object, to examine diligently into the force of the several testimonies collected, in support of his assertions; since should these be found to fail, the superstructure built upon them, must fall in consequence. I shall attend particularly also, to such short but significant reflections, not immediately relating to the subject of his history, as our author has occasionally indulged himself in, in the course of his general notes. From these, perhaps the true temper and design of our historian may best be collected, since in attending to them, we follow him as it were, into his most secret recesses, and hear him speaking in his own person. For all such reflexions too, he is more immediately accountable, should it be found, that the history itself can by no means be said to have required them.

Much stress is laid by our author, on his first supposed cause of the rapid growth of the christian church. Yet how "an inflexible, and intolerant zeal,"[4] such as condemned even the most harmless ceremonies of paganism, could invite Pagans, amidst all their prejudices, to embrace christianity, does not seem altogether easy to explain. It might indeed produce the only effect, our author, in the recapitulation of his argument,[5] has assigned to it; it might supply Christians with that invincible valour, which should keep them firm to their received principles, but it could hardly be of service in converting Pagans. Is not then this secondary cause, inadequate to its declared effect?

To the next cause alleged, we may certainly attribute more force; and the friends of christianity, will very readily acknowledge the doctrine of a future life, brought to light by

[4] P. 450.
[5] P. 502.

the gospel, to have had its share in spreading the belief of it. But with what propriety can this be considered, as an human cause? Is not this distinguished excellence of the Christian revelation, to be considered rather as a part of "the convincing evidence of the doctrine itself,"[6] and as belonging to the very essence of the gospel? If so, it is altogether improperly enumerated, among "the secondary causes which assisted the truth of the Christian religion."[7]

The miraculous powers ascribed to the primitive church, are assigned as a third cause. We may here also readily join issue with our author. But we may at the same time remind him, that he gains no step towards accounting for the growth of Christianity, from "human causes,"[8] while he sets before us, the supposed extraordinary interposition, of the hand of God.

Thus much, of his general delineation of the causes of the growth of the Christian church. Let us proceed now to consider such disquisitions, as present themselves in his particular display of them.

Among the first objects of his researches, the sects of the Ebionites and Gnostics, hold a distinguished place.

It will not be matter of much wonder to any one, who considers the authoritative and express decision, of the great Apostle of the Gentiles – who considers the general tenor and spirit of the gospel – that in process of time at least, those who like the Ebionites, contended for the retaining the ceremonies of the Mosaic law, as a part of the system of Christianity, should be openly condemned and rejected, by every true Christian.

If an intemperate degree of zeal, exerted in a good cause, unhappily transported many into a culpable extreme, and led them not only to "exclude their judaizing brethren from the hope of salvation," but to decline also, "any intercourse with them, in the common offices of social life,"[9] we have certainly to lament, the error of those who knew not what spirit they were of.

But on the other hand, to have treated those, who, while they professed themselves Christians in principle, were Jews in

[6] P. 450.
[7] P. 502.
[8] P. 479.
[9] P. 459.

practice, as real and perfect Christians, would have been to forego the plain and decisive precepts of the gospel, which, when that which was perfect was now come, enjoined, that, that which was imperfect, should be done away.

The history of the Gnostics, were it fully displayed, would afford room for several important observations. It might be shown, that their knowledge was not indeed according to truth, was rather in many instances in direct opposition to it, and that their objections seem to have flowed principally, from that fruitful source of error, even in later times, a vain affectation of science, falsely so called. Let us for the present, content ourselves, with collecting such scattered features of their true portraiture, as even our author himself, who must be allowed certainly to have done full justice to their objections, may supply us with.

I cannot however but make mention of the profane derision of the Gnostics, in one instance. There is something so extremely daring and horrible, in giving the soft epithet of "venial,"[10] to an offence committed in defiance to the express command of God, delivered by himself; – there is such a flagrant want of truth, in asserting "eternal condemnation to have been pronounced against human kind"[11] for this offence of their first progenitors, when every circumstance of God's sentence, relates to this life only; when no mention whatsoever, is made, of human kind in general,[12] that we may well wonder, to find such objections, repeated, by the too-faithful historian.

For the rest, let us avail ourselves of his own acknowledgments, that the objections of the Gnostics, were "petulantly urged, thro' vain science,[13] that they delivered themselves to the guidance of a disordered imagination; that they degraded the honour of religion,[14] and impiously represented the God of Israel"[15] under a character, which cannot indeed belong to him.

We may well apply on this occasion, a very judicious remark, which we borrow from our author himself. "The

---

[10] P. 460.
[11] P. 469.
[12] See Genesis, ch. 3. v. 16-20.
[13] P. 461.
[14] P. 462.
[15] P. 460.

enemies of a religion, never understand it, because they hate it; and they often hate it, because they do not understand it. They adopt the most atrocious calumnies against it."[16]

If notwithstanding all this, the Gnostics "contributed to assist, rather than retard, the progress of Christianity,"[17] they seem at least to have formed their converts, very imperfectly, while "they required not any belief of that antecedent revelation,"[18] which duly understood, forms an indispensable part of the genuine system of Christianity.

An extreme abhorrence of idolatry, is described to us, as a striking feature, of the character of the first Christians. This will not surely be condemned by those, who are themselves turned from vain idols, to the living God.

It is indeed impossible to worship God and Jupiter; and if the zeal of Christians sometimes carried them to a scrupulous abhorrence of the very appearance of idolatry, even in its most harmless forms, it may be remembered, that they were expressly enjoined to abstain from all appearance of evil.

What wonder then, if those, who were peculiarly called upon, not to serve vain idols, fled even from "the most sacred festivals of the Roman ritual, if they abhorred even the humane licence of the Saturnalia, and refused to hail the genial powers of fecundity;"[19] when these festivals were destined to indulge the pious remembrance of the dead, with idolatrous ceremonies, when, to partake of them, implied necessarily, a belief of the system of Polytheism!

What wonder, if devoted as they were, to worship the deity, in spirit and in truth, they remained unmoved by the splendor and pomp of external ceremonies, if even "the elegant forms,

---

[16] "Les ennemis d'une religion ne la connoissent jamais, parceq'ils la haissent, et souvent ils la haissent, parcequ'ils ne la connoissent pas. Ils adoptent contre elle les calomnies les plus atroces." GIBBON, Essai sur l'etude de la litterature. Lond. 1761. p. 111.

I am happy to seize an opportunity of acknowledging, that, that attention to the Belles Lettres, which is displayed in the course of this work, forms its least merit. It is preceded by an English dedication, which does the utmost honour to the author's heart. A dedication from A SON, distinguishing himself in literature, at an early period of life, addressed in the warmest terms of affection, to A RESPECTED FATHER. I had almost said, LET THIS EXPIATE!

[17] P. 462.

[18] Ibid.

[19] P. 465.

and agreeable fictions of the Greeks," and the "beautiful mythology"[20] of the poets, made no impression on those who were not engaged in the search of what was alluring to the eye, or pleasing to the imagination, but dedicated only, to the solemn study of pure religion!

In the course of a display, of the doctrines of a future state among the Pagans of Greece and Rome, we find it acknowledged that even "the most sublime efforts of philosophy" cannot ascertain its existence.[21] We are obliged to our author, for confirming anew, the important arguments of others, in favour of the necessity of that revelation, which in the general course of his disquisitions, he seems insensible of the value of. I shall not detain you long on this head. It seems only necessary to offer a few remarks in vindication of the canonical authority of the Apocalypse.

"In the council of Laodicea, we are told, the Apocalypse was tacitly excluded from the sacred canon, by the same churches of Asia, to which it was addressed."[22] No new objection this! But since it has been thought proper, to bring it forward again into view, why is it not introduced, with a more exact state of the case? From this, it must for ever appear, at the very worst, that the point in question, is strictly problematical, and that in the course of the debate, at least, neither side, can claim a decisive victory. If it cannot be shewn absolutely, that the Apocalypse was tacitly approved by the council, so neither can it be shewn, that it was tacitly excluded.

The true state of the case, is briefly this. It should be remarked, that it seems plainly to have been the immediate object of the council, not, to establish a complete canon of the scriptures, but to ascertain only, what books, among those that were deemed canonical, should be publickly read, in the churches. They decree first, that no books which were composed only by private persons, should be read, nor any other that were not canonical; but only those, which belonged to the canon of the Old and New Testament.[23] They then

---

[20] P. 465. Our author's description of Paganism, in his former work, already quoted, is somewhat more accurate. Ce systeme riant, mais *absurde*. p. 109.

[21] P. 468.

[22] Note 65. p. lxix.

[23] Can. 59. Conc. Laod. Beveregii Synodicon, Ox. 1672. Tom. 1. p. 480.

proceed to determine,[24] which of these should be read, and in their list of the books of the New Testament, the Apocalypse is not found included.

No direct reason, is given then for the omitting to make mention of the Apocalypse. It is not proscribed, but it is not enjoined to be read.[25] It has been conjectured, therefore, not without seeming probability, that this was occasioned only, by its being thought, too mysterious to be rightly understood by common hearers.[26]

But of such importance does this problematical objection appear to our author, that he is able to assign no other cause, for the Apocalypse's having been received by the Protestant churches, than, "the advantage of turning its mysterious prophecies against the see of Rome."

We cannot indeed adopt the cause he has assigned, but we will supply him, not with one reason in the place of it, but with many and abundant reasons.

In less than threescore years after the council of Laodicea, the Synod of Carthage, reckons the Apocalypse by name, among the canonical books of the New Testament.[27] And in the seventh century, the sixth general council, fully established the authority of this Synod, and confirmed its decrees.[28]

The testimonies of the Fathers in favour of the authenticity of this book are numerous.

We may allege, those of Justin Martyr, Irenæus, Clemens, Tertullian, Origen, Cyprian, and Lactantius; to omit mentioning several others.[29] We need not therefore seemingly be at a loss, as our author is, to account for the reception of the Apocalypse, even in the Greek churches, when we find so many of the Greek, as well as the Latin Fathers, bearing testimony to

[24] Can. 60. ibid. 481.

[25] See Twell's critical examen of the new text and version of the New Testament, p. 3. where this point is fully considered.

[26] See Bp. Cosin's scholastical history, of the canon of scripture, ch. vi. lxii.

[27] Cone, Carthag. can. 47. tom. 2. Conc. Labbe.

[28] Bev. Synod. Can. 2. tom. 1. p. 158.

[29] I. Martyr dial. xx. 4 or 6. Irenæus, 1.4.c. 37. Origen Comment in Joann. xiv. 6, 7. Cyprian de bon. pudicit. xxii. 9. Lact. Ep. c. xlii. Tertull. adv. Marc. 1. 3 c. xiv.

The several passages of the Fathers, that bear testimony to the scriptures, may be seen under one view, in a very useful work, by the Rev. Mr. Atkinson, entitled, a Table of the Evidence of the Sacred Canon.

it. Much less need we assign, an unworthy, and interested reason for its reception in the protestant churches.

Indeed the very eminent writer, whom our author has chosen to refer to, (not surely for a confirmation of the whole of his remark) might have suggested to his thoughts, the reasons that have led the several churches, to receive the Apocalypse, as canonical. On consulting his elegant discourses, we shall find the use of the apocalyptic prophecies, against the church of Rome, touched on, by the hand of a master;[30] but we shall find the same able interpreter of these prophecies, agreeing with those who consider this book, as more strongly attested, than even any other book, of the New Testament.[31]

One word, concerning, "the condemnation of the wisest and most virtuous of the pagans," stated by our author, as the unanimous doctrine of the primitive church.[32] It may not be improper to remark, that "the vehement Tertullian," is here, the only evidence appealed to. Nor is it on this occasion only, but on many others also,[33] that he is brought forward to view, as if we were to consider him, as our author's favourite witness. It must be confessed, that the writings of this "zealous African," however they may on many accounts deserve our respect, sometimes also, breathe a spirit, altogether contrary to the plain dictates of Christian charity, and still oftener exhibit instances of a mistaken piety, that is rather enthusiastic, than rational. How far it became our author to select diligently, the blemishes that stain the writings of this intemperate advocate of Christianity; how far even "the melancholy duty imposed on the historian," on this, as well as other occasions, may serve to plead his apology, we have ventured to assert, is at least uncertain.

There may be those among the fathers of the church, who have openly asserted the crime of "obstinately persisting," in the worship of false deities, when they had it in their power to know the true God. St. Paul had declared men inexcusable, for their idolatry, even under a reference to the light of nature

---

30 Bp. Hurd's Sermon xii. vol. 2. p. 208.

31 Sermon x. p. 111. (note) vol. 2. 2d. edit. 12mo. 1773. The observation introduced there, ought not to be passed over. – "If the authority of this momentous book be indeed questionable, the church of Rome could hardly have failed long since to make the discovery, or to triumph in it."

32 P. 473.

33 See notes 39. 41. 45. 47. 49. 83, &c. and p. 484.

only.[34] But to warn men of their sins, and to pronounce their absolute condemnation, in consequence of those sins, are distinct things. It might well be said, that those obstinate idolaters, who wilfully shut their eyes against the light of nature and revelation, did not *"deserve pardon"* of the deity. If our author means to assert, that the fathers taught that neither could such pardon *"be expected"* by any means, this requires further proof; and cannot be granted on the sole evidence of the inhuman and uncharitable declamation, of "the stern Tertullian."

But it is not the faith of the primitive church alone, that undergoes the severity of our author's censure. The same offensive doctrine, he asserts, is still "the *public* doctrine of *all* the christian churches."[35] But he asserts it wholly without proof. I cannot but presume to enter a protest against our author's judgment, at least in the name of one church, the church of England; and am bold to affirm, that her mild decisions, are not stained with so foul a blot, as "the condemnation of the wisest and most virtuous Pagans."

In the mean time let him blush at the remembrance, of having included that church of which he is himself a member, in so severe a censure, without even attempting to bring proof of the truth of his assertion.

I should be but ill inclined to take any notice of our author's disquisitions concerning the miraculous powers of the primitive church, had not some reflections fallen from him (not perhaps necessarily suggested by his immediate subject) which affect materially, the faith of modern Christians. "That very free and ingenious inquiry," which, in his own words, "appears to have excited a general scandal among the divines of our own, as well as of the other churches of Europe," met with many learned antagonists. To enter again into so recent a controversy, to repeat answers, so easy to be consulted, would be altogether superfluous.

But the description that he gives us of the faith of modern times, is indeed melancholy and alarming.

"A latent, and even involuntary scepticism adheres to the most pious dispositions. Their admission of supernatural truths, is much less an active consent, than a cold and passive

---

[34] Rom. i. 20. 21.

[35] Note 68. p. lxx.

acquiescence. Accustomed long since to observe and to respect the invariable order of nature, our reason, or at least our imagination is not sufficiently prepared to sustain the visible action of the deity."[36]

I would willingly hope, that there can be but little reason to think that such scepticism adheres to, "the most pious dispositions," or that they admit "the supernatural truths of the gospel but with a cold and passive acquiescence." An active inquiry into the authenticity of Revelation, (and such surely we must expect from pious dispositions) will not fail to produce an active, ready, and willing consent. Later histories do indeed set before us, "the invariable order of nature" rather than "the visible action of the deity" employed, in changing its course, for the purpose of sealing his authentic instructions, in the sight of his creatures. But this affords no argument against our believing fully, the wonders of former ages, when sufficiently attested to us. In such case the space of time, which has passed since, may well be said, to be, in a manner, annihilated. Thro' the medium of authentic history, we are set in the place, as it were, of actual spectators of the events, and no "respect" can be due, "to the invariable order of nature" that is not far exceeded by the respect due to "the authentic wonders of the evangelic history,"[37] when the end plainly seems worthy of the interposition of God. A rational faith thus acquired, will indeed become naturally, "a deep impression," and may be justly celebrated, as the Christian's truest boast.

But the objection we have been considering, is in reality no other than the well known argument of Mr. Hume, clothed in a new form, for the present occasion. It has been so often and so fully answered, that it is needless to take further notice of it.[38] We shall readily acknowledge, that the doctors of the church of England, are to be reckoned among those, "more rigid," but orthodox teachers, who consider "the moral virtues as destitute of any value, or efficacy, in the work of our justification."

We will only add, that these rigid doctors, tho' they exclude the moral virtues from the office of justifying, teach at the same time, the absolute necessity of practising them.

[36] P. 478.
[37] P. 479.
[38] See Dr. Adam's Essay on miracles, – Dr. Campbell's inquiry, &c. and the late Dr. Powell's sermons.

The well-known reproach of Celsus, "when it is cleared from misrepresentation, contributes, says our author, to the honour of the church." We readily acquiesce in the observation.

But we may not perhaps be willing to acknowledge, that, the influx of "the most abandoned of sinners,"[39] contributed so much to the increase of the church, as he seems to imagine.

That many abandoned sinners were converted in the first ages of Christianity, may readily be granted; but that the number of those who needed no repentance was greater, may likewise be asserted.

The testimony of Origen, who in the opinion even of our author, "was intimately acquainted with the history of the Christians"[40] is express,

"If any one, says he, will candidly consider us Christians, we can produce him more who have been converted from a life not the worst, than from a very wicked course. For they whose conscience speaks favourably in their behalf, are disposed to wish, that our doctrine concerning the future rewards of the good, may be true; and so are more ready to assent to the gospel, than profligate men."[41]

---

[39] P. 480.

[40] Ch. 16. p. 546. However Origen may sometimes meet with respect from our author, he stands elsewhere accused of the most disingenuous conduct in *mutilating* the objection of his adversary Celsus (see note 101. p. lxxi.) I am not able to discover the least traces of mutilation; but had there even been room for suspicion, I should have thought candour had obliged me to be very cautious in exhibiting the accusation, in an instance in which there is no opportunity of comparing the passage, with the original. – I should have been the more cautious because the method which Origen has pursued, bespeaks the utmost fairness in his proceedings. He does not interweave the objections of his adversary, as he might have done, into the body of his text, but states them separately, to all appearance at least, in his own words. But to pass by all this. I am sorry to be obliged to add, that the charge of *mutilation*, in this case, lies at our author's door. Origen expressly denies the accusation of Celsus, and does not attempt to answer his objection, because, as he asserts, it proceeds wholly on a false supposition. — Ειτα παλιν, ως εθος τω Κελσω, φυρει εν τοις εξης, λεγων α ουδεις ημων ανεγραψε, και φησι τοιαυτα: and then, (having quoted the objection), προς τουτων ουχ ερει λογος, ου γαρ λεγει τις ημων.

After this, we at least cannot agree with our author, that Celsus has urged his objection, *with great candour*; and we may ask, how it can be supposed, that Origen, even had he been shewn to be capable of it, would *mutilate* an objection, which he meant to expose, as founded on a *false* assertion!

[41] Origen contra Cels. Lib 3.

Nor do we think indeed, that "the sudden emotions of shame, of grief, and of terror," can be looked upon as necessary, towards a rational conversion; nor is the general question concerned about "wonderful conversions," when we treat of the many thousands that were converted in the first ages of Christianity.

That Christ also, as well as his Apostles, did indeed often address themselves to "those who were oppressed by the consciousness of their vices," is indisputably true. But we do not find however, that such alone were converted, tho' the saving truths of the gospel were often more immediately urged to them, because they stood most in need, of having them peculiarly enforced. Our divine master, may best apologize for his own conduct, in a manner worthy of himself. "They that are whole, need not a physician, but they that are sick."

That some of the first Christians were averse to the business of war and government, cannot be disputed.

But we must not admit this as a general description of their conduct, or as the common practice, or determination of the church.

Many, it is certain, bore arms, and discharged public offices. A variety of testimonies might be produced, to shew that they were at least in all respects, as useful to society, as their consciences would permit. That they contributed in many respects, to promote the business of civil society, even our author may assure us, when he remarks that the converts of the new religion "were permitted to increase their separate property, by all the lawful means of trade and industry."[42]

It should be remarked too, that these offices and employments which some declined, were usually clogged with such circumstances and conditions, as in their opinions interfered wholly with the precepts of Christianity. The reason of their conduct will therefore, in such cases, be as evident, as it is honourable.

Our author's attempt to account for the growth of Christianity, from secondary causes, does not end with the display of those five principal causes, which he has chosen to insist on. One circumstance is yet behind, which as we find it stated, is to be looked upon as almost alone sufficient, to explain its rapid and extended propagation.

[42] P. 495.

But should we be inclined, to attribute some part of the success of Christianity, to the sceptical state, of the minds of Pagans, it surely cannot be thought, to have had any great share, in the work. If the minds of many were already estranged from their own numberless deities, can it be conceived yet, that they would be altogether willing to embrace a new religion, in which they could discern *no deity* at all, for the object of their worship? That the first Christians, were for this very reason, in general considered as Atheists, our author, has afforded us sufficient proof. If the generality, had conceived an aversion for the absurd customs of their own external rites, would they yet, readily become converts to a form of worship, simple and unadorned, without temples,[43] and without images, and undoubtedly very ill calculated, to attract the servile veneration of the people? If, as it should seem, our author's character of Christianity, considered as "a revelation, adorned with all, that could attract the curiosity, the wonder, and the veneration of the people,"[44] must be understood to relate to its form of worship, and its external ceremonies, I cannot but wholly differ from him in opinion, as the contrary, I think may be undeniably proved. The New Testament itself is an unanswerable proof of it, the only authority, by which such a testimony can be decided, and the only one to which a protestant at least can appeal, to determine the question.

Nor have we as yet descended in the course of our author's history, into those times, in which the spirit of Christianity became corrupted, and the pure religion of Jesus, unhappily received into its bosom, the treacherous pageantry of paganism. The natural simplicity of its worship, could not but be preserved, while it still continued at open war, even with the most harmless ceremonies of idolatry.

But why too, conclude, that the incredulity of the speculative philosopher, would so readily communicate itself to the multitude; that the people, incapable surely in general, of comprehending the refined scepticism of their superiors, would yet at once forsake those doctrines "to which they had yielded

---

[43] This is well known, for some time, to have been literally the case; and when afterwards churches were erected, they were wholly destitute of the splendor of heathen temples.

[44] P. 505.

the most implicit belief?"[45] If we may argue from present facts (and it is a position of our author's, that the human heart is still the same)[46] it is fully seen, that the same deluding ceremonies, as have unhappily produced in our own times, the melancholy effect of precipitating, the higher ranks of men, into a total desertion of religion, still retain at the same time, their full hold, on the minds of the people. The multitude has not in any sort shaken off, the chains of bigotry, in consequence of the free, and avowed principles, of their superiors.

It is granted too that the higher ranks of the pagans, in practice, still "affected to treat with respect and decency, the religious institutions of their country."[47] And it would require surely, more penetration, than usually falls to the lot, of the people, to discern "their secret contempt."[48]

I cannot indeed but consider, the system of reasoning, which seeks to account for the growth of Christianity, from the scepticism of pagans, as materially affected by fact, by the repeated proceedings of the pagan multitude. "The impatient clamours of the multitude, dooming the Christians to the severest tortures, on the stated returns of the public games and festivals,"[49] but ill agree with the idea of an actual disposition to receive the religion of Christians, and to forsake the Gods, to whose memory, these games and festivals were dedicated. On the whole, surely our author must at least be said, to have drawn far too general an inference, when he ventures to assert, that those who are inclined to pursue such reflections, as a consideration of the scepticism of the pagan world, suggests, "instead of viewing with astonishment, the rapid progress of Christianity, will perhaps be surprised, that its success was not still more rapid and still more universal."[50]

That the peace and union of the Roman empire facilitated the progress of Christianity, will readily be granted; and it has been ingeniously remarked, that this circumstance, may serve to point out, to those who are curious, to enquire into the reason of the late appearance of Christianity, the propriety of

[45] P. 504.
[46] N. 112. p. lxii.
[47] P. 504.
[48] P. 504.
[49] Ch. xvi. p. 543.
[50] Ch. xv. p. 505.

that fullness of time which was fixed on, by the providence of the Almighty, for the introduction of Revelation.

I shall not follow our author, through all his nicer calculations of the numbers of the first Christians. They must at least be allowed, to be in part conjectural, and the testimonies of Tacitus and Pliny, afford us positive and unsuspected evidence. Nor do I see, why that candid allowance,[51] should so humanely be extended to their "vague expressions" which is not in any sort granted to the "splendid exaggeration" of Justin Martyr.[52] Their testimonies certainly do not so much stand in need of it, and it cannot be said, that "the measure of their belief was regulated by that of their wishes."[53]

But, the language of Tacitus "is almost similar to the stile employed by Livy, when he relates the introduction and suppression of the rites of Bacchus."[54] Perhaps the similitude, on an accurate comparison, will not be easily discovered. It is a common indefinite mode of expression, to speak of "a great multitude,"[55] and it does not seemingly stand in need of the aid of conjecture, to justify it. The reason that may be given for the stile of Livy, will not at all apply to the narrative of Tacitus. In the former case, the Roman government, was really alarmed, on account of the reputed numbers of the Bacchanals, who might well be expected to rise in arms. And the historian accordingly relates the real apprehensions of the senate. In the latter case, in however criminal a light, the unhappy victims of Nero's cruelty, might otherwise be regarded, they had at least uniformly shewn themselves obedient subjects, and they are expressly described, as selected only, as so many destined sacrifices, to suppress, if possible, the rumour that had prevailed against the emperor. Tacitus therefore could have no occasion for adopting a language, suited to express the fears of the Roman people.

Much less can this reasoning be applied to the testimony of Pliny. His letter shews, that he was alarmed only, by the

[51] P. 509.
[52] P. 512.
[53] P. 512.
[54] P. 509.
[55] Ingens multitudo. Tacit. 15. 44.

number of those that would be in danger of *suffering*,⁵⁶ should a rigid persecution be enforced, not of those, who might endanger the peace of the Roman government, through a rebellious disposition. His conduct is evidently that of the prudent politician, desirous of saving the lives of his master's subjects, not of the affrighted magistrate, dreading an insurrection.⁵⁷

But perhaps it will still be contended, that allowance must be made for an oratorical stile. It should be remarked here, that he acquaints Trajan, that "the temples which were almost forsaken, *begin* to be frequented, that the sacred solemnities, after a long intermission, *are revived*, and that the victims likewise are every where bought up, whereas for some time, there *were* few purchasers.⁵⁸ So that could he be supposed to have been at all influenced by fear, it appears that at the actual time of his writing, the prospect of affairs was such, as might inspire him with fresh hopes. What appearances are there then, of exaggeration? But the very improbability of the supposition, duly considered, might otherwise serve to refute it.⁵⁹

The discussion of one point more, shall conclude my examination of this chapter.

The inattention of the sages of Greece and Rome, to the convincing evidence of miracles, is stated by our author, as matter of much surprise. And the omission of the darkness of

---

⁵⁶ Visa est enim mihi res digna consultatione, maxime propter *periclitantium* numerum. Plin. Epist. xcvii. Lib. x.

⁵⁷ The candour of our author, celebrates the Roman governour, by the title of the *humane* Pliny. Yet this humane governour, dissatisfied with the testimony that even those, who had *revolted* from the religion of the Christians, had given of the innocence of their worship, and the purity of their manners, judges it even the more necessary, to examine, *by torture*, two unhappy *women*. Surely he exhibits a bad specimen of his own *humanity*. See his letter already quoted.

⁵⁸ See the letter, as before.

⁵⁹ This argument is placed in a strong light, by a late able writer. "These are," says he, Pliny's expressions, and we must "either suppose, that the governor of a province, writing to an emperor about a difficulty which embarrassed his administration, and requesting his directions how he should proceed, uses the arts of oratory, and totally misleads *him* whom he will be obliged to follow, or we must confess that the Christians, in that extensive and remote country, on the border of the Euxine sea, *far exceeded in number, the other inhabitants.*" Dr. Powell's sermons, disc. x. p. 161.

the passion, in the works of two distinguished philosophers, is made the occasion of a problem, which those who maintain the certainty of the event, seem called upon to solve.

The former of these difficulties, will not, at least be found, wholly inexplicable. The miracles that were performed during the age of Christ, were performed at a distance from the residence of these sages, and while as yet, no other circumstances had contributed to direct their attention to the obscure and despised sect of Christians. In the age of the apostles, Judea still continued the chief scene of their miracles; nor does the preaching of St. Paul, appear to have been accompanied by signs and wonders, either at Corinth, at Athens, or at Rome. It cannot therefore be affirmed strictly during these ages at least, that the evidence of miracles, was addressed to "their senses;"[60] they could only become acquainted with them, thro' the medium of the scriptures, or by common report; and how little attention, the sages of antiquity paid to all that concerned the history of Christianity, need not be insisted on.[61]

In the time of the first disciples of the apostles, the miracles that are said to have been wrought, must be considered as falling more immediately under their inspection. – But it may well be conjectured, from the reigning fashion of the times, that the minds of these sages were still filled with such early prejudices, as would effectually prevent their lying open to conviction. – It is acknowledged to be doubtful at least, whether they condescended to peruse the apologies of the first Christians; and if a variety of circumstances combined to fix in them a rooted contempt for the very name of Christianity,[62]

---

[60] P. 517.

[61] The scepticism of the Pagan world, in the opinion of a good judge, may be alleged rather, as a reason for their disbelief of Christianity, than as a circumstance favourable to its propagation. "Such were many of the heathen. – They thought, and they had reason to think, that the religion of their country was fable and forgery, which inclined them to suppose that other religions were no better, and deserved not to be examined." (JORTIN's truth of the Christian religion. p. 57.) "The careless glance which men of wit and learning condescended to cast on the Christian revelation," is borne witness to by our author (ch. xvi. p. 125.) And Dr. Lardner conjectures that Epictetus's silence with regard to the Christians, may be accounted for, from this consideration. (Collection of testimonies, vol. ii. p. 105.)

[62] It was a common complaint of the first Christians, that they were persecuted on account of *the name* only. Pliny's letter to Trajan, very

and to withhold them from studying the pure morality of its doctrines, it may afford but little cause for wonder, that they either carelessly overlooked, or obstinately rejected, even its more sensible proofs.

The other difficulty proposed to us, is founded on this circumstance.

Both Seneca and Pliny, "have recorded all the great phenomena of nature, earthquakes, meteors, comets, and *eclipses*, which their indefatigable curiosity could collect."[63] But they "have omitted to mention" that particular eclipse which is related to have happened at the time of the crucifixion.[64]

Of the three chapters referred to in Seneca, two of them treat only of comets and meteors, and one of earthquakes. But his disquisitions in this chapter, relate only to such earthquakes as had produced their usual and dreadful effects in destroying cities, and burying thousands. His attention therefore, cannot properly be supposed to have been directed, towards a far different kind of earthquake, which tho' it rent the rocks, and divided the vail of the temple in twain, does not appear to have occasioned any such damage as might entitle it to a place, among that class of earthquakes, which the philosopher, alone considers. Of *eclipses*, the more immediate subject of the present argument, *no one*, of these chapters treats; nor have I been fortunate enough, to discover, even elsewhere, in the course of Seneca's laborious work, any enumeration of eclipses, "collected by his indefatigable curiosity."[65] But in Pliny, we are told "a distinct chapter, is devoted to eclipses of an extraordinary nature, and unusual duration," "who contents himself nevertheless, with describing the singular defect of light, which followed the murder of Cesar." As the best solution of the difficulty, I will repeat to you, this *important* chapter, "devoted" as it is, to eclipses of that kind, among

---

remarkably confirms this; "NOMEN IPSUM, ETIAMSI FLAGITIIS CAREAT, an flagitia cohærentia nomini puniantur."

[63] P. 518.

[64] A similar objection, drawn from the silence of heathen writers in general, is urged by *Mons'r. de Voltaire*, in his Dictionaire philosophique. But he proceeds wholly on the idea, that the darkness was universal, a position that may well be contested, from the evidence of the evangelists, themselves.

[65] P. 518.

which, it is contended, the preternatural darkness, in question, ought to have found a place. It will not detain you long.

"There are, says our philosopher, eclipses of an extraordinary nature, and unusual duration, such as that which followed the murder of Cesar, and in the war with Anthony; when a perpetual paleness covered the sun, almost throughout the whole year."[66] You have the whole chapter laid before you.

You will now perhaps be surprized at the serious manner, in which this objection is proposed. It must appear surely from the whole of the chapter, that it was not the philosopher's design, to record all the most remarkable eclipses, that might be collected, but merely to confirm the general truth of his proposition, so far, as not to leave it wholly without proof. Why he should have fixed particularly on a traditional instance, relating to Cesar, will easily be conceived, when it is recollected, how flattering the mention of it might prove, and that "this season of obscurity, had already been celebrated by most of the poets, and historians of that memorable age".[67]

Had this latter objection, been really formidable, it yet might have been sufficient perhaps, to have remarked, that a mere silence, concerning any fact, in persons at least, but accidentally called on, to make mention of it, cannot properly be considered as of any weight, in opposition to the positive evidence of those, whose express business it is to record it.

And we might have insisted farther on that "careless indifference," which it is acknowledged, "the most copious and the most minute of the Pagan writers have shewn to the affairs of the Christians."[68]

But we have no need to recur to such solutions, when it appears, that of the two philosophers, appealed to, the one has not any where designedly recorded eclipses, and the other has only treated of them in such a manner, as to give us no reason to expect the mention of the darkness of the passion, in preference, to that of other instances, which the history of his own nation, supplied him with.

The remaining pages of our author's disquisitions, while they treat of the conduct of the Roman government towards the

---

[66] P. 158. Fiunt prodigiosi & longiores defectus; qualis occiso Cæsare, & Antoniano bello, totius fere anni pallore perpetuo. Plin. nat. hist. lib. II. c. 30. fol. edit. Paris. 1723.

[67] P. 518.

[68] P. 530.

Christians, contain in reality a laboured apology for it, rather than a disinterested relation of mere facts.

The guilt of the princes and magistrates of Rome, is industriously palliated; the most stubborn proofs occasionally turned aside from their plain and natural signification, and the persecuted Christians considered in that light *only*, in which the most bigotted of their persecutors would have placed them. It is every where supposed, according to the spirit of the argument adopted, that the Christians were acknowledged criminals, and without doubt, merited the punishments inflicted on them. On this idea, the conduct of their persecutors is apologized for, and "the indulgent spirit of Rome, and of Polytheism"[69] is extolled, either on account of the nature of the punishments they inflicted, or of the occasional cessation of their cruelties.

Yet many of those emperors, who distinguished themselves in the persecution of Christianity, were tyrants of so odious a character, were themselves so lost to all ideas of religion, that even the pretence of their having persecuted the Christians in defence of the religion of their country, can scarcely be urged in their favour. The inoffensive principles of the Christians, considered as subjects, soon became sufficiently known and experienced; and it behoved *every* sovereign, who regarded them as objects of punishment, to have inquired, previously into their religious principles, into the validity of those reasons, which had induced them, in the language of our author, to reject "the religion of *nature*, of Rome, and of their ancestors."[70] Had they made this inquiry, the Christians might have replied, that they conformed themselves strictly to the *genuine* religion of Nature, and that they had received a new divine revelation, founded on the religion of nature, in consequence of every possible proof of its authenticity.

But it is not probable, that the pagans themselves, would have attempted to defend their system, by an appeal to the religion of nature, which they had long lost sight of amidst the fictions of their poets, and their customary worship, of deified *human* personages. They would have contented themselves rather, with their favourite plea of following the religion of their ancestors, and their country.[71] The ingenuity of modern

---

[69] P. 568.

[70] P. 570.

[71] What deference was usually paid to this consideration amongst the

times has advanced those laboured sophisms in defence of polytheism, which seem never to have occurred to polytheists themselves.[72]

It is certain, that the persecutors of Christianity, did not inquire, with that candour which reason itself might have suggested, into the grounds of that *obstinacy*, which they so hastily condemned. And even their own proceedings, their omission of punishment at one time, (while the principles and conduct of the Christians, still remained the same,) nay, their mitigation of it, at another, serve to shew, that they were in general conscious of the injustice of inflicting punishment.[73]

It ought not to be omitted, that our historian ascends beyond the proper limits of his history, to state to us, the persecution under Nero. It is easier to see the reason of this digression from his subject, than to justify the propriety of it. The intent is, to blot out, if possible from the page of history, one distinguished persecution of the Christians, by the assistance, of a refined conjecture.[74]

To admit willingly that Tacitus composed his description of Nero's cruelty, at the distance of sixty years from the event – still let it be remembered, that the event happened in his own life time, tho' it might be in his infancy. Would the true history of such signal cruelty, detested even by the Romans themselves,

 ancients may appear from the doctrine, even of the enlightened Socrates; who amidst the most just and exalted ideas of the one true God, at the same time unhappily gave countenance to every various absurdity of idolatry, by his well-known decision, that the Gods ought to be worshipped, according to the customs of the state. (Νομω πολεως.) See Xenoph. mem.

72 See the late Mr. Hume's Natural History of religion.

73 It was on this ground, and surely with much reason, that Tertullian attacked the inconsistency of Trajan's proceedings. "O sententiam necessitate confusam! negat inquirendos, ut innocentes, et mandat puniendos, ut nocentes. Parcit et sævit; dissimulat, et animadvertit. Quid temet ipsum censurâ circumvenis? Si damnas, cur non et inquiris? Si non inquiris, cur non & absolvis?" Apolog. c. 2. Our author considers this censure (note 58. p. lxxx) as inconsistent with his acknowledgment, that Trajan's rescript was a relaxation of the ancient penal laws. But what inconsistency is there, in acknowledging candidly what the emperor *had* done, but insisting at the same time, that he ought to have done *more?*

74 "Most of the moderns," says our author (note 124. p. lxxxiv) "have seized the occasion" (arising from the uncertainty with regard to Aurelian's proceedings) "of *gaining* a few extraordinary martyrs." It must be allowed, that he himself uses no less diligence on every occasion, in trying to *abolish* the memory of reputed martyrs.

have been forgotten even in the course of one man's life? If this supposition cannot be admitted, if "THE ANNALIST,"[75] must have been informed of the real truth, from "the narratives of contemporaries," the character of "the PHILOSOPHER"[76] will but ill excuse him for having disguised it, in complaisance to the "knowledge, or prejudices of the time of Hadrian."

By this mode of arguing, if the conjecture should be established, the character of the historian is sacrificed.

Let us turn now to the conjecture itself. It depends wholly, on the uncertain position, that the Christians in the time of Nero, were called GALILÆANS. I call it, at least, uncertain, because the testimony appealed to,[77] will not support it, sufficiently for our author's purpose. It is rather in some sort proved that the Christians could not be called Galilæans in the reign of Nero.

Suidas informs us "that in the time of the emperor Claudius, (the predecessor of Nero) they who had *before* been called Nazareans and Galilæans, received a new name at Antioch, and were called Christians."[78] There is no positive evidence to prove our author's assertion, and there is very probable evidence, to contradict the supposition.

Pliny,[79] Suetonius, and the emperor Adrian, at the beginning of the second century, all use the appellation of Christians.

And in the course of the same century, the two Antonines, Celsus, and Galen, in their several testimonies, each adopt the same title of distinction.[80] If we suppose the name of Galilæans to have been still in use, even after the times of Claudius, either during the reign of Nero or his successors, this difficulty remains to be accounted for, how such a variety of heathen writers should all have made use of a different term.

But were we even to admit the supposition, the conjecture would still be perplexed with material difficulties. Can it yet be conceived, that the innocent Galilæans at *Rome* would be

[75] P. 536.

[76] P. 536.

[77] Dr. Lardner who is appealed to, has only proved that the Christians were called GALILÆANS, *before the time of Nero*, and again after it (on the testimony of one writer only) in the third century.

[78] Lardner (Jewish and Heathen testimonies) vol. 2. p. 102 and 103. Suidas. V. Ναζηραιος.

[79] See Lardner.

[80] See the same author.

confounded with the guilty zealots in *Judea*, whose rebellious conduct could not but distinguish them from those whose peaceable principles, gave no offence?

The one were "the friends," the other, "the enemies of human kind."[81] A difference of character too remarkable to be lost, under one general name, when the followers of Judas had their own proper *distinction*, of zealots, if not, as some think of GAULONITES also.

May we not say too, that a conjecture started in opposition to the most express testimony, rests on very slight grounds, when it is to be supported by "the *extreme conciseness*"[82] of the stile of the historian, however remarkable his conciseness may be, in matters of less importance? It must be esteemed a very remarkable conciseness in the historian, and surely a very culpable one, if in relating a fact, which stood in need of every apology, he has trusted "to the curiosity or reflexion of his readers" to supply the only apology that could be suggested for it. Here the character of Tacitus, is again sacrificed in order to maintain a favourite conjecture, (in behalf of one, "whose rage, it is confessed," had been usually directed "against virtue and innocence"[83]) at all events.[84]

We must not yet dismiss this celebrated passage. The mention of its integrity, has served to introduce a severe decision concerning another celebrated testimony (not indeed on the same subject) in the works of Josephus. "The passage concerning Jesus Christ, which was inserted into the text of Josephus, between the time of Origen, and that of Eusebius, may furnish," we are told, "an example, of no vulgar forgery."[85] Perhaps we may borrow an argument from our author himself, in defence of this passage. If "the reputation of

---

[81] Ch. xvi. p. 537.

[82] P. 536. "we may therefore (that is on account of Tacitus's extreme conciseness) presume to imagine some probable cause, which could direct the cruelty of Nero, against the Christians of Rome."

[83] The expression of Tertullian, is of the same kind. P. 537. "Qui scit illum, intelligere potest, non nisi grande bonum, a Nerone damnatum."

[84] "The difficulties with which it is perplexed," (p. 534) are made a plea for the introduction of our author's observations on this passage. But these difficulties, are not pointed out to us; and other commentators, the accurate Lardner in particular, do not appear to have discovered any. One only difficulty seems to attend the passage, that it cannot be thought capable of the new interpretation put upon it.

[85] Note 35. p. lxxviii.

26   *Religious Scepticism*

Tacitus, guarded his text from the interpolations of pious fraud,"[86] something also ought to be attributed, in this respect, to the reputation of Josephus. Both himself and his works were so well received among the Romans, that he was enrolled a citizen of Rome, and had a statue erected to his memory.[87] His writings also were admitted into the imperial library. It should be remembered too, that not only the Romans, may be looked upon as the guardians of the integrity of his text, but that the Jews also, would certainly use all diligence, to prevent any interpolation, in favour of the Christian cause. Yet it cannot be discovered that any objection, was ever made to this passage in the earlier ages.

The various arguments of many learned writers, will serve still better to protect this passage from suspicion.[88] And had our author been careful to avoid, either the imputation of interposing his own judgment, too dogmatically, or of concealing studiously the important observations of others, he should have spoken of the question, as being still undetermined.[89]

For my own part, when I consider its agreement with the general stile of Josephus,[90] the long undisputed title it enjoyed,

[86]   Ch. 16. p. 535.

[87]   Minucius Felix, in the very next age, mistook him for a ROMAN. "De Judæis, scripta eorum require; vel si ROMANI mavis, FLAVII JOSEPHI.

[88]   See in particular, among many other authors on this subject, Cave's historia literaria – Dr. Willes's two dissertations prefixed to L'Estrange's Josephus, and Whiston's first dissertation, prefixed to his own translation. In each of these latter writers there may be found a critical analysis of the passage. – That in Whiston, is quoted from Daubuz de testimonio Josephi. Lond. 1706. – See also, Bp. Parker's demonstration of the laws of nature and Christianity, which Dr. Lardner does not appear to have consulted. It contains perhaps the best answer, that can be found, to such objections, as are principally insisted on.

[89]   Dr. Lardner, while he openly controverts the authenticity of the passage, by many laboured arguments, adopts however, a very different language. "This passage is received by many learned men, as genuine. By others it is rejected, as an interpolation. It is allowed on all hands, THAT IT IS IN ALL THE COPIES OF JOSEPHUS'S WORKS NOW EXTANT, BOTH PRINTED AND MANUSCRIPT. Nevertheless it may be for several reasons called in question." Vol. 1. ch. iv. p. 151. – A very candid and complete state of the arguments on *each* side, may be found in Vernet, Traité de la religion Chretienne. Sect. VII. ch. 11. Dr. Lardner has not given us the answers that have been offered to his objections.

[90]   See this accurately stated by Daubuz, whose criticism may be found in Havercamp's edition, as well as Whiston's translation.

through the course of fifteen centuries,[91] and how much every objection raised against it rests only on presumptive proofs,[92] while positive evidence may be produced in its favour, from the consent of the most ancient manuscripts, I cannot but incline to the side of those writers, who are satisfied, that it is not an interpolation. If it be a forgery, I agree with our author, that it is, "no vulgar forgery."[93] But to return from the digression which this note has occasioned.

"Whatever opinion may be entertained of his conjecture," says our author, "it is evident that the effects, as well as the cause of Nero's persecution, were confined to the walls of Rome."[94] This is by no means evident, when the matter is fully stated.

[91] It appears to have been first publickly attacked by Tanaquil Faber, about the middle of last century. Perhaps the character that Mr. Gibbon has given of this author, in his former work, may on this occasion, be applied, in a bad sense, rather than a good one. - "La *Finesse* de Taneguy le Fevre." Essai, &c. p. 13.

[92] One of the principal objections insisted on, is drawn from the *silence* of Origen, and other of the fathers, concerning this passage. The words of Bp. Parker, seem to deserve attention. "This is the hard condition that our critics have of late put upon all authors, to quote all that ever they read, and to think of every thing that is pertinent to their cause; but this seems too severe an imposition upon the memories of mankind." What too if some of these Fathers could not have quoted this passage with propriety, according to the nature of their design? It is the evident design of Justin Martyr, and Tertullian, to dispute against the Jews, purely out of the writings of the *prophets*. Our author *laments* that the fathers *in general* draw their arguments principally from the prophecies. (see p. 517) - Perhaps too the reasoning of Dr. Lardner himself, mutatis mutandis, may well be applied on this occasion. "Supposing Josephus not to have said any thing of Jesus Christ, some may ask, what could be the reason of it? And how can it be accounted for? To which I might answer, that such a question is rather more *curious* than judicious and important." (Testimonies, vol. i. ch. iv. p. 168.)

[93] Some of the objections that seem principally to have influenced our author in forming his opinion, are perhaps easily removed. Why should it excite our wonder so particularly that Josephus has born witness to the miracles and resurrection of Jesus, when Celsus himself has done the same? That Josephus acknowledges him to be the Messiah, we cannot grant. St. Jerome's version (in the fourth century) renders this part of the passage, not, hic *erat Christus*, but hic *credebatur* esse Christus. And Josephus elsewhere doubts, whether Moses as well as Christ, was not more than man. (Antiq. l.3.c.15.) It is a common form of speech too, with such Greek and Latin writers, as Josephus often imitates, to give the title of Gods, to all great and extraordinary persons.

[94] P. 537.

His own proof (and the only proof) is, that the Spanish inscription in Gruter, is a manifest and acknowledged imposition.[95] But this is at least not *universally* acknowledged.[96]

Admit however, that the inscription is spurious, there are other evidences from divers antient Christian writers, which ought not to have been suppressed, and which tend to prove that the Christians suffered in the *provinces*, as well as the city.[97] Nero's laws against the Christians must be understood to have been general laws. And those who contend that these laws were repealed by the senate after his death, acknowledge nevertheless, that there were such laws.[98]

Should it be thought therefore, that Nero's persecution was not confined to the walls of Rome (an opinion which Suetonius's testimony strongly countenances)[99] it will be probable also in opposition to another assertion of our author's, "that the religious tenets of the Christians, *were* made a subject of inquiry."[100]

His attempt to defend the cause of Nero is succeeded by an apology for Domitian. It is doubted whether this emperor, any more than Nero, can be ranked among the persecutors of Christianity. We will refer the question wholly, to the unsuspected testimony of an heathen historian, which, important as it is, our author hath passed over in silence. He has produced his testimony, so far only as it relates to Clemens and Domitilla; yet in the very same passage, it follows immediately, that "on a like accusation, MANY OTHERS also were condemned. Some of whom, were put to death, others suffered the confiscation of their goods."[101] It should seem now, that the

[95] Note 42. on Ch. xvi. p. lxxix.

[96] Dr. Lardner acknowledges the authenticity of this inscription to be doubtful, but is himself strongly inclined to receive it as genuine. vol. 1. ch. 3.

[97] Lardner, as above.

[98] For instance, Mosheim de rebus Christianis ante C. M. Sect. 2. vii. Suetonius also mentions Nero's proceedings against the Christians, along with other *ordinances* and *institutions* of Nero, in ROME. Dr. Lardner also hesitates not to affirm, that there *had* been laws in force against the Christians, in the time of Nero and Domitian.

[99] See Lardner's argument from it.

[100] P. 537.

[101] Επενηχθη δε αμφοιν εγκλημα αθεοτητος, εφ ης και ΑΛΛΟΙ ες τα των Ιουδαιων ηθη εποκελλοντες ΠΟΛΛΟΙ κατεδικαοθησαν. Και οι μεν απεθανον, οι δε των ουσιων εσερηθησαν. Dion. Hist. l. 67.

cruelty of Domitian, may justly, be "branded with the name of the second persecution."[102]

We come now to consider the conduct of the Roman princes and magistrates, as to the nature of the punishments they inflicted.

Their bold apologist, has not scrupled to affirm, that "they were moderate in the use of their punishments."

It is indeed true, that the Christian, often had the alternative of life and death, set before him. It is true, he might meet with pardon; but it was a pardon offered to one, who had committed no crime. It was a pardon offered on terms, however they may appear "easy"[103] to our author, which could not be complied with. It mattered not to him, whose conscience forbad his compliance altogether, whether he was called upon to make open sacrifice of his faith, "by casting a few grains of incense upon the altar"[104] or by prostrating himself solemnly before some detested idol. In either case the very "applause"[105] which he might expect, would in effect prove that he was equally understood, to have made an explicit renunciation of his faith. The proper question therefore will be, whether those who imposed on their inoffensive subjects, the cruel necessity of betraying their consciences, in order to save their life, can be at all defended; not whether the terms proposed, might in some sort be considered rather as "a legal evasion"[106] than a formal declaration. It should ever be remembered, that it was not the profligate criminal, but the inoffensive citizen; it was not the daring enemy of society, but the friend of mankind, that was the victim of the various punishments of Roman cruelty.

But there are yet other striking instances of clemency, which in our author's opinion, decorate the annals of Roman persecution. Death was by no means the punishment, on all occasions. These *humane* judges, "contented themselves for

[102] P. 539. From the criticism of Mosheim already refer'd to, and from the opinion of Dodwell (Diff. Cyprianicæ Diff. xi.) both founded on a remarkable passage of Tertullian (eæ leges quas Trajanus ex parte frustratus est) it may be collected with much probability, that DOMITIAN as well as NERO had passed edicts against the Christians.

[103] P. 543.

[104] ibid.

[105] P. 543.

[106] P. 545.

the most part, with the milder chastisements of imprisonment, exile, or slavery in the mines;"[107] nay more than this, those who endured this last *mild* punishment[108] "were permitted, by the humanity, or the *negligence* of their keepers, to build chapels, and freely to profess their religion, in the midst of those dreary habitations."[109]

There may be those, we conclude, who are not so sensible of the virtues of the princes and magistrates of Rome; who find no comfort for the persecuted, in the reflection that "the several transient persecutions that were carried on, served only to revive the zeal, and restore the discipline of the faithful"[110] (through the peculiar virtue of the faithful themselves) who think it no apology for unjust cruelty, that "the moments of extraordinary rigour were compensated by much longer intervals of peace and security."[111]

Such will perhaps remark, that to contend for the humanity of the Roman magistrates, by alleging that they inflicted only imprisonment, exile, or slavery, on their inoffensive subjects, when they might have inflicted death, can only be considered, as an attempt to prove that they were not inhuman, by shewing that they might have been more inhuman.[112]

But in fact the premises as well as the conclusion, of such an argument, may be denied. In the latter persecutions of the Christians, the refined cruelty of their enemies purposely avoided inflicting death on them in order to inflict punishments

---

[107] P. 545.

[108] P. 583.

[109] From Eusebius (de Mart. Palæst. c. 13.) it appears, that even this indulgence gave offence. The governor of Palestine complained to Maximin of their enjoying this liberty. In consequence of the complaint, they were dispersed into different parts, and treated with additional cruelty.

[110] P. 555.

[111] P. 555.

[112] Other insufficient arguments of the same kind, or rather palpable fallacies, might be pointed out. Our author argues elsewhere, in favour of the judicial proceedings of the Roman Magistrates, by turning our attention to the proceedings of a *modern inquisitor*. (p. 553) And he closes his work, by reminding us, that Christians in later times, "have inflicted far greater severities on each other, than they had experienced from the zeal of infidels." That is, he attempts to justify *infidels* for having done wrong, by shewing that *Christians* have acted still more wrongly.

on them, which they themselves, thought more formidable. The words of a learned writer, who while he has laboured to lessen the number of actual martyrs, among the first Christians, has not been insensible of their real sufferings, may serve to place this matter in its proper light.

"The conduct of their persecutors, in studiously avoiding to inflict death, that they might make their torments more cruel, and protract them to a longer duration, produced this effect, that the fewer martyrdoms there were, the more illustrious the confessions became, and rivaled the fame of the martyrdoms of other times. And as the persecutors thought to elude by this art of inflicting the most dreadful tortures,"[113] but no deaths, the infamy of a "bloody administration, they indulged their native cruelty the more freely, without the hazard of losing their character."[114]

Amidst the horrors of such scenes, one is rather inclined, to wish the number of martyrs lessened, and the received faith of history, shaken and overturned. But while we avoid carefully the legendary inventions of later ages, while we at least wish not to extend the number of holy martyrs beyond the strictest letter of authentic evidence, we owe it to their memory, not to abandon the testimony that is afforded us, or admit too hastily such objections as are not valid. While I shall not therefore in any sort enter fully into the question of the numbers of the primitive martyrs, I shall yet so far attempt a discussion of it, as to point out the uncertainty, if not, fallacy of such arguments, as our author has alleged in support of his calculations. The testimony of Origen, with regard to the small number of martyrs, that had died, for the sake of the Christian religion, naturally attracts our attention. But it will cease to astonish us, when we recollect, that he lived before the time of the severest and longest

[113] The various cruelties of sometimes burning the sinews of the knees, and sometimes burning out the eyes, as is particularly related by Eusebius, (De vità Const. l. 1. c. 58. and elsewhere) were in general adopted, instead of inflicting death. Lactantius's words are too remarkable to be omitted. "Illud vero pessimum genus est, cui clementiæ species falsa blanditur; ille gravior, ille sævior carnifex qui neminem statuit *occidere*. Exquisitos dolores corporibus immittunt, & nihil aliud evitant quam ut ne torti moriantur. Non curassent tam solicitè quos amàssent."

[114] Dodwelli Dissertationes Cyprianicæ. Diss. xi. It should be observed that his arguments tend chiefly, to lessen only, the numbers of *modern* martyrologies.

persecutions that the church experienced, and that his testimony must not therefore be received as generally, as it is stated to us.[115] It cannot extend to the persecutions either of Decius or Diocletian.

That, under Decius is acknowledged to have been one of the most rigid that the Christians suffered. And that a far greater number of martyrs, than had suffered under any one prince before, must have perished in the course of the long persecution, under Diocletian, may naturally be concluded.

But even during this persecution, if we adopt our author's calculation, the number of martyrs was far less, than has been usually imagined. His calculation is founded on Eusebius's catalogue of the Martyrs of Palestine. It may perhaps appear, that the superstructure, is too weighty for the foundation. It may at least be disputed, whether the passage of Eusebius, can be said to contain that positive evidence, which our author has collected from it. It is certain, that he does not expressly say *no more than* ninety two Christians suffered.

His words are, "these were" (not there were *no more than these*) the martyrdoms inflicted in Palestine.[116] A probable argument may be advanced from his method, on other occasions, to evince, that he does not mean his catalogue should be looked upon as complete. He sometimes selects out of many martyrdoms a few only distinguished by some eminent circumstances, for particular mention. But I do not insist particularly on this conjecture, though it may receive countenance from our observing, that the martyrs of Palestine, whom he has enumerated, are all distinguished either by their superior characters, or by the peculiar circumstances of their sufferings, and their exemplary fortitude in enduring them.

A stronger argument may be derived from his own words, as they immediately follow the passage in question. He proceeds,

---

[115] Dodwell in the use of this testimony, has been more accurate than our author; he has added the words, "*ante suam ætatem.*" However obvious such a distinction is, it yet may be forgotten; and we see, it is a distinction of importance.

It is the opinion of the judicious Mosheim, that this passage can only be understood to relate to the number of martyrs, as compared with the whole body of Christians, not as considered collectively, in themselves. In the one sense, they might well be said to be few, in the other, perhaps they were justly to be called, many.

[116] Ταυτα μεν τα κατα παλαισινην εν ολοις τοις οκτω ετεσιν συμπαραθ εντα μαρτυρια. c. 13.

"such was the persecution, which began amongst us with the destruction of the Churches, and which afterwards rose to a great height, by the successive persecutions of the governors, in which the various trials of those who contended for the faith, raised up an *innumerable multitude of Martyrs* in *every* province, in the countries that reach from Africa, and throughout all *Egypt*, and Syria, and from the East, and round about, to the region of Illyricum."[117]

If then the sense of the passage, in respect of the support that has been borrowed from it, for our author's hypothesis, be, but uncertain, let it be remembered, that "the important conclusion" he draws concerning the number of martyrs, is in consequence uncertain; if it should be thought that the testimony of Eusebius, considered altogether, necessarily leads us to conclude that there were either more than ninety-two who suffered in Palestine, or that very great numbers suffered in other provinces, let it be remembered that the conclusion is false.

The declaration of Eusebius, elsewhere indeed, appears even to our author "to contradict his moderate computation,"[118] but he endeavours to obviate this objection by exhibiting a severe accusation, against the historian.

We shall willingly take for granted that the words ιστορησαμεν and υπομειναντας are altogether as ambiguous as he has represented them. Concerning the sense attributed to the first, it matters little indeed, whether we admit it or not. If Eusebius only *heard* of the many martyrs that he makes mention of, instead of *seeing* them suffer, his testimony is still sufficient, while his general character remains unimpeached. Nay it must be allowed that, as he was himself on the spot, he

[117] Τοιουτος ο καθ' ημας διωγμος, αρξαμενος μεν απο της των εκκλησιων καθαιρεσεως, εις μεγα δε προκοψας, εν ταις κατα χρονους των αρχοντων επαναστεσιν· εν αις πολυτροποι και πολυειδεις των υπερ ευσεβειας ηθλθχοτων αγωνες ανηριθμον τι πληθος μαρτυρων κατα πασαν επαρχιον συνερτησαντο· εν τοις απο λιβυης και δι' ολης αιγυπτου, συριας τε, και της' απ' ανατολης, και κυκλω, μεχρι το κατα το ιλλυρικον κλιμα παρατεινουσι. Euseb. de mart. Palœst. c. 13.

[118] Note 181. p. lxxxvii - Even before we enter into a particular review of the accusation, by looking back to a passage already quoted, from Eusebius, in which he treats of the same persecution, we may observe how little reason there can be for supposing him to have adopted "*a cautious language*" in speaking of the martyrdoms of Egypt, when he has elsewhere, so positively asserted the great number of them.

must have possessed the very best means of information. Indeed the word signifies, to hear, only so far as it signifies to hear in consequence of *enquiry*. After this state of the real force of the word, surely Eusebius may be acquitted of the charge of having adopted it, as being capable of a double sense, merely from considering how little advantage could be gained, by such equivocation. Respecting the latter word, we presume, that the historian will at once stand acquitted, of the severe charge of "providing to himself a secure evasion"[119] in the equivocal sense of it, when it is shewn, that one of the two senses attributed to it, is palpably inconsistent, even to a degree of absurdity, with the rest of the sentence. To evince this, let us adopt for a moment, the sense which it is supposed capable of, and apply it to the passage in question. It will then stand thus:

"We ourselves also, when we were on the spot, saw (or heard of) many in one day, some of whom EXPECTED to be beheaded, and some to suffer by fire; so that the murderer's sword became blunted, and unable to perform its office, and the executioners themselves, thro' fatigue, succeeded one another, by turns."[120]

The rhetorical figure in the latter part of this passage, must be considered as altogether extraordinary, if it can be maintained, that the historian meant to provide himself a secure evasion, by persuading his readers, if necessary, that the executioners were tired, and their swords blunted, from their *attendance*, to execute the punishments, which others EXPECTED but never underwent.

It ought to be added too, that in the beginning of the very same chapter, and in that preceding it, Eusebius has again made use of the same word, in such a manner, that if we give a like sense to it, we must fall into a like absurdity. In the one passage we must understand him to speak only of calamities which the MARTYRS[121] in Thebais EXPECTED, tho' he adds

[119] Note 181 p. lxxxvii.

[120] Ιστορησαμεν δε και αυτοι, επι των τοπων γενομενοι πλειους αθροως κατα μιαν ημεραν, τους μεν της κεφαλης αποτομην υπομειναντας, τους δε την δια πυρος τιμωριαν· ως αμβλυνεσθαι φονευοντα τον σιδηρον, ατονουντα τε διαθλασθαι· αυτους τε τους αναιρουμενους υποκαμνοντας αμοιβαδον αλληλους διαδεχεσθαι. Euseb. Lib. viii. cap. 9. (De iis qui in Thebaide passi sunt.)

[121] The very word μαρτυρες might be sufficient to ascertain the sense of this passage, since Eusebius is remarkably accurate in distinguishing between martyrs and confessors. (ομολογηται)

immediately, that they were tormented to death; and in the other to assert only, that numbers EXPECTED different deaths, tho' it is subjoined, that some of these were *drowned*, some *starved*, some *burnt*, and some *crucified*.

May we not conclude then, that this accusation serves to refute itself, by its own absurdity, and to exhibit a very unhappy instance of refined criticism?[122]

But a yet heavier attack on the venerable historian, remains behind. "He very frankly confesses, says our author, that he has related whatsoever might redound to the glory, and that he has suppressed all that could tend to the disgrace of religion."[123] Let us at least hear Eusebius, in his own defence, before we utterly condemn him. We may however, venture to assert, that there is an inconsistency in the accusation, even at first sight, upon the strength of an authority, that even the critical exactness of our author, will not condemn. When he *himself* informs us "of THE CORRUPTION OF MANNERS AND PRINCIPLES" (among the first Christians) "so FORCIBLY LAMENTED by Eusebius,"[124] I am totally at a loss to reconcile the historian's conduct on this occasion, with that of one, who suppresses all that can tend to the disgrace of his cause. For once at least, even his accuser must confess, that the historian has been very remarkably inconsistent with himself.

Still however, his own words, as *they stand represented to us*, must upon the whole serve to condemn him, if no more favourable interpretation of them, can justly be adopted. Some alleviation of the charge at least, I presume, rather an entire refutation of it, may be derived from permitting Eusebius to speak for himself more fully, in the passages refered to. As his character is at stake, in the translation I shall give, I shall prefer exactness to elegance.

After describing a variety of affecting circumstances that had attended the persecutions of the first Christians, as *seen by himself*, in the first passage, he proceeds thus:

"But it is not our part to describe the sad calamities which at last befel them, since it does not agree with our plan, to

---

[122] I do not take notice of our author's reflection on the *artful management of the historian*, in choosing Thebais for his scene, since till it can be *proved* that Thebais was not the scene of such cruelty, the whole is a mere begging of the question: nor can I make a compliment of *granting* it.

[123] P. 583.

[124] P. 564.

36 *Religious Scepticism*

relate their dissentions and wickedness, before the persecution; on which account we have determined to relate nothing more concerning them, than may serve to justify the divine judgment. We therefore have not been induced to make mention either of those who were tempted in the persecution, nor of those who made utter shipwreck of their salvation, and were sunk of their own accord in the depths of the storm; but shall only add those things to our general history, which may in the first place be profitable to ourselves, and afterwards to posterity."[125]

On a candid examination of this passage, may we not say, that no just accusation against Eusebius, can be deduced from it? He explains his own plan consistently; he considers himself according to it, not as a complete historian of the times, but rather as a *didactic*[126] writer, whose main object it is, to make his work, like the scriptures themselves, "profitable for doctrine." As he treats only of the affairs of the church, the plan surely is at least excusable, perhaps peculiarly proper; and if he has been but faithful, in relating those facts which fall within the compass of his design (nor is any direct accusation as yet brought against him in this respect) he is so far at least, consistent with himself, and may so far be depended on, for his relation of facts. Nay more, he will appear even to have conformed himself to that just idea of the principal duty of history, according to which, as elegantly stated by our author, "it undertakes to record the transactions of the past, for the INSTRUCTION of future ages."[127] And let it be remarked still farther, that neither can he well be said to have "suppressed all

---

[125] Αλλα τουτων μεν ουχ ημετερον διαγραφειν τας επι τελει σκυθρωπας συμφορας· επει και τας προσθεν τον διωγμου διαστασεις τε αυτων εις αλληλους, και ατοπιας, ουχ ημιν οικειον μνημη παραδιδοναι· διο και πλεον ουδεν ιστορησαι περι αυτων εγνωμεν, η δι' ων αν την θειαν δικαιωσαιμεν κρισιν· ουκουν ουδε των προς τον διωγμου πεπειραμενων, η των εις απαν της σωτηριας νεναυαγηκοτων, αυτη τε γνωμη τους του κλυδωνος εναπορριφεντων βυθοις μνημην ποιησασθαι προηχθημεν, μονα δε εκεινα τη καθολου προσθνσομεν ιστορια, α πρωτον μεν ημιν αυτοις, επειτα δε και τοις μεθ' ημας, γενοιτ' αν προς ωφελειας. Euseb. Lib. viii. c. 2.

[126] His own declaration, made elsewhere, of his reasons for principally relating the martyrdoms that had been inflicted, confirms this idea. - ουχ ιστορικην αυτο μονον, αλλα και ΔΙΔΑΣΚΑΛΙΚΗΝ περιεχον διηγησιν· Proæm. ad Lib. 5. E. H.

[127] P. 529.

that could tend to the disgrace of religion," who, while according to his more immediate design, he has not indeed particularly related such transactions, has yet openly and fully acknowledged them.

This, as well as the express nature of his design, will appear yet farther, on considering the other passage.

Eusebius here again, expressly mentions "dissentions among the confessors themselves," but again declares that it is his intent "to pass over all these things" agreeably to his former declaration. He then quotes the very words of scripture, as best descriptive of his immediate design, "Whatsoever things are honest, whatsoever things are of good report, if there be any virtue, and if there be any praise, these things he thinks it most suitable to an history of martyrs, to lay before his readers."[128]

I shall add but one remark more. It should be remembered, that while Eusebius omits the particular history of such transactions, as were disgraceful to the first Christians, he omits also the particular history of many of the oppressions, of their enemies.

I trust now, Eusebius, may still lay claim to the character of a faithful historian. Unless an author's right to choose his own subject can be contested, (and that too, for the particular benefit of his reader) no accusation can lie against him, from his own declaration, *fairly interpreted*.

But the character of this pious historian, seems indeed to have been peculiarly obnoxious to our author. At the close of his work, he is transported beyond the usual temper of his writings, and rises into a stile of the severest declamation, against "the courtly bishop."[129]

---

[128] It is impossible to reconcile the express words of the charge exhibited, with any part of either of the passages appealed to. There is a remarkable agreement between the interpretation which Mr. Gibbon has adopted, and the French translation of Monsʳ. Cousin. "He (Eusebius) has related whatever MIGHT REDOUND TO THE GLORY, and suppressed all that could tend to the disgrace of RELIGION," are the words of the former. "Ne voulant donc rien mettre devant les yeux de fideles, que ce qui peut RELEVER L'HONNEUR DE NOTRE RELIGION," are the words in which, the latter, according to his loose method of interpretation, has chosen to express what forms the substance of full three preceding sentences; and has at the same time misled, his readers, wholly as to the true sense of his author.

I leave it to others, to account for this striking similarity between the interpretations of Mr. Gibbon and Monsʳ Cousin.

[129] Dr. Jortin, whom, those who know the free turn of his writings, will not

He has however fortunately himself furnished us with a strong case in point, that may serve to free the character of Eusebius, from the vague imputation thrown upon him.

In the very same instance, in which, to adopt our author's phrase, "*it suited the purpose*[130] of Lactantius, to place the death of Maxentius, among those of the persecutors," Eusebius has exempted even this "*vanquished rival*" of Constantine, from the charge of persecution.

Yet how natural was it for "*the passionate declaimer,*"[131] according to the idea our author has given us of him, to have caught fire on the occasion and availed himself of his "*exclusive privilege*"[132] to stain the memory of this most distinguished rival of his "gracious sovereign" with all possible infamy.

Lactantius was distinguished by the favour of Constantine, as well as Eusebius; but it could not certainly have *suited the purpose* of the one, less than of the other, to place Maxentius in the most odious light. It may not perhaps be impossible, to reconcile, in some degree, the different accounts of these two authors. Though the prudence of the tyrant, led him to tolerate the Christians, as a sect, yet his acknowledged cruelties towards his subjects, in general,[133] may well be conceived, to have been occasionally exercised, on some at least among the Christians. Lactantius, perhaps thought that facts of this kind justified him in placing his death among those of the persecutors; Eusebius, even *courtly* and *passionate* as he was, chose rather to relate his general conduct, than to dwell on particular facts.

> suspect of partiality, nor those who know his learning and diligence, of judging hastily, gives us a far different idea of Eusebius's character. "He had the favour and friendship of Constantine, which he seems never to have used in depressing or hurting others, *or in getting any thing for himself; and he refused to change his bishoprick for a better.*" (Remarks on E. H. Vol. iii. p. 161.)

[130] Note 167. p. lxxxvii. – The same phrase is elsewhere applied to the writings of the truly-respectable Bp. Pearson. (See note 92. p. lxxxiii.) They that are well read in the *Free Enquiry, &c.* will not perhaps be at a loss to discover the disciple of Dr. Middleton, on this, as well as other occasions. "Forged *for a particular purpose,*" and "*singularly adapted to his argument,*" are some of the phrases, which the *Free Enquirer* applies to the writings of the most venerable of the Fathers of the Church.

[131] P. 584.

[132] P. 584.

[133] See our author's idea of his character, and of the motives of his conduct towards the Christians, P. 577.

Having now accompanied our author to the close of his laborious work, let us turn back to estimate the true nature and force of his disquisitions, by supposing for a moment, the utmost success to have attended them.

They contain an attempt to account for the growth of Christianity, from the end of the *second*[134] century, by the aid of human causes. They tend to lessen the supposed numbers of the first Christians, while they unavoidably shew, at the same time, that their numbers were considerable. Other testimonies not adduced by our author, confirm the same idea.[135] They tend to apologize for the conduct of the Roman government, towards their persecuted subjects, but they no where assert that the Christians in general, were guilty of such crimes as deserved the severest punishments. They tend to censure the uncharitable sentiments and the private vices of a few individuals, but they bear witness, in a general view, to "the pure, and austere morals of the Christians."[136]

What then if our historian had succeeded, even, in every one of his positions?

We had still remained in full possession of all the most important evidences of our Religion, of the evidence even of its MIRACULOUS PROPAGATION, during the age of the Apostles, and of the extraordinary continuance of it, for at least a century afterwards. We had still surveyed with pleasure the general characters of the first Christians, and we had had sufficient occasion to admire the amazing fortitude of some

---

[134] See remarks at the beginning of this tract, p. 2.

[135] There is a very remarkable testimony, in particular, of the *Apostate* Julian, the declared enemy of Christianity. He supposes, that there were in *many cities of Greece and Italy multitudes of believers in Jesus*, before John wrote his gospel. See the passage quoted by Dr. Lardner, vol. iv, ch. xlvi. Though we may have some reason to suspect the zealous temper of Tertullian, of a degree of exaggeration, his testimony is yet too striking to be omitted. "Hesterni sumus, & vestra omnia implevimus, urbes, insulas, castella, municipia, conciliabula, castra ipsa, tribus, decurias, senatum, forum; sola vobis relinquimus templa." Apolog. c. 36.

[136] To this *human* cause, much certainly may be attributed. Julian, the avowed enemy of Christianity bears honourable testimony to the manners of the first Christians, in attributing the success of the gospel, *principally* to this circumstance. He reproaches the Gentiles for not imitating their philanthropy, and their distinguished charity, in maintaining, besides their own poor, the poor of their *enemies* also. Τρεφουσι δε οι δυσσεβεις Γαλιλαιοι, προς τοις εαυτων, και τους ημετερους. Epist. xlix. edit. Paris 1630, 4to.

40 *Religious Scepticism*

thousands of martyrs,[137] and of a far greater number of confessors.

In any case, it would remain yet, to achieve many other, still more difficult labours, before the melancholy triumph, of having eradicated Christianity out of the minds of men, could be enjoyed by any one.

But what then, shall we say, if our author be found to have failed altogether in his attempts; if his several *human* causes, are either inadequately, or improperly alleged;[138] if his conjectures are ill supported, and his arguments in general, weak and fallacious? Christianity surely derives a new triumph on this, as well as on former occasions, from the unsuccessful attack that has been made upon it. However we may admire the talents of our author, we have but too much reason to lament the use he has made of them. His extensive researches into antiquity, and his polished stile, interest us in his favour. But he is the less entitled to our thanks for the agreeable entertainment he has set before us, while it is our duty to complain, of his ungenerous treatment of Christianity. The characters of his history, at one time utter the most false imputations,[139] at another, oppose, even the sacred truths of religion, with ridicule, instead of argument; and use those

---

[137] Our author's own calculation (the certainty of which we have had occasion to call in question) according to *the annual consumption*, of martyrs which he supposes to have taken place, in the course of *one* persecution only, amounts to near two thousand. (See p. 585) Taking in every other persecution, we may safely say, *many* thousands.

[138] It may perhaps be remarked justly, that our author's own recapitulation of the five causes principally insisted on (p. 502) does not give that force to them, which the use they were intended for, requires. They are summoned (p. 450) to account for the rapid *growth* of the Christian church. It appears in the end, that at the most, they can account only for the continuance, and *defence* of it. The first, we are told, inspired the Christians with that valour, which *disdained to capitulate*; the three succeeding causes, "supplied their valour, with the most formidable arms" the last, "united their courage, and directed their arms." Through the whole of this delineation, no other idea can be discovered, but that of a successful *resistance* to a persecuting enemy, not of a triumphant victory over them, without bloodshed, by making friends, of enemies.

[139] Besides some other similar instances already pointed out, our author has not hesitated to *close* a sentence of praise, with the impious railleries of Celsus. In the offensive language of this virulent enemy of Christianity, the *miraculous* birth of Christ, is represented to us as "equivocal" and the life of him WHO WENT ABOUT DOING GOOD, is stigmatized as a "*wandering life.*" (See p. 526.)

weapons, which are alone to be dreaded, because they are indirectly aimed.

We have seen him, influenced too often, by the same malicious spirit; we have seen him, aiming the most deadly and unmerited blows, at the respectable character of a grave historian, and pleading the cause of paganism, with his utmost eloquence, as if retained in its service, by some lawful obligation. He has not however, failed to remember that "the wise" of this world "abuse in doubt and dispute, their vain superiority of reason and knowledge."[140] And this melancholy instance of human frailty, might perhaps have afforded an useful caution. May he enjoy, unenvied, the honourable triumph of being justly distinguished, in the republic of letters! I cannot but add a wish, that he had secured to himself also, the far nobler, heart-felt triumph of having benefited mankind, by using his endeavours to promote among them, the only true "system of love and harmony."

An opportunity will yet present itself, in the intended prosecution of his work, for making some atonement to the injured Genius of Christianity. The remarkable period of its first civil establishment, may naturally suggest, the respect that is due to it, from every good citizen, who lives under the protection of those laws, of which it is the only firm support.

But the friend of mankind, will be still more strongly influenced by the reflection, that should his writings, have been the means of depriving but one honest man of his faith in Christianity, he has robbed that man of all his better hopes, and has taken from him, that source of comfort, for which he can offer him no equivalent.

Such considerations may properly be urged even to those, who doubt of the truth of Revelation.

But I may add, that in any cause, to form decisions on a slight examination, to adopt unwarrantable censures, and to follow servilely the objections of others,[141] is utterly repugnant

---

[140] P. 474.

[141] Our author's too fond attachment to Dr. Middleton, appears to have betrayed him into one very remarkable misrepresentation. "Irenæus" he informs us, (p. 475) in an age in which the gift of tongues was common, "was left to struggle with the difficulties of a barbarous dialect." The objection is urged, more openly, in the Free Enquiry (p. 119) and is founded on an utter misrepresentation of the passage in Irenæus. (Præf. adv. Hær. l. 1. 2.) Far from acknowledging either the want of the language of Gaul, or any *difficulties* respecting it, Irenæus apologizes only

to that natural duty, which obliges us to employ our faculties, in the discovery of truth. When important passages are misrepresented, when the characters of venerable writers are sacrificed to false criticism, neither the diligence of an impartial inquirer, the discernment of a scholar, nor the fidelity of an historian, are discoverable.

I have now only to address myself, for the last time, more immediately to you. Did not I know, your regard for truth, above all, for religious truth, I might think, I owed you an apology for having so long detained you, with researches far more important, than amusing. The plan I have followed, neither admitted, nor required, the pleasing ornaments of stile. To contend with an ingenious writer, step by step, is a painful employment, even to him that undertakes it. But it was necessary, and it might prove useful, to expose fallacious reasoning, to detect insufficient proofs, and to point out the suppression of material evidence. If it should be thought, that I have been in any degree, useful in an important cause, I shall have succeeded to the utmost of my wishes.

I cannot however conclude, without lamenting, the hard fate of those, who from sincere conviction, think it incumbent on them to oppose the attacks of infidelity. The enemies of religion assume at pleasure, a variety of shapes; and they scruple not to repeat the most partial objections, nay to collect them studiously, under the delusive appearance of novelty.

The apologist of religion, can adopt but one mode of defence; conclusive indeed, and satisfactory to those who search patiently after truth, but simple and unadorned, and destitute of the charms, either of variety or novelty, for those who seek only to be amused. He is obliged sometimes to repeat the observations of others; and he may to some perhaps, seem altogether to insist on obvious and well-known truths. It is too often forgotten, that repeated attacks require repeated answers; and that the cause of religion is too sacred and

for his want of eloquence, of the knowledge of composition, and of the ornaments of stile, in his writings, from his residence among the Celtæ, and his being for the most part used to a *barbarous* dialect. It should be observed, that our author does not refer to the passage itself, in Irenæus, for the support of assertion, but introduces only in his note, (as on many other occasions) a *new* remark. (Note 72. p. lxx.) Had he either examined the passage itself, or attended fairly to both sides of the question, by reading the answers to Dr. Middleton's work, he could not have fallen into so gross a mistake.

important, not to lay claim to continual defence. Not to be ready to oppose the enemy, as often as he returns to the charge, would be in some sort to abandon the field, and to acknowledge tacitly, the superiority of his forces.

One comfort, however, remains to the apologist of religion, amidst every disadvantage arising from the conduct of its adversaries; amidst the use of those arts which he disdains to imitate, and of those indirect censures, which it is difficult to refute. He cannot but be conscious to himself, that he endeavours to defend those truths, which are of the highest importance to mankind.

I am, &c.

AN APOLOGY FOR CHRISTIANITY, IN A SERIES OF LETTERS, ADDRESSED TO EDWARD GIBBON
by Richard Watson

LETTER FIRST.

SIR,
It would give me much uneasiness to be reputed an Enemy to free inquiry in religious matters, or as capable of being animated into any degree of personal malevolence against those who differ from me in opinion. On the contrary, I look upon the right of private judgment, in every concern respecting God and ourselves, as superior to the control of human authority; and have ever regarded free disquisition, as the best mean of illustrating the doctrine, and establishing the truth of Christianity. Let the followers of Mahomet, and the zealots of the church of Rome, support their several religious systems by damping every effort of the human intellect to pry into the foundations of their faith; but never can it become a Christian, to be afraid of being asked a *reason of the faith that is in him*; nor a Protestant, to be studious of enveloping his religion in mystery and ignorance; nor the church of England, to abandon that moderation, by which she permits every individual *et sentire quæ velit, et quæ sentiat dicere*.

It is not, Sir, without some reluctance, that, under the influence of these opinions, I have prevailed upon myself to address these letters to you; and you will attribute to the same motive, my not having given you this trouble sooner. I had moreover an expectation, that the task would have been undertaken by some person, capable of doing greater justice to the subject, and more worthy of your attention. Perceiving however, that the two last chapters, the fifteenth in particular, of your very laborious and classical history of the Decline and Fall of the Roman empire, had made upon many an impression not at all advantageous to Christianity; and that the silence of others, of the Clergy especially, began to be looked upon as an acquiescence in what you had therein advanced; I have thought it my duty, with the utmost respect and good-will towards you, to take the liberty of suggesting to your consideration, a few remarks upon some of the passages, which have been esteemed, (whether you meant, that they should be so esteemed, or not) as powerfully militating against that revelation, which still is to many, what it formerly was *to the Greeks, Foolishness*; but which we deem to be true, to *be the power of God unto salvation to every one that believeth*.

To the inquiry, by what means the Christian faith obtained so remarkable a victory over the established religions of the earth, you rightly answer, By the evidence of the doctrine itself, and the ruling providence of it's Author. But afterwards, in assigning for this astonishing event five secondary causes, derived from the passions of the human heart and the general circumstances of mankind, you seem to some to have insinuated, that Christianity, like other Impostures, might have made it's way in the world, though it's origin had been as human as the means by which you suppose it was spread. It is no wish or intention of mine, to fasten the odium of this insinuation upon you; I shall simply endeavour to shew, that the causes you produce, are either inadequate to the attainment of the end proposed; or that their efficiency, great as you imagine it, was derived from other principles than those, you have thought proper to mention.

Your first cause is "the inflexible, and, if you may use the expression, the intolerant zeal of the Christians, derived, it is true, from the Jewish religion, but purified from the narrow and unsocial spirit, which instead of inviting, had deterred the Gentiles from embracing the law of Moses." – Yes, Sir, we are agreed, that the zeal of the Christians was inflexible, *neither death, nor life, nor principalities, nor powers, nor things present, nor things to come*, could bend it into a separation *from the love of God, which was in Christ Jesus their Lord*; it was an inflexible obstinacy, in not blaspheming the name of Christ, which every where exposed them to persecution; and which even your amiable and philosophic Pliny thought proper, for want of other crimes, to punish with death in the Christians of his province. – We are agreed too, that the zeal of the Christians was intolerant; for it denounced *tribulation and anguish upon every soul of man that did evil, of the Jew first, and also of the Gentile*; it would not tolerate in Christian worship, those who supplicated the image of Cæsar, who bowed down at the altars of Paganism, who mixed with the votaries of Venus, or wallowed in the filth of Bacchanalian festivals.

But though we are thus far agreed, with respect to the inflexibility and intolerance of Christian zeal; yet as to the principle from which it was derived, we are *toto cœlo* divided in opinion. You deduce it from the Jewish religion; I would refer it to a more adequate and a more obvious source, a full persuasion of the truth of Christianity. What! think you that it was a zeal derived from the unsociable spirit of Judaism, which inspired Peter with courage to upbraid the whole people of the Jews in the very capital of Judea, with having *delivered up Jesus, with having denied him in the presence of Pilate, with having desired a murderer to be granted them in his stead, with having killed the Prince of life*? Was it from this principle, that the same Apostle in conjunction with John, when summoned, not before the dregs of the people, (whose judgments they might have been supposed capable of misleading, and whose resentment they might have despised,) but before the rulers and the elders and the scribes, the dread Tribunal of the Jewish nation, and commanded by them to teach no more in the name of Jesus; boldly answered, *that they could not but speak the things, which they had seen and heard? - they had seen with their eyes, they had handled with their hands the word of life*; and no human jurisdiction could deter them from being faithful witnesses of what they had seen and heard. Here then you may perceive the genuine and undoubted origin of that zeal, which you ascribe to what appears to me a very insufficient cause; and which the Jewish rulers were so far from considering as the ordinary effect of their religion, that they were exceedingly at a loss how to account for it; - *now when they saw the boldness of Peter and John, and perceived that they were unlearned and ignorant men, they marvelled*. The Apostles, heedless of consequences, and regardless of every thing but truth, openly every where professed themselves witnesses of the resurrection of Christ; and with a confidence, which could proceed from nothing but conviction, and which pricked the Jews to the heart, bade *the house of Israel know assuredly, that God had made that same Jesus, whom they had crucified, both Lord and Christ.*

I mean not to produce these instances of apostolic zeal, as direct proofs of the truth of Christianity; for every religion, nay, every absurd sect of every religion, has had it's zealots, who have not scrupled to maintain their principles at the expence of their lives; and we ought no more to infer the truth of Christianity from the mere zeal of it's propagators, than the truth of Mahometanism from that of a Turk. When a man suffers himself to be covered with infamy, pillaged of his property, and dragged at last to the block or the stake, rather than give up his opinion; the proper inference is, not that his opinion is true, but that he believes it to be true; and a question of serious discussion immediately presents itself, – upon what foundation has he built his belief? This is often an intricate inquiry, including in it a vast compass of human learning; a Bramin or a Mandarin, who should observe a missionary attesting the truth of Christianity with his blood, would, notwithstanding, have a right to ask many questions, before it could be expected, that he should give an assent to our faith. In the case indeed of the Apostles, the inquiry would be much less perplexed; since it would briefly resolve itself into this, – whether they were credible reporters of facts, which they themselves professed to have seen: – and it would be an easy matter to shew, that their zeal in attesting what they were certainly competent to judge of, could not proceed from any alluring prospect of worldly interest or ambition, or from any other probable motive than a love of truth.

But the credibility of the Apostles' testimony, or their competency to judge of the facts which they relate, is not now to be examined; the question before us simply relates to the principle, by which their zeal was excited; and it is a matter of real astonishment to me, that any one conversant with the history of the first propagation of Christianity, acquainted with the opposition it every where met with from the people of the Jews, and aware of the repugnancy which must ever subsist between it's tenets and those of Judaism, should ever think of deriving the zeal of the primitive Christians from the Jewish religion.

Both Jew and Christian, indeed, believed in one God, and abominated idolatry; but this detestation of idolatry, had it been unaccompanied with the belief of the resurrection of Christ, would probably have been just as inefficacious in exciting the zeal of the Christian to undertake the conversion of the Gentile world, as it had for ages been in exciting that of the Jew. But supposing, what I think you have not proved, and what I am certain cannot be admitted without proof, that a zeal derived from the Jewish religion inspired the first Christians with fortitude to oppose themselves to the institutions of Paganism; what was it, that encouraged them to attempt the conversion of their own countrymen? Amongst the Jews they met with no superstitious observances of idolatrous rites; and therefore amongst them, could have no opportunity of "declaring and confirming their zealous opposition to Polytheism, or of fortifying by frequent protestations their attachment to the Christian faith." Here then at least, the cause you have assigned for Christian zeal ceases to operate; and we must look out for some other principle than a zeal against idolatry, or we shall never be able satisfactorily to explain the ardour, which which the Apostles pressed the disciples of Moses, to become the disciples of Christ.

Again, does a determined opposition to, and an open abhorrence of, every the minutest part of an established religion, appear to you to be the most likely method of conciliating to another faith those who profess it? The Christians, you contend, could neither mix with the Heathens in their convivial entertainments, nor partake with them in the celebration of their solemn festivals; they could neither associate with them in their hymenæal, nor funereal rites; they could not cultivate their arts, or be spectators of their shews; in short, in order to escape the rites of Polytheism, they were, in your opinion, obliged to renounce the commerce of mankind, and all the offices and amusements of life. Now, how such an extravagant and intemperate zeal as you here describe, can, humanly speaking, be considered as one of the chief causes of the quick propagation of Christianity, in opposition to all the established powers of Paganism, is a circumstance I can by no means comprehend. The Jesuit missionaries, whose human prudence no one will question, were quite of a contrary way of thinking; and brought a deserved censure upon themselves, for not scrupling to propagate the faith of Christ, by indulging to their Pagan converts a frequent use of idolatrous ceremonies. Upon the whole it appears to me, that the Christians were in no wise indebted to the Jewish religion, for the zeal with which they propagated the gospel amongst Jews as well as Gentiles; and that such a zeal as you describe, let its principle be what you please, could never have been devised by any human understanding, as a probable mean of promoting the progress of a reformation in religion; much less could it have been thought of, or adopted by a few ignorant and unconnected men.

In expatiating upon this subject you have taken an opportunity of remarking, that "the contemporaries of Moses and Joshua had beheld with careless indifference the most amazing miracles – and that in contradiction to every known principle of the human mind, that singular people (the Jews) seems to have yielded a stronger and more ready assent to the traditions of their remote ancestors, than to the evidence of their own senses." This observation bears hard upon the veracity of the Jewish scriptures; and, was it true, would force us either to reject them, or to admit a position as extraordinary as a miracle itself; – that the testimony of others produced in the human mind, a stronger degree of conviction concerning a matter of fact, than the testimony of the senses themselves. – It happens however, in the present case, that we are under no necessity of either rejecting the Jewish scriptures, or of admitting such an absurd position; for the fact is not true, that the contemporaries of Moses and Joshua beheld with careless indifference, the miracles related in the Bible to have been performed in their favour. That these miracles were not sufficient to awe the Israelites into an uniform obedience to the Theocracy, cannot be denied; but, whatever reasons may be thought best adapted to account for the propensity of the Jews to idolatry, and their frequent defection from the worship of the one true God, a "stubborn incredulity" cannot be admitted as one of them.

To men, indeed, whose understandings have been enlightened by the Christian revelation, and enlarged by all the aids of human learning; who are under no temptations to idolatry from without, and whose reason from within, would revolt at the idea of worshipping the infinite Author of the universe under any created symbol;– to men who are compelled, by the utmost exertion of their reason, to admit as an irrefragable truth, what puzzles the first principles of all reasoning – the eternal existence of an uncaused Being; – and who are conscious, that they cannot give a full account of any one phænomenon in nature, from the rotation of the great orbs of the universe to the germination of a blade of grass, without having recourse to him, as the primary incomprehensible cause of it; – and who from seeing him every where, have, by a strange fatality, (converting an excess of evidence into a principle of disbelief) at times doubted concerning his existence any where, and made the very universe their God; – to men of such a stamp, it appears almost an incredible thing, that any human being which had seen the order of nature interrupted, or the uniformity of it's course suspended, though but for a moment, should ever afterwards lose the impression of reverential awe, which, they apprehend, would have been excited in their minds. But whatever effect the visible interposition of the Deity might have in removing the scepticism, or confirming the faith of a few Philosophers, it is with me a very great doubt, whether the people in general of our days, would be more strongly affected by it, than they appear to have been in the days of Moses.

Was any people under heaven, to escape the certain destruction impending over them, from the close pursuit of an enraged and irresistible enemy, by seeing the waters of the Ocean *becoming a wall to them on their right hand and on their left*; they would, I apprehend, be agitated by the very same passions we are told the Israelites were, when they saw the sea returning to his strength, and swallowing up the host of Pharaoh; they *would fear the Lord, they would believe the Lord*, and they would express their faith and their fear by praising the Lord: – they would not behold such a great work with *careless indifference*, but with astonishment and terror; nor would you be able to detect the slightest vestige of *stubborn incredulity* in their song of gratitude. No length of time would be able to blot from their minds the memory of such a transaction, or induce a doubt concerning it's Author, though future hunger and thirst might make them call out for water and bread, with a desponding and rebellious importunity.

But it was not at the Red Sea only, that the Israelites regarded with something more than a *careless indifference* the amazing miracles which God had wrought; for when the law was declared to them from mount Sinai, *all the people saw the thunderings, and the lightenings, and the noise of the tempest, and the mountain smoking; and when the people saw it, they removed and stood afar off, and they said unto Moses, Speak thou with us, and we will hear; but let not God speak with us, lest we die.* – This again, Sir, is the Scripture account of the language of the contemporaries of Moses and Joshua; and I leave it to you to consider, whether this is the language of *stubborn incredulity, and careless indifference.*

We are told in Scripture too, that whilst any of the *contemporaries* of Moses and Joshua were alive, the whole people served the Lord, the impression, which a sight of the miracles had made, was never effaced; nor the obedience, which might have been expected as a natural consequence, refused, till Moses and Joshua, and all their contemporaries, were gathered unto their fathers; till *another generation after them arose, which knew not the Lord, nor yet the works which he had done for Israel.* – But *the people served the Lord all the days of Joshua, and all the days of the elders that outlived Joshua, who had seen all the great works of the Lord that he did for Israel.*

I am far from thinking you, Sir, unacquainted with Scripture, or desirous of sinking the weight of it's testimony; but as the words of the history, from which you must have derived your observation, will not support you, in imputing *careless indifference* to the contemporaries of Moses, or *stubborn incredulity* to the forefathers of the Jews; I know not what can have induced you to pass so severe a censure upon them, except that you look upon a lapse into idolatry as a proof of infidelity. In answer to this, I would remark, that with equal soundness of argument we ought to infer, that every one who transgresses a religion, disbelieves it; and that every individual, who in any community incurs civil pains and penalties, is a disbeliever of the existence of the authority by which they are inflicted. The sanctions of the Mosaic law were, in your opinion, terminated within the narrow limits of this life; in that particular then, they must have resembled the sanctions of all other civil laws: *transgress and die* is the language of every one of them, as well as that of Moses; and I know not what reason we have to expect, that the Jews, who were animated by the same hopes of temporal rewards, impelled by the same fears of temporal punishments with the rest of mankind, should have been so singular in their conduct, as never to have listened to the clamours of passion before the still voice of reason; as never to have preferred a present gratification of sense, in the lewd celebration of idolatrous rites, before the rigid observance of irksome ceremonies.

Before I release you from the trouble of this letter, I cannot help observing, that I could have wished you had furnished your reader with Limborch's answers to the objections of the Jew Orobio, concerning the perpetual obligation of the law of Moses; you have indeed mentioned Limborch with respect, in a short note; but though you have studiously put into the mouths of the Judaising Christians in the Apostolic days, and with great strength inserted into your text, whatever has been said by Orobio, or others against Christianity, from the supposed perpetuity of the Mosaic dispensation; yet you have not favoured us with any one of the numerous replies, which have been made to these seemingly strong objections. You are pleased, it is true, to say, "that the industry of our learned divines has abundantly explained the ambiguous language of the old Testament, and the ambiguous conduct of the Apostolic teachers." It requires, Sir, no learned industry, to explain what is so obvious and so express, that he who runs may read it: The language of the old Testament is this; *Behold, the days come, saith the Lord, that I will make a new covenant with the house of Israel, and with the house of Judah; not according to the covenant that I made with their fathers, in the day that I took them by the hand to bring them out of the land of Egypt.* This, methinks, is a clear and solemn declaration, there is no ambiguity at all in it, that the covenant with Moses was not to be perpetual, but was in some future time to give way to a *new covenant*. I will not detain you with an explanation of what Moses himself has said upon this subject; but you may try, if you please, whether you can apply the following declaration, which Moses made to the Jews, to any prophet or succession of prophets, with the same propriety that you can to Jesus Christ; – *The Lord thy God will raise up unto thee a Prophet, from the midst of thee, of thy brethren, like unto me, unto him shall ye hearken.* If you think this ambiguous or obscure, I answer, That it is not a history, but a prophecy; and as such unavoidably liable to some degree of obscurity, till interpreted by the event.

Nor was the conduct of the Apostles more ambiguous, than the language of the old Testament; they did not indeed at first comprehend the whole of the nature of the new dispensation; and when they did understand it better, they did not think proper upon every occasion to use their Christian liberty; but, with true Christian charity, accommodated themselves in matters of indifference to the prejudices of their weaker brethren. But he who changes his conduct with a change of sentiments, proceeding from an increase of knowledge, is not ambiguous in his conduct; nor should he be accused of a culpable duplicity, who in a matter of the last importance endeavours to conciliate the good-will of all, by conforming in a few innocent observances to the particular persuasions of different men.

One remark more, and I have done. In your account of the Gnostics, you have given us a very minute catalogue of the objections, which they made to the authority of Moses, from his account of the creation, of the patriarchs, of the law, and of the attributes of the Deity: I have not leisure to examine, whether the Gnostics of former ages really made all the objections you have mentioned. I take it for granted, upon your authority, that they did: but I am certain if they did, that the Gnostics of modern times have no reason to be puffed up with their knowledge, or to be had in admiration as men of subtile penetration or refined erudition; they are all miserable copiers of their brethren of antiquity; and neither Morgan, nor Tindal, nor Bolingbroke, nor Voltaire, have been able to produce scarce a single new objection. You think, that the Fathers have not properly answered the Gnostics. I make no question, Sir, you are able to answer them to your own satisfaction; and informed of every thing, that has been said by our *industrious divines* upon the subject: and we should have been glad, if it had fallen in with your plan to have administered together with the poison it's antidote; but since that is not the case, lest it's malignity should spread too far, I must just mention it to my younger readers, that Leland and others, in their replies to the modern Deists, have given very full, and, as many learned men apprehend, very satisfactory answers to every one of the objections, which you have derived from the Gnostic heresy.

I am, &c.

LETTER SECOND.

SIR,

"The doctrine of a future life, improved by every additional circumstance, which could give weight and efficacy to that important truth," is the second of the causes to which you attribute the quick increase of Christianity. Now if we impartially consider the circumstances of the persons, to whom the doctrine, not simply of a future life, but of a future life accompanied with punishments as well as rewards; not only of the immortality of the soul, but of the immortality of the soul accompanied with that of the resurrection, was delivered; I cannot be of opinion that, abstracted from the supernatural testimony by which it was enforced, it could have met with any very extensive reception amongst them.

It was not that kind of future life, which they expected; it did not hold out to them the punishments of the infernal regions, as *aniles fabulas*: to the question, *Quid si post mortem maneant animi*? they could not answer with Cicero and the philosophers, – *Beatos esse concedo*; – because there was a great probability, that it might be quite otherwise with them. I am not to learn, that there are passages to be picked up in the writings of the antients, which might be produced as proofs of their expecting a future state of punishment for the flagitious; but this opinion was worn out of credit, before the time of our Saviour: the whole disputation in the first book of the Tusculan Questions, goes upon the other supposition: nor was the absurdity of the doctrine of future punishments confined to the writings of the philosophers, or the circles of the learned and polite; for Cicero, to mention no others, makes no secret of it in his public pleadings before the people at large. You yourself, Sir, have referred to his oration for Cluentius; in this oration, you may remember, he makes great mention of a very abandoned fellow, who had forged I know not how many wills, murdered I know not how many wives, and perpetrated a thousand other villainies; yet even to this profligate, by name Oppianicus, he is persuaded, that death was not the occasion of any evil[1]. Hence, I think, we may conclude, that such of the Romans, as were not wholly infected with the annihilating notions of Epicurus, but entertained, (whether from remote tradition, or enlightened argumentation,) hopes of a future life, had no manner of expectation of such a life, as included in it the severity of punishment, denounced in the Christian scheme against the wicked.

---

[1] Nam nunc quidem quid tandem mali illi mors attulit? nisi forte ineptiis ac fabulis ducimur, ut existimemus apud inferos impiorum supplicia perferre; ac plures illic offendisse inimicos quam hic reliquisse – quæ si falsa sint, id quod omnes intelligunt, &c.

Nor was it that kind of future life, which they wished; they would have been glad enough of an Elysium, which could have admitted into it men who had spent this life, in the perpetration of every vice, which can debase and pollute the human heart. To abandon every seducing gratification of sense, to pluck up every latent root of ambition, to subdue every impulse of revenge, to divest themselves of every inveterate habit, in which their glory and their pleasure consisted; to do all this and more, before they could look up to the doctrine of a future life, without terror and amazement, was not, one would think, an easy undertaking; nor was it likely, that many would forsake the religious institutions of their ancestors, set at nought the gods, under whose auspices the Capitol had been founded, and Rome made mistress of the world, and suffer themselves to be persuaded into the belief of a tenet, the very mention of which made Felix tremble, by any thing less than a full conviction of the supernatural authority of those who taught it.

The several schools of Gentile philosophy had discussed, with no small subtlety, every argument, which reason could suggest, for and against the immortality of the soul; and those uncertain glimmerings of the light of nature, would have prepared the minds of the learned for the reception of the full illustration of this subject by the gospel, had not the resurrection been a part of the doctrine therein advanced. But that this corporal frame, which is hourly mouldering away, and resolved at last into the undistinguished mass of elements, from which it was at first derived, should ever be *clothed with immortality; that this corruptible should* ever *put on incorruption*, is a truth so far removed from the apprehension of philosophical research, so dissonant from the common conceptions of mankind, that amongst all ranks and persuasions of men it was esteemed an impossible thing. At Athens the philosophers had listened with patience to St. Paul, whilst they conceived him but a *setter forth of strange gods*; but as soon as they comprehended, that by the αναστασις, he meant the resurrection, they turned from him with contempt. It was principally the insisting upon the same topic, which made Festus think, *that much learning had made him mad:* and the questions, *how are the dead raised up? and, with what body do they come?* seem, by Paul's solicitude to answer them with fullness and precision, to have been not unfrequently proposed to him, by those who were desirous of becoming Christians.

The doctrine of a future life then, as promulged in the gospel, being neither agreeable to the expectations, nor corresponding with the wishes, nor conformable to the reason of the Gentiles, I can discover no motive, (setting aside the true one, the divine power of it's first preachers) which could induce them to receive it; and in consequence of their belief, to conform their loose morals to the rigid standard of gospel purity, upon the mere authority of a few contemptible fishermen of Judea. And even you yourself, Sir, seem to have changed your opinion, concerning the efficacy of the expectation of a future life in converting the Heathens, when you observe in the following chapter, that "the Pagan multitude reserving their gratitude for temporal benefits alone, rejected the inestimable present of life and immortality, which was offered to mankind by Jesus of Nazareth."

Montesquieu is of opinion, that it will ever be impossible for Christianity to establish itself in China and the east, from this circumstance, that it prohibits a plurality of wives: how then could it have been possible for it to have pervaded the voluptuous Capitol, and traversed the utmost limits of the empire of Rome, by the feeble efforts of human industry, or human knavery?

But the Gentiles, you are of opinion, were converted by their fears; and reckon the doctrines of Christ's speedy appearance, of the millennium, and of the general conflagration, amongst those additional circumstances, which gave weight to that concerning a future state. Before I proceed to the examination of the efficiency of these several circumstances, in alarming the apprehensions of the Gentiles, what if I should grant your position? Still the main question recurs, From what source did they derive the fears, which converted them? Not surely from the mere human labours of men, who were every where spoken against, made a spectacle of, and considered as the filth of the world, and the offscouring of all things – not surely from the human powers of him, who professed himself *rude in speech, in bodily presence contemptible*, and a despiser of *the excellency of speech, and the enticing words of men's wisdom.* No, such wretched instruments were but ill fitted, to inspire the haughty, and the learned Romans, with any other passions than those of pity, or contempt.

Now, Sir, if you please, we will consider that universal expectation of the approaching end of the world, which, you think, had such great influence in converting the Pagans to the profession of Christianity. The near approach, you say, of this wonderful event had been predicted by the Apostles, "though the revolution of seventeen centuries has instructed us, not to press too closely the mysterious language of prophecy and revelation". That this opinion, even in the times of the Apostles, had made it's way into the Christian church, I readily admit; but that the Apostles ever, either predicted this event to others, or cherished the expectation of it in themselves, does not seem probable to me. As this is a point of some difficulty and importance, you will suffer me to explain it at some length.

It must be owned, that there are several passages in the writings of the Apostles, which, at the first view, seem to countenance the opinion you have adopted. *Now*, says St. Paul, in his epistle to the Romans, *it is high time to awake out of sleep; for now is our salvation nearer than when we believed: the night is far spent, the day is at hand.* And in his first epistle to the Thessalonians, he comforts such of them as were sorrowing for the loss of their friends, by assuring them, that they were not lost for ever; but that the Lord when he came, would bring them with him; and that they would not, in the participation of any blessings, be in any wise behind those, who should happen then to be alive; *we*, says he, (the Christians of whatever age or country, agreeable to a frequent use of the pronoun *we*) *which are alive, and remain unto the coming of the Lord, shall not prevent them which are asleep; for the Lord himself shall descend from heaven with a shout, with the voice of the archangel, and with the trump of God, and the dead in Christ shall rise first: then, we which are alive and remain, shall be caught up together with them in the clouds, to meet the Lord.* In his epistle to the Philippians, he exhorts his Christian brethren, not to disquiet themselves with carking cares about their temporal concerns, from this powerful consideration, that the Lord was at hand; *let your moderation be known unto all men; the Lord is at hand; be careful about nothing.* The apostle to the Hebrews, inculcates the same doctrine, admonishing his converts *to provoke one another to love, and to good works; and so much the more, as they saw the day approaching.* The age in which the Apostles lived, is frequently called by them the end of the world, the last days, the last hour. I think it unnecessary, Sir, to trouble you with an explication of these and other similar texts of scripture, which are usually adduced in support of your opinion; since I hope to be able to give you a direct proof, that the Apostles neither comforted themselves, nor encouraged others with the delightful hope of seeing their master coming again into the world. It is evident then, that St. John, who survived all the other Apostles, could not have had any such expectation; since in the Book of the Revelation, the future events of the Christian church, which were not to take place, many of them, till a long series of years after his death, and some of which have not yet been accomplished, are there minutely described. St. Peter, in like manner, strongly intimates, that the day of the Lord might be said to be at hand, though it was at the distance of a thousand years or more; for in replying to the taunt of those who did then, or should in future ask, *Where is the promise of his coming?* he says, *Beloved, be not ignorant of this one thing, that one day is with the Lord as a thousand years, and a thousand years as one day: the Lord is not slack concerning his promise, as some men count slackness.* And he speaks of putting off his tabernacle, as the Lord had shewed him; and of his endeavour, that the Christians after his decease, might be able to have these things in remembrance: so that it is past a doubt, he could not be of opinion, that the Lord would come in his time. As to St. Paul, upon a partial view of whose writings the doctrine concerning the speedy coming of Christ is principally founded; it is manifest, that he was conscious he should not live to see it, notwithstanding the expression before mentioned, *we which are alive*; for he foretels his own death in express terms – *the time of my departure is at hand*; and he speaks of his reward, not as immediately to be conferred on him; but as laid up, and reserved for him till some future day – *I have fought a good fight, I have finished my course; henceforth there is laid up for me a crown of righteousness, which the Lord, the righteous judge, shall give me at that day.* There is moreover one passage in his writings, which is so express, and full to the purpose, that it will put the matter, I think, beyond all doubt; it occurs in his second Epistle to the Thessalonians: They, it seems, had either by misinterpreting some parts of his former letter to them, or by the preaching of some, who had not the spirit of truth; by some means or other, they had been led to expect the speedy coming of Christ, and been greatly disturbed in mind upon that account: To remove this error, he writes to them in the following very solemn and affectionate manner; *We beseech you, brethren, by the coming of our Lord Jesus Christ, and by our gathering together unto him, that ye be not soon shaken in mind, or be troubled, neither by spirit, nor by word, nor by letter as from us, as that the day of the Lord is at hand; let no man deceive you by any means.* He then goes on to describe a falling away, a great corruption of the Christian church, which was to happen before the day of the Lord: now by this revelation of the man of sin, this mystery of iniquity, which is to be consumed with the spirit of his mouth, destroyed with the brightness of his coming, we have every reason to believe, is to be understood the past and present abominations of the church of Rome. How then can it be said of Paul, who clearly foresaw this corruption above seventeen hundred years ago, that he expected the coming of the Lord in his own day? Let us press, Sir, the mysterious language of prophecy and revelation, as closely as you please; but let us press it truly; and we may, perhaps, find reason from thence to receive, with less reluctance, a religion, which describes a corruption, the strangeness of which, had it not been foretold in unequivocal terms, might have amazed even a friend to Christianity.

I will produce you, Sir, a prophecy, which, the more closely you press it, the more reason you will have to believe, that the speedy coming of Christ could never have been *predicted* by the Apostles. Take it, as translated by Bishop Newton: *But the Spirit speaketh expressly, that in the latter times, some shall apostatize from the faith; giving heed to erroneous spirits, and doctrines concerning demons, through the hypocrisy of liars; having their conscience seared with a red hot iron; forbidding to marry, and commanding to abstain from meats.* - Here you have an express prophecy - the Spirit hath spoken it - that in the latter times - not immediately, but at some distant period - some should apostatize from the faith - some, who had been Christians, should in truth be so no longer - but should give heed to erroneous spirits, and doctrines concerning demons; - Press this expression closely, and you may, perhaps, discover in it the erroneous tenets, and the demon, or saint worship of the church of Rome; - through the hypocrisy of liars: - you re-recognize, no doubt, the priesthood, and the martyrologists; - having their conscience seared with a red hot iron: - callous, indeed, must his conscience be, who trafficks in indulgences; - forbidding to marry, and commanding to abstain from meats:

– this language needs no pressing; it discovers, at once, the unhappy votaries of monastic life, and the mortal sin of eating flesh on fast days.

If, notwithstanding what has been said, you should still be of opinion, that the Apostles expected Christ would come in their time; it will not follow, that this their error ought in any wise to diminish their authority as preachers of the gospel. I am sensible, this position may alarm even some well-wishers to Christianity; and supply it's enemies with, what they will think, an irrefragable argument: the Apostles, they will say, were inspired with the spirit of truth; and yet they fell into a gross mistake, concerning a matter of great importance; how is this to be reconciled? Perhaps, in the following manner: When the time of our Saviour's ministry was nearly at an end, he thought proper to raise the spirits of his disciples, who were quite cast down with what he had told them about his design of leaving them; by promising, that he would send to them the holy Ghost, the Comforter, the Spirit of truth; who should teach them all things, and lead them into all truth. And we know, that this his promise was accomplished on the day of Pentecost, when they were all filled with the holy Ghost; and we know farther, that from that time forward, they were enabled to speak with tongues, to work miracles, to preach the word with power, and to comprehend the mystery of the new dispensation, which was committed unto them. But we have no reason from hence to conclude, that they were immediately inspired with the apprehension of whatever might be known; that they became acquainted with all kinds of truth: they were undoubtedly led into such truths, as it was necessary for them to know, in order to their converting the world to Christianity; but in other things, they were probably left to the exercise of their understandings, as other men usually are. But surely they might be proper witnesses of the life and resurrection of Christ, though they were not acquainted with every thing, which might have been known; though in particular, they were ignorant of the precise time, when our Lord would come to judge the world. It can be no impeachment, either of their integrity as men, or their ability as historians, or their honesty as preachers of the gospel, that they were unacquainted with what had never been revealed to them; that they followed their own understandings, where they had no better light to guide them; speaking from conjecture, when they could not speak from certainty; of themselves, when they had no commandment of the Lord. They knew but in part, and they prophesied but in part; and concerning this particular point, Jesus himself had told them, just as he was about finally to leave them, that it was not for them to *know the times and the seasons, which the Father had put in his own power.* Nor is it to be wondered at, that the Apostles were left in a state of uncertainty, concerning the time in which Christ should appear; since Beings, far more exalted and more highly favoured of heaven they they, were under an equal degree of ignorance; *Of that day,* says our Saviour, *and of that hour, knoweth no one; no, not the angels which are in heaven, neither the Son, but the Father only.* I am afraid, Sir, I have tired you with scripture quotations; but if I have been fortunate enough to convince you, either that the speedy coming of Christ was never expected, much less *predicted*, by the Apostles; or that their mistake in that particular expectation, can in no degree diminish the general weight of their testimony as historians, I shall not be sorry for the *ennui* I may have occasioned you.

The doctrine of the Millennium, is the second of the circumstances which you produce, as giving weight to that of a future state; and you represent this doctrine as having been "carefully inculcated by a succession of the fathers, from Justin Martyr and Irenæus down to Lactantius;" and observe, that when "the edifice of the church was almost completed, the temporary support was laid aside;" and in the notes, you refer us, as a proof of what you advance, to "Irenæus, the disciple of Papias, who had seen the Apostle St. John," and to the second Dialogue of Justin with Trypho.

I wish, Sir, you had turned to Eusebius, for the character of this Papias, who had seen the Apostle St. John; you would there have found him represented as little better than a credulous old woman; very averse from reading, but mightily given to picking up stories and traditions next to fabulous; amongst which Eusebius reckons this of the Millennium one. Nor is it, I apprehend, quite certain, that Papias ever saw, much less discoursed, as seems to be insinuated, with the Apostle St. John. Eusebius thinks rather, that it was John the presbyter he had seen. But what if he had seen the Apostle himself? many a weak-headed man had undoubtedly seen him, as well as Papias; and it would be hard indeed upon Christians, if they were compelled to receive as apostolical traditions, the wild reveries of ancient enthusiasm, or such crude conceptions of ignorant fanaticism, as nothing but the rust of antiquity can render venerable.

As to the works of Justin, the very Dialogue you refer to contains a proof, that the doctrine of the Millennium had not, even in his time, the universal reception you have supposed; but that many Christians of pure and pious principles rejected it. I wonder, how this passage escaped you; but it may be, that you followed Tillotson, who himself followed Mede, and read in the original ου, instead of αυ; and thus unwarily violated the idiom of the language, the sense of the context, and the authority of the best editions.[2] In the note you observe, that it is unnecessary for you to mention all the intermediate fathers between Justin and Lactantius, as the fact, you say, is not disputed. In a man, who has read so many books, and to so good a purpose, he must be captious indeed, who cannot excuse small mistakes: that unprejudiced regard to truth, however, which is the great characteristic of every distinguished historian, will, I am persuaded, make you thank me for recalling to your memory, that Origen, the most learned of all the fathers, and Dionysius, bishop of Alexandria, usually for his immense erudition surnamed the Great, were both of them prior to Lactantius, and both of them impugners of the Millennium doctrine. Look, Sir, into Mosheim, or almost any writer of ecclesiastical history; and you will find the opposition of Origen and Dionysius to this system, particularly noticed: look into so common an author as Whitby; and in his learned treatise upon this subject, you will find he has well proved these two propositions; first, that this opinion of the Millennium was never generally received in the church of Christ: secondly, that there is no just ground to think it was derived from the Apostles. From hence, I think, we may conclude, that this

[2] Justin, in answering the question proposed by Trypho, Whether the Christians believed the doctrine of the Millennium, says, Ωμολογησα ουν σοι και προτερον, οτι εγω μεν και αλλοι πολλοι ταυτα φρονουμεν, ως και παντως επισταθε, τουτο γενησομενον. Πολλους δ' αυ και των της ΚΑΘΑΡΑΣ ΚΑΙ ΕΥΣΕΒΟΥΣ οντων Χριστιανων ΓΝΩΜΗΣ τουτο μη γνωριζειν, εσημανα σοι. The note subjoined to this passage out of Justin, in Thirlby's Ed. an. 1722. is, Πολλους δ'αυ και των της καθαρας Medus (quem sequitur Tillotsonus, Reg. Fidei per. iii. sect, 9. p. 756. & seq.) legit των ου της καθαρας. Vehementer errant viri præclari.

And in Jebb's Edit. an. 1719. we have the following note: Doctrina itaque de Millennio, neque erat universalis ecclesiæ traditio, nec opinio de fide recepta, &c.

An Apology for Christianity 63

Millennium doctrine, (which, by the bye, though it be new modelled, is not yet thrown aside) could not have been any very serviceable scaffold, in the erection of that mighty edifice, which has crushed by the weight of it's materials, and debased by the elegance of it's structure, the stateliest temples of heathen superstition. With these remarks, I take leave of the Millennium; just observing, that your third circumstance, the general conflagration, seems to be effectually included in your first, the speedy coming of Christ.
       I am, Sir,

LETTER THIRD.

SIR,
You esteem "the miraculous powers ascribed to the primitive church," as the third of the secondary causes of the rapid growth of Christianity; I should be willing to account the miracles, not merely ascribed to the primitive church, but really performed by the Apostles, as the one great primary cause of the conversion of the Gentiles. But waving this consideration, let us see whether the miraculous powers, which you ascribe to the primitive church, were in any eminent degree calculated to spread the belief of Christianity amongst a great, and an enlightened people.

They consisted, you tell us, "of divine inspirations, conveyed sometimes in the form of a sleeping, sometimes of a waking vision; and were liberally bestowed on all ranks of the faithful, on women as on elders, on boys as well as upon Bishops." "The design of these visions, you say, was for the most part either to disclose the future history, or to guide the present administration of the church."

"You speak of the expulsion of Demons as an ordinary triumph of religion, usually performed in a public manner; and when the patient was relieved by the skill or the power of the Exorcist, the vanquished Demon was heard to confess, that he was one of the fabled gods of antiquity, who had impiously usurped the adoration of mankind"; and you represent even the miracle of the resurrection of the dead, as frequently performed on necessary occasions. - Cast your eye, Sir, upon the church of Rome, and ask yourself, (I put the question to your heart, and beg you will consult that for an answer; ask yourself,) whether her absurd pretensions to that very kind of miraculous powers, you have here displayed as operating to the increase of Christianity, have not converted half her numbers to Protestantism, and the other half to Infidelity? Neither the sword of the civil magistrate, nor the possession of the keys of heaven, nor the terrors of her spiritual thunder, have been able to keep within her Pale, even those who have been bred up in her faith; how then should you think, that the very cause, which hath almost extinguished Christianity amongst Christians, should have established it amongst Pagans? I beg, I may not be misunderstood; I do not take upon me to say, that all the miracles recorded in the history of the primitive church after the apostolical age, were forgeries; it is foreign to the present purpose to deliver any opinion upon that subject; but I do beg leave to insist upon this, that such of them as were forgeries, must in that learned age, by their easy detection, have rather impeded, than accelerated the progress of Christianity: and it appears very probable to me, that nothing but the recent prevailing evidence, of real, unquestioned, apostolical miracles, could have secured the infant church from being destroyed by those, which were falsely ascribed to it.

It is not every man, who can nicely separate the corruptions of religion from religion itself; nor justly apportion the degrees of credit due to the diversities of evidence; and those, who have ability for the task, are usually ready enough to emancipate themselves from gospel restraints, (which thwart the propensities of sense, check the ebullitions of passion, and combat the prejudices of the world at every turn,) by blending it's native simplicity with the superstitions, which have been derived from it. No argument so well suited to the indolence or the immorality of mankind, as that priests of all ages and religions are the same; we see the pretensions of the Romish priesthood to miraculous powers, and we know them to be false; we are conscious, that they at least must sacrifice their integrity to their interest, or their ambition; and being persuaded, that there is a great sameness in the passions of mankind, and in their incentives to action; and knowing, that the history of past ages is abundantly stored with similar claims to supernatural authority, we traverse back in imagination the most distant regions of antiquity; and finding, from a superficial view, nothing to discriminate one set of men, or one period of time from another; we hastily conclude, that all revealed religion is a cheat, and that the miracles attributed to the Apostles themselves, are supported by no better testimony, nor more worthy our attention, than the prodigies of Pagan story, or the lying wonders of papal artifice. I have no intention in this place, to enlarge upon the many circumstances, by which a candid inquirer after truth might be enabled to distinguish a pointed difference between the miracles of Christ and his Apostles, and the tricks of antient or modern superstition. One observation I would just suggest to you upon the subject; the miracles recorded in the old and new Testament, are so intimately united with the narration of common events, and the ordinary transactions of life, that you cannot, as in profane history, separate the one from the other. My meaning will be illustrated by an instance; Tacitus and Suetonius have handed down to us an account of many great actions performed by Vespasian; amongst the rest, they inform us of his having wrought some miracles, of his having cured a lame man, and restored sight to one that was blind. But what they tell us of these miracles, is so unconnected with every thing that goes before and after, that you may reject the relation of them without injuring, in any degree, the consistency of the narration of the other circumstances of his life: On the other hand, if you reject the relation of the miracles said to have been performed by Jesus Christ, you must necessarily reject the account of his whole life, and of several transactions, concerning which we have the undoubted testimony of other writers besides the Evangelists. But if this argument should not strike you, perhaps the following observation may tend to remove a little of the prejudice, usually conceived against gospel miracles, by men of lively imaginations, from the gross forgeries attributed to the first ages of the church.

The phænomena of physicks are sometimes happily illustrated by an Hypothesis; and the most recondite truths of Mathematical science not unfrequently investigated, from an absurd position; what if we should try the same method of arguing in the case before us. Let us suppose then, that a new revelation was to be promulged to mankind, and that twelve unlearned and unfriended men, inhabitants of any country most odious and despicable in the eyes of Europe, should by the power of God be endowed with the faculty of speaking languages they had never learned, and performing works surpassing all human ability; and that being strongly impressed with a particular truth, which they were commissioned to promulgate, they should travel, not only through the barbarous regions of Africa, but through all the learned and polished states of Europe; preaching every where with unremitted sedulity a new religion, working stupendous miracles in attestation of their mission, and communicating to their first converts (as a seal of their conversion) a variety of spiritual gifts; does it appear probable to you, that after the death of these men, and probably after the deaths of most of their immediate successors, who had been zealously attached to the faith they had seen so miraculously confirmed, that none would ever attempt to impose upon the credulous or the ignorant, by a fictitious claim to supernatural powers? would none of them aspire to the gift of tongues? would none of them mistake phrensy for illumination, and the delusions of a heated brain for the impulses of the spirit? would none undertake to cure inveterate disorders, to expel Demons, or to raise the dead? As far as I can apprehend, we ought, from such a position, to deduce, by every rule of probable reasoning, the precise conclusion, which was in fact verified in the case of the Apostles; every species of miracles, which heaven had enabled the first preachers to perform, would be counterfeited, either from misguided zeal, or interested cunning; either through the imbecility, or the iniquity of mankind; and we might just as reasonably conclude, that there never was any piety, charity, or chastity in the world, from seeing such plenty of pretenders to these virtues, as that there never were any real miracles performed, from considering the great store of those, which have been forged.

But, I know not how it has happened, there are many in the present age (I am far from including you, Sir, in the number) whose prejudices against all miraculous events have arisen to that height, that it appears to them utterly impossible for any human testimony, however great, to establish their credibility. I beg pardon for stiling their reasoning, prejudice; I have no design to give offence by that word; they may, with equal right, throw the same imputation upon mine; and I think it just as illiberal in Divines, to attribute the scepticism of every Deist to wilful infidelity; as it is in the Deists, to refer the faith of every Divine to professional biass. I have not had so little intercourse with mankind, nor shunned so much the delightful freedom of social converse, as to be ignorant, that there are many men of upright morals and good understandings, to whom, as you express it, "a latent and even involuntary scepticism adheres;" and who would be glad to be persuaded to be Christians: and how severe soever some men may be in their judgements concerning one another; yet we Christians at least, hope, and believe, that the great Judge of all will make allowance for "our habits of study and reflection," for various circumstances, the efficacy of which in giving a particular bent to the understandings of men, we can neither comprehend, nor estimate. For the sake of such men, if such should ever be induced to throw an hour away in the perusal of these letters, suffer me to step for a moment out of my way, whilst I hazard an observation or two upon the subject.

Knowledge is rightly divided by Mr. Locke into intuitive, sensitive, and demonstrative; it is clear, that a past miracle can neither be the object of sense, nor of intuition, nor consequently of demonstration; we cannot then, philosophically speaking, be said to know, that a miracle has ever been performed. But in all the great concerns of life, we are influenced by probability, rather than knowledge: and of probability, the same great author establishes two foundations; a conformity to our own experience, and the testimony of others. Now it is contended, that by the opposition of these two principles, probability is destroyed; or, in other terms, that human testimony can never influence the mind to assent to a proposition repugnant to uniform experience. – Whose experience do you mean? you will not say, your own; for the experience of an individual reaches but a little way; and no doubt, you daily assent to a thousand truths in politicks, in physicks, and in the business of common life, which you have never seen verified by experience. – You will not produce the exprience of your friends; for that can extend itself but a little way, beyond your own. – But by uniform experience, I conceive, you are desirous of understanding the experience of all ages and nations since the foundation of the world. I answer, first; how is it, that you become acquainted with the experience of all ages and nations? You will reply, from history. – Be it so: – peruse then, by far the most antient records of antiquity; and if you find no mention of miracles in them, I give up the point. Yes; – but every thing related therein respecting miracles, is to be reckoned fabulous. – Why? – Because miracles contradict the experience of all ages and nations. Do you not perceive, Sir, that you beg the very question in debate? for we affirm, that the great and learned nation of Egypt, that the Heathen inhabiting the land of Canaan, that the numerous people of the Jews, and the nations, which, for ages, surrounded them, have all had great experience of miracles. You cannot otherways obviate this conclusion, than by questioning the authenticity of that book; concerning which, Newton, when he was writing his Commentary on Daniel, expressed himself to the person,[3] from whom I had the anecdote, and which deserves not to be lost; "I find more sure marks of authenticity in the Bible, than in any profane history whatsoever."

However, I mean not to press you with the argument *ad verecundiam*; it is needless to solicit your modesty, when it may be possible, perhaps, to make an impression upon your judgment: I answer therefore, in the second place, that the admission of the principle, by which you reject miracles, will lead us into absurdity. The laws of gravitation, are the most obvious of all the laws of nature; every person in every part of the globe, must of necessity have had experience of them: There was a time, when no one was acquainted with the laws of magnetism; these suspend in many instances the laws of gravity; nor can I see, upon the principle in question, how the rest of mankind could have credited the testimony of their first discoverer; and yet to have rejected it, would have been to reject the truth. But that a piece of iron should ascend gradually from the earth, and fly at last with an increasing rapidity through the air; and attaching itself to another piece of iron, or to a particular species of iron ore, should remain suspended in opposition to the action of it's gravity, is consonant to the laws of nature. – I grant it; but there was a time, when it was contrary, I say not to the laws of nature, but to the uniform experience of all preceding ages and countries; and at that particular point of time, the testimony of an individual, or of a dozen individuals, who should have reported themselves eye witnesses of such a fact, ought, according to your argumentation, to have been received as fabulous. And what are those laws of nature, which, you think, can never be

---

[3] Dr. Smith, late Master of Trinity College.

suspended? are they not different to different men, according to the diversities of their comprehension and knowledge? and if any one of them, (that, for instance, which rules the operations of magnetism or electricity,) should have been known to you or to me alone, whilst all the rest of the world were unacquainted with it; the effects of it would have been new, and unheard of in the annals, and contrary to the experience of mankind; and therefore ought not, in your opinion, to have been believed.
Nor do I understand, what difference, as to credibility, there could be, between the effects of such an unknown law of nature and a miracle; for it is a matter of no moment, in that view, whether the suspension of the known laws of nature be effected, that is, whether a miracle be performed, by the mediation of other laws that are unknown, or by the ministry of a person divinely commissioned; since it is impossible for us to be certain, that it is contradictory to the constitution of the universe, that the laws of nature, which appear to us general, should not be suspended, and their action overruled by others, still more general, though less known; that is, that miracles should not be performed before such a Being as Man, at those times, in those places, and under those circumstances, which God, in his universal providence, had preordained.
I am, &c.

LETTER FOURTH.

SIR,
I readily acknowledge the utility of your fourth cause, "the virtues of the first Christians," as greatly conducing to the spreading their religion; but then you seem to quite mar the compliment you pay them, by representing their virtues, as proceeding either from their repentance for having been the most abandoned sinners, or from the laudable desire of supporting the reputation of the society, in which they were engaged.

That repentance is the first step to virtue, is true enough; but I see no reason for supposing, according to the calumnies of Celsus and Julian, "that the Christians allured into their party, men, who washed away in the waters of baptism the guilt, for which the temples of the gods refused to grant them any expiation." The Apostles, Sir, did not, like Romulus, open an asylum for debtors, thieves, and murderers; for they had not the same sturdy means of securing their adherents from the grasp of civil power; they did not persuade them to abandon the temples of the gods, because they could there obtain no expiation for their guilt; but because every degree of guilt, was expiated in them with too great facility; and every vice practised, not only without remorse of private conscience, but with the powerful sanction of public approbation.

"After the example, you say, of their Divine Master, the missionaries of the gospel addressed themselves to men, and especially to women, oppressed by the consciousness, and very often by the effects of their vices." – This, Sir, I really think, is not a fair representation of the matter; it may catch the applause of the unlearned, embolden many a stripling to cast off for ever the sweet blush of modesty, confirm many a dissolute veteran in the practice of his impure habits, and suggest great occasion of merriment and wanton mockery to the flagitious of every denomination and every age; but still it will want that foundation of truth, which alone can recommend it to the serious and judicious. The Apostles, Sir, were not like the Italian *Fratricelli* of the thirteenth, nor the French *Turlupins* of the fourteenth century; in all the dirt that has been raked up against Christianity, even by the worst of it's enemies, not a speck of that kind have they been able to fix, either upon the Apostles, or their Divine Master. The gospel of Jesus Christ, Sir, was not preached in single houses, or obscure villages, not in subterraneous caves and impure brothels, not in lazars and in prisons; but in the synagogues and in the temples, in the streets and in the market-places of the great capitals of the Roman provinces; in Jerusalem, in Corinth, and in Antioch, in Athens, in Ephesus, and in Rome. Nor do I any where find, that it's missionaries were ordered particularly to address themselves to the shameless women you mention; I do indeed find the direct contrary; for they were ordered to turn away from, to have no fellowship or intercourse with such, as were wont *to creep into houses, and lead captive silly women laden with sins, led away with divers lusts.* And what if a few women, who had either been seduced by their passions, or had fallen victims to the licentious manners of their age, should be found amongst those, who were most ready to receive a religion that forbad all impurity? I do not apprehend, that this circumstance ought to bring an insinuation of discredit, either upon the sex, or upon those who wrought their reformation.

That the majority of the first converts to Christianity, were of an inferior condition in life, may readily be allowed; and you yourself have in another place given a good reason for it; those who are distinguished by riches, honours, or knowledge, being so very inconsiderable in number, when compared with the bulk of mankind: But though not many mighty, not many noble, were called; yet some mighty, and some noble, some of as great reputation as any of the age in which they lived, were attached to the Christian faith. Short indeed are the accounts, which have been transmitted to us, of the first propagating of Christianity; yet even in these, we meet with the names of many, who would have done credit to any cause; I will not pretend to enumerate them all, a few of them will be sufficient to make you recollect, that there were, at least, some converts to Christianity, both from among the Jews and the Gentiles, whose lives were not stained with inexpiable crimes. Amongst these we reckon Nicodemus, a ruler of the Jews, Joseph of Arimathea, a man of fortune and a counsellor, a nobleman and a centurion of Capernaum, Jairus, Crispus, Sosthenes, rulers of synagogues, Apollos an eloquent and learned man, Zenas a Jewish lawyer, the treasurer of Candace queen of Æthiopia, Cornelius, a centurion of the Italian band, Dionysius a member of the Areopagus at Athens, and Sergius Paulus, a man of proconsular or prætorian authority, of whom it may be remarked, that if he resigned his high and lucrative office in consequence of his turning Christian, it is a strong presumption in it's favour; if he retained it, we may conclude, that the profession of Christianity was not so utterly incompatible with the discharge of the offices of civil life, as you sometimes represent it. This Catalogue of men of rank, fortune, and knowledge, who embraced Christianity, might, was it necessary, be much enlarged; and probably another conversation with St. Paul would have enabled us to grace it with the names of Festus, and King Agrippa himself; not that the writers of the Books of the new Testament seem to have been at all solicitous, in mentioning the great or the learned, who were converted to the faith: had that been part of their design, they would, in the true stile of impostors, have kept out of sight the publicans and sinners, the tanners and the tentmakers with whom they conversed and dwelt; and introduced to our notice none but those, who had been *brought up with Herod, or the chief men of Asia* – whom they had the honour to number amongst their friends.

That the Primitive Christians took great care to have an unsullied reputation, by abstaining from the commission of whatever might tend to pollute it, is easily admitted; but we do not so easily grant, that this care is a "circumstance, which usually attends small assemblies of men, when they separate themselves from the body of a nation, or the religion to which they belong." It did not attend the Nicolaitanes, the Simonians, the Menandrians, and the Carpocratians in the first ages of the church, of which you are speaking; and it cannot be unknown to you, Sir, that the scandalous vices of these very early Sectaries, brought a general and undistinguished censure upon the Christian name; and so far from promoting the increase of the church, excited in the minds of the Pagans an abhorrence of whatever respected it; it cannot be unknown to you, Sir, that several Sectaries both at home and abroad might be mentioned, who have departed from the religion to which they belonged; and which, unhappily for themselves and the community, have taken as little care to preserve their reputation unspotted, as those of the first and second centuries. If then the first Christians did take the care you mention, (and I am wholly of your opinion in that point;) their solicitude might as candidly, perhaps, and as reasonably be derived from a sense of their duty, and an honest endeavour to discharge it, as from the mere desire of increasing the honour of their confraternity by the illustrious integrity of it's members.

You are eloquent in describing the austere morality of the primitive Christians, as adverse to the propensities of sense, and abhorrent from all the innocent pleasures and amusements of life; and you enlarge, with a studied minuteness, upon their censures of luxury, and their sentiments concerning marriage and Chastity; – but in this circumstantial enumeration of their errors or their faults, (which I am under no necessity of denying or excusing,) you seem to forget the very purpose, for which you profess to have introduced the mention of them; for the picture you have drawn is so hideous, and the colouring so dismal, that instead of alluring to a closer inspection, it must have made every man of pleasure or of sense turn from it with horror or disgust; and so far from contributing to the rapid growth of Christianity by the austerity of their manners, it must be a wonder to any one, how the first Christians ever made a single convert. – It was first objected by Celsus, that Christianity was a mean religion, inculcating such a pusillanimity and patience under affronts, such a contempt of riches and worldly honours, as must weaken the nerves of civil government, and expose a society of Christians to the prey of the first invaders. This objection has been repeated by Bayle; and though fully answered by Bernard and others, it is still the favourite theme of every Esprit fort of our own age: even you, Sir, think the aversion of Christians to the business of war and government, "a criminal disregard to the publick welfare." To all that has been said upon this subject, it may with justice, I think, be answered, that Christianity troubles not itself with ordering the constitutions of civil societies; but levels the weight of all it's influence at the hearts of the individuals which compose them; and as Celsus said to Origen, was every individual in every nation a gospel Christian, there would be neither internal injustice, nor external war; there would be none of those passions, which imbitter the intercourses of civil life, and desolate the globe. What reproach then can it be to a religion, that it inculcates doctrines, which, if universally practised, would introduce universal tranquillity, and the most exalted happiness amongst mankind?

It must proceed from a total misapprehension of the design of the Christian dispensation, or from a very ignorant interpretation of the particular injunctions, forbidding us to make riches or honours a primary pursuit, or the prompt gratification of revenge a first principle of action, to infer, – that an individual Christian is obliged by his religion to offer his throat to an assassin, and his property to the first plunderer; or that a society of Christians may not repel, in the best manner they are able, the unjust assaults of hostile invasion.

I know of no precepts in the gospel, which debar a man from the possession of domestic comforts, or deaden the activity of his private friendships, or prohibit the exertion of his utmost ability in the service of the publick; the – *nisi quietum nihil beatum* – is no part of the Christian's Creed; his virtue, is an active virtue; and we justly refer to the school of Epicurus, the doctrines concerning abstinence from marriage, from the cultivation of friendship, from the

management of publick affairs, as suited to that selfish indolence, which was the favourite tenet of his philosophy.
I am, Sir,

LETTER FIFTH.
SIR,
"The union and the discipline of the Christian church," or, as you are pleased to stile it, of the Christian republic, is the last of the five secondary causes, to which you have referred the rapid and extensive spread of Christianity. It must be acknowledged, that union essentially contributes to the strength of every association, civil, military, and religious; but unfortunately for your argument, and much to the reproach of Christians, nothing has been more wanting amongst them, from the apostolic age to our own, than union. *I am of Paul, and I of Apollos, and I of Cephas, and I of Christ*, are expressions of disunion, which we meet with in the earliest period of church history; and we cannot look into the writings of any, either friend or foe to Christianity, but we find the one of them lamenting, and the other exulting in an immense catalogue of sectaries; and both of them thereby furnishing us with great reason to believe, that the divisions with respect to doctrine, worship, and discipline, which have ever subsisted in the church, must have greatly tended to hurt the credit of Christianity, and to alienate the minds of the Gentiles from the reception of such a various and discordant faith.

I readily grant, that there was a certain community of doctrine, an intercourse of hospitality, and a confederacy of discipline established amongst the individuals of every church; so that none could be admitted into any assembly of Christians, without undergoing a previous examination into his manner of life[4], (which shews by the bye, that every reprobate could not, as the fit seized him, or his interest induced him, become a Christian) and without protesting in the most solemn manner, that he would neither be guilty of murder, nor adultery, nor theft, nor perfidy; and it may be granted also, that those who broke this compact, were ejected by common consent from the confraternity into which they had been admitted; it may be

---

[4] Nonnulli præpositi sunt, qui in vitam et mores eorum, qui admittuntur, inquirant, ut non concessa facientes candidatos religionis arceant a suis conventibus. Orig. Con. Cel. Lib. 2.

further granted, that this confederacy extended itself to independent churches; and that those who had, for their immoralities, been excluded from Christian community in any one church, were rarely, if ever admitted to it by another; just as a member, who has been expelled any one College in an University, is generally thought unworthy of being admitted by any other: But it is not admitted, that this severity and this union of discipline could ever have induced the Pagans to forsake the gods of their country, and to expose themselves to the contemptuous hatred of their neighbours, and to all the severities of persecution exercised, with unrelenting barbarity, against the Christians.

The account you give of the origin and progress of episcopal jurisdiction, of the pre-eminence of the Metropolitan churches, and of the ambition of the Roman Pontiff, I believe to be in general accurate and true; and I am not in the least surprised at the bitterness, which now and then escapes you in treating this subject; for, to see the most benign religion that imagination can form, becoming an instrument of oppression; and the most humble one administering to the pride, the avarice, and the ambition of those, who wished to be considered as it's guardians, and who avowed themselves it's professors, would extort a censure from men more attached probably to church authority than yourself: Not that I think it, either a very candid, or a very useful undertaking, to be solely and industriously engaged in portraying the characters of the professors of Christianity in the worst colours; it is not candid, because "the great law of impartiality, which obliges an historian to reveal the imperfections of the uninspired teachers and believers of the gospel," obliges him also not to conceal, or to pass over with niggard and reluctant mention, the illustrious virtues of those, who gave up fortune and fame, all their comforts, and all their hopes in this life, nay, life itself, rather than violate any one of the precepts of that gospel, which, from the testimony of inspired teachers, they conceived they had good reason to believe; it is not useful, because "to a careless observer," (that is, to the generality of mankind) "*their* faults may seem to cast a shade on the faith, which they professed;" and may really infect the minds of the young and unlearned especially, with prejudices against a religion, upon their rational reception or rejection of which, a matter of the utmost importance may (believe me, Sir, it may, for ought you or any person else can prove to the contrary,) entirely depend. It is an easy matter to amuse ourselves and others with the immoralities of priests, and the ambition of prelates, with the absurd virulence of synods and councils, with the ridiculous doctrines, which visionary enthusiasts or interested churchmen have sanctified with the name of Christian; but a display of ingenuity, or erudition upon such subjects is much misplaced; since it excites almost in every person, an unavoidable suspicion of the purity of the source itself, from which such polluted streams have been derived. Do not mistake my meaning; I am far from wishing, that the clergy should be looked up to with a blind reverence, or their imperfections screened by the sanctity of their function, from the animadversion of the world: quite the contrary; their conduct, I am of opinion, ought to be more nicely scrutinized, and their deviation from the rectitude of the gospel, more severely censured, than that of other men; but great care should be taken, not to represent *their* vices, or *their* indiscretions, as originating in the principles of their religion. Do not mistake me; I am not here begging quarter for Christianity; or contending, that even the principles of our religion should be received with implicit faith, or that every objection to Christianity should be stifled, by a representation of the mischief it might do, if publicly promulged: on the contrary, we invite, nay, we challenge you to a direct and liberal attack; though oblique glances, and disingenuous insinuations, we are willing to avoid; well knowing, that the character of our religion, like that of an honest man, is defended with greater difficulty against the suggestions of ridicule, and the secret malignity of pretended friends, than against positive accusations, and the avowed malice of open enemies.

In your account of the primitive church, you set forth, that "the want of discipline and human learning, was supplied by the occasional assistance of the prophets; who were called to that function, without distinction of age, of sex, or of natural abilities." – That the gift of prophecy was one of the spiritual gifts, by which some of the first Christians were enabled to cooperate with the Apostles, in the general design of preaching the Gospel; and that this gift, or rather, as Mr. Locke thinks, the gift of tongues, (by the ostentation of which, many of them were prompted to speak in their assemblies at the same time,) was the occasion of some disorder in the church of Corinth, which required the interposition of the Apostle to compose, is confessed on all hands. But if you mean, that the prophets were ever the sole pastors of the faithful; or that no provision was made by the Apostles for the good government and edification of the church, except what might be accidentally derived from the occasional assistance of the prophets, you are much mistaken; and have undoubtedly forgot, what is said of Paul and Barnabas having ordained elders in Lystra, Iconium, and Antioch; and of Paul's commission to Titus, whom he had left in Crete, to ordain elders in every city; and of his instructions both to him and Timothy, concerning the qualifications of those, whom they were to appoint bishops: one of which was, that a bishop should be able by sound doctrine, to exhort and to convince the gain-sayer; nor is it said, that this sound doctrine was to be communicated to the bishop by prophecy, or that all persons, without distinction, might be called to that office; but a bishop was *to be able to teach*, not what he had learned by prophecy, but what Paul had publicly preached; *the things that thou hast heard of me among many witnesses, the same commit thou to faithful men, who shall be able to teach others also.* And in every place almost, where prophets are mentioned, they are joined with Apostles and teachers, and other ministers of the gospel; so that there is no reason for your representing them as a distinct order of men, who were by their occasional assistance to supply the want of discipline and human learning in the church. It would be taking too large a field, to inquire, whether the prophets, you speak of, were endowed with ordinary or extraordinary gifts; whether they always spoke by the immediate impulse of the Spirit, or according to *the analogy of faith*; whether their gift consisted in the foretelling of future events, or in the interpreting of scripture to the edification and exhortation and comfort of the church, or in both: I will content myself with observing, that he will judge very improperly concerning the prophets of the apostolic church, who takes his idea of their office or importance, from your description of them.

In speaking of the community of goods, which, you say, was adopted for a short time in the primitive church, you hold as inconclusive the arguments of Mosheim; who has endeavoured to prove, that it was a community, quite different from that recommended by Pythagoras or Plato; consisting principally in a common use, derived from an unbounded liberality, which induced the opulent to share their riches with their indigent brethren; there have been others, as well as Mosheim, who have entertained this opinion; and it is not quite so indefensible, as you represent it; but whether it be reasonable or absurd, need not now be examined: it is far more necessary to take notice of an expression, which you have used, and which may be apt to mislead unwary readers into a very injurious suspicion, concerning the integrity of the Apostles. In process of time, you observe, "the converts, who embraced the new religion, were permitted to retain the possession of their patrimony." – This expression, *permitted to retain*, in ordinary acceptation, implies an antecedent obligation to part with: now, Sir, I have not the shadow of a doubt in affirming, that we have no account in scripture of any such obligation being imposed upon the converts to Christianity, either by Christ himself, or by his Apostles, or by any other authority: nay, in the very place, where this community of goods is treated of, there is an express proof, (I know not how your impartiality has happened to overlook it,) to the contrary. When Peter was about to inflict an exemplary punishment upon Ananias (not for keeping back a part of the price, as some men are fond of representing it, but) for his lying and hypocrisy, in offering a part of the price of his land, as the whole of it; he said to him, *whilst it remained* (unsold), *was it not thine own? and after it was sold, was it not in thine own power?* From this account it is evident, that Ananias was under no obligation to part with his patrimony; and after he had parted with it, the price was in his own power; the Apostle would have *permitted him to retain* the whole of it, if he had thought fit; though he would not permit his prevarication to go unpunished.

You have remarked, that "the feasts of love, the agapæ, as they were called, constituted a very pleasing and essential part of public worship." – Lest any one should from hence be led to suspect, that these feasts of love, this pleasing part of the public worship of the primitive church, resembled the unhallowed meetings of some impure sectaries of our own times, I will take the liberty to add to your account, a short explication of the nature of these agapæ. Tertullian, in the 39th chapter of his Apology, has done it to my hands. The nature of our supper, says he, is indicated by it's name; it is called by a word, which, in the Greek language, signifies Love. We are not anxious about the expence of the entertainment; since we look upon that as gain, which is expended with a pious purpose, in the relief and refreshment of all our indigent. – The occasion of our entertainment being so honourable, you may judge of the manner of it's being conducted; it consists in the discharge of religious duties; it admits nothing vile, nothing immodest. Before we sit down, prayer is made to God. The hungry eat as much as they desire, and every one drinks as much as can be useful to sober men. We so feast, as men, who have their minds impressed with the idea of spending the night in the worship of God; we so converse, as men, who are conscious that the Lord heareth them, &c. Perhaps you may object to this testimony, in favour of the innocence of Christian meetings, as liable to partiality, because it is the testimony of a Christian; and you may, perhaps, be able to pick out from the writings of this Christian, something that looks like a contradiction of this account: however, I will rest the matter upon this testimony for the present; forbearing to quote any other Christian writer upon the subject, as I shall in a future letter, produce you a testimony, superior to every objection. You speak too of the agapæ, as an essential part of the public worship; this is not according to your usual accuracy; for, had they been essential, the edict of an heathen magistrate would not have been able to put a stop to them; yet Pliny, in his letter to Trajan, expressly says, that the Christians left them off, upon his publishing an edict prohibiting assemblies; and we know, that in the council of Carthage, in the fourth century, on account of the abuses which attended them, they began to be interdicted, and ceased almost universally in the fifth.

I have but two observations to make upon what you have advanced, concerning the severity of ecclesiastical pennance; the first is, that even you yourself do not deduce it's institution from the scripture; but from the power, which every voluntary society has over it's own members; and therefore, however extravagant, or however absurd; however opposite to the attributes of a commiserating God, or the feelings of a fallible man, it may be thought; or upon whatever trivial occasion, such as that, you mention, of calumniating a Bishop, a Presbyter, or even a Deacon, it may have been inflicted; Christ and his Apostles are not answerable for it. The other is, that it was of all possible expedients, the least fitted to accomplish the end, for which you think it was introduced, the propagation of Christianity. The sight of a penitent humbled by a public confession, emaciated by fasting, clothed in sackcloth, prostrated at the door of the assembly, and imploring for years together the pardon of his offences, and a readmission into the bosom of the church, was a much more likely means of deterring the Pagans from Christian community, than the pious liberality you mention, was of alluring them into it. This pious liberality, Sir, would exhaust, even your elegant powers of description, before you could exhibit it in the amiable manner it deserves; it is derived from the *new commandment of loving one another*; and it has ever been the distinguishing characteristic of Christians, as opposed to every other denomination of men, Jews, Mahometans, or Pagans. In the times of the Apostles, and in the first ages of the church, it shewed itself in voluntary contributions for the relief of the poor and the persecuted, the infirm and the unfortunate; as soon as the church was permitted to have permanent possessions in land, and acquired the protection of the civil power, it exerted itself in the erection of hospitals of every kind; institutions these, of charity and humanity, which were forgotten in the laws of Solon and Lycurgus; and for even one example of which, you will, I believe, in vain explore the boasted annals of Pagan Rome. Indeed, Sir, you will think too injuriously of this liberality, if you look upon it's origin as superstitious; or upon it's application as an artifice of the priesthood, to seduce the indigent into the bosom of the church; it was the pure and uncorrupted fruit of genuine Christianity.

You are much *surprised*, and not a little *concerned*, that Tacitus and the younger Pliny, have spoken so slightly of the Christian system; and that Seneca and the elder Pliny, have not vouchsafed to mention it at all. This difficulty seems to have struck others, as well as yourself; and I might refer you to the conclusion of the second volume of Dr. Lardner's Collection of Ancient Jewish and Heathen Testimonies to the Truth of the Christian Religion, for full satisfaction in this point; but perhaps an observation or two, may be sufficient to diminish your surprise.

Obscure sectaries of upright morals, when they separate themselves from the religion of their country, do not speedily acquire the attention of men of Letters. The Historians are apprehensive of deprecating the dignity of their learned labour, and contaminating their splendid narration of illustrious events, by mixing with it a disgusting detail of religious combinations; and the philosophers are usually too deeply engaged in abstract science, or in exploring the infinite intricacy of natural appearances, to busy themselves with what they, perhaps hastily, esteem popular superstitions. Historians and philosophers, of no mean reputation, might be mentioned, I believe, who were the cotemporaries of Luther and the first reformers; and who have passed over in negligent or contemptuous silence, their daring and unpopular attempts to shake the stability of St. Peter's Chair. Opposition to the religion of a people, must become general, before it can deserve the notice of the civil magistrate; and till it does that, it will mostly be thought below the animadversion of distinguished writers. This remark is peculiarly applicable to the case in point. The first Christians, as Christ had foretold, were *hated of all men for his name's sake:* it was the name itself, not any vices adhering to the name, which Pliny punished; and they were every where held in exceeding contempt, till their numbers excited the apprehension of the ruling powers. The philosophers considered them as enthusiasts, and neglected them; the priests opposed them as innovators, and calumniated them; the great overlooked them, the learned despised them, and the curious alone, who examined into the foundation of their faith, believed them. But the negligence of some half dozen of writers, (most of them however bear incidental testimony to the truth of several facts respecting Christianity,) in not relating cirumstantially the origin, the progress, and the pretentions of a new sect, is a very insufficient reason for questioning, either the evidence of the principles upon which it was built, or the supernatural power by which it was supported.

The Roman historians, moreover, were not only culpably incurious concerning the Christians; but unpardonably ignorant of what concerned either them, or the Jews: I say, unpardonably ignorant; because the means of information were within their reach; the writings of Moses were every where to be had in Greek; and the works of Josephus were published, before Tacitus wrote his History; and yet, even Tacitus has fallen into great absurdity, and self contradiction in his account of the Jews; and though Tertullian's zeal carried him much too far, when he called him *Mendaciorum loquacissimus,* yet one cannot help regretting the little pains he took to acquire proper information upon that subject. He derives the name of the Jews by a forced interpolation from mount Ida in Crete[5]; and he represents them as abhorring all kinds of images in public worship, and yet accuses them of having placed the image of an Ass in the holy of holies; and presently after he tells us, that Pompey, when he profaned the temple, found the sanctuary entirely empty. Similar inaccuracies might be noticed in Plutarch and other writers, who have spoken of the Jews; and you yourself have referred to an obscure passage in Suetonius, as offering a proof how strangely the Jews and Christians of Rome were confounded with each other. Why then should we think it remarkable, that a few celebrated writers, who looked upon the Christians as an obscure sect of the Jews, and upon the Jews as a barbarous and detested people, whose history was not worth the perusal, and who were moreover engaged in the relation of the great events, which either occasioned or accompanied the ruin of their eternal empire; why should we be surprised, the men occupied in such interesting subjects, and influenced by such inveterate prejudices, should have left us but short and imperfect descriptions of the Christian system?

"But how shall we excuse, you say, the supine inattention of the pagan and philosophic world, to those evidences, which were presented by the hand of omnipotence, not to their reason, but to their senses?" – "The laws of nature were perpetually suspended, for the benefit of the church: But the sages of Greece and Rome turned aside from the awful spectacle." – To their shame be it spoken, that they did so – "and pursuing the ordinary occupations of life and study, appeared unconscious of any alterations in the moral or physical government of the world." – To this objection, I answer in the first place, that we have no reason to believe, that miracles were performed, as often as philosophers deigned to give their attention to them; or that, at the period of time you allude to, the laws of nature were *perpetually* suspended, for the benefit of the church. It may be, that not one of the few heathen writers, whose books have escaped the ravages of time, was ever present, when a miracle was wrought; but will it follow, because Pliny, or Plutarch, or Galen, or Seneca, or Suetonius, or Tacitus, had never seen a miracle, that no miracles were ever performed? They indeed were learned, and observant men; and it may be a matter of surprise to us, that

---

[5] Inclytum in Creta Idam montem, accolas Idæos aucto in barbarum cognomento Judæos vocitari. Tac. Hist. L. 5. sub. Init.

miracles so celebrated, as the friends of Christianity suppose the Christian ones to have been, should never have been mentioned by them though they had not seen them; and had an Adrian or a Vespasian been the authors of but a thousandth part of the miracles, you have ascribed to the primitive church, more than one probably of these very historians, philosophers as they were, would have adorned his history with the narration of them: for though they turned aside from the awful spectacle of the miracles of a poor despised Apostle – yet they beheld with exulting complacency, and have related with unsuspecting credulity, the ostentatious tricks of a Roman Emperor. It was not for want of faith in miraculous events, that these Sages neglected the Christian miracles, but for want of candour, and impartial examination.

I answer in the second place, that in the Acts of the Apostles, we have an account of a great multitude of Pagans of every condition of life, who were so far from being inattentive to the evidences, which were presented by the hand of omnipotence to their senses, that they contemplated them with reverence and wonder; and forsaking the religion of their ancestors, and all the flattering hopes of worldly profit, reputation, and tranquillity, adhered with astonishing resolution to the profession of Christianity. From the conclusion of the Acts, till the time in which some of the Sages you mention flourished, is a very obscure part of church history; yet we are certain, that many of the Pagan, and we have some reason to believe, that not a few of the Philosophic world, during that period, did not turn aside from the awful spectacle of miracles, but saw and believed; and that a few others should be found, who probably had never seen, and therefore would not believe, is surely no very extraordinary circumstance. Why should we not answer to objections, such as these, with the boldness of St. Jerome; and bid Celsus, and Porphyry, and Julian, and their followers, learn the illustrious characters of the men, who founded, built up, and adorned the Christian church[6]? why should we not tell them, with Arnobius, of the orators, the grammarians, the rhetoricians, the lawyers, the physicians, the

---

[6] Discant Celsus, Porphyrius, Julianus, rabidi adversus Christum canes, discant eorum sectatores, qui putant Ecclesiam nullos Philosophos et eloquentes, nullos habuisse Doctores; quanti et quales viri eam fundaverint, extruxerint, ornaverintque; et desinant fidem nostram rusticæ tantum simplicitatis arguere, suamque potius imperitiam agnoscant. Jero. Prœ. Lib. de Illus. Eccl. Scrip.

philosophers, "who appeared conscious of the alterations in the moral and physical government of the world;" and from that consciousness, forsook the ordinary occupations of life and study, and attached themselves to the Christian discipline[7]?

I answer in the last place, that the miracles of Christians were falsely attributed to magic; and were for that reason thought unworthy the notice of the writers, you have referred to. Suetonius, in his life of Nero, calls the Christians, Men of a new and magical superstition:[8] I am sensible, that you laugh at those "sagacious commentators," who translate the original word by magical; and adopting the idea of Mosheim, you think it ought to be rendered mischievous or pernicious: Unquestionably it frequently has that meaning; with due deference, however, to Mosheim and yourself, I cannot help being of opinion, that in this place, as descriptive of the Christian religion, it is rightly translated magical. The Theodosian Code must be my excuse, for dissenting from such respectable authority; and in it, I conjecture, you will find good reason for being of my opinion.[9] Nor ought any friend to Christianity, to be astonished or alarmed at Suetonius applying the word Magical to the Christian religion; for the miracles wrought by Christ and his Apostles, principally consisted in alleviating the distresses, by curing the obstinate diseases of human kind; and the proper meaning of magic, as understood by the ancients, is a higher and more holy branch of the art of healing.[10] The elder Pliny lost his life in an eruption of Vesuvius, about forty seven years after the death of Christ; some fifteen years before the death of Pliny, the Christians were persecuted at Rome for a crime, of which every person knew them innocent; but from the description, which Tacitus gives, of the low estimation they were held in at that time, (for which, however, he assigns no cause; and therefore we may reasonably conjecture it was the

---

[7] Arnob. Con. Gen. L. 11.

[8] Genus hominum, superstitionis novæ et *maleficæ*. Suet. in Nero. c. 16.

[9] Chaldæi, ac *Magi*, et cæteri quos vulgus *maleficos* ob facinorum magnitudinem appellat. – Si quis *magus* vel magicis contaminibus adsuetus, qui *maleficus* vulgi consuetudine nuncupatur. IX Cod. Theodo. Tit. xvi

[10] Pliny, speaking of the origin of magic, says, Natam primum e medicina nemo dubitat, ac specie salutari irrepsisse velut *altiorem sanctioremque medicinam*. – He afterwards says, that it was mixed with mathematical arts; and this *magici* and *mathematici* are joined by Pliny, as *malefici* and *mathematici* are in the Theodosian Code. Plin. Nat. Hist. Lib. 30. c. 1.

same, for which the Jews were every where become so odious, an opposition to polytheism) and of the extreme sufferings they underwent, we cannot be much surprised, that their name is not to be found in the works of Pliny, or of Seneca; the sect itself must, by Nero's persecution, have been almost destroyed in Rome; and it would have been uncourtly, not to say unsafe, to have noticed an order of men, whose innocence an emperor had determined to traduce, in order to divert the dangerous, but deserved stream of popular censure from himself. Notwithstanding this, there is a passage in the Natural History of Pliny; which, how much soever it may have been overlooked, contains, I think, a very strong allusion to the Christians; and clearly intimates, he had heard of their miracles. In speaking concerning the origin of magic, he says, – there is also another faction of magic, derived from the Jews, Moses and Lotopea, and subsisting at present.[11] – The word faction, does not ill denote the opinion the Romans entertained of the religious associations of the Christians;[12] and a magical faction implies their pretensions, at least, to the miraculous gifts of healing; and it's descending from Moses, is according to the custom of the Romans, by which they confounded the Christians with the Jews; and it's being then subsisting, seems to have a strong reference to the rumours Pliny had negligently heard reported of the Christians.

Submitting each of these answers to your cool and candid consideration; I proceed to take notice of another difficulty in your fifteenth chapter, which some have thought one of the most important in your whole book – The silence of profane historians, concerning the preternatural darkness at the crucifixion of Christ. – You know, Sir, that several learned men are of opinion, that profane history is not silent upon this subject; I will, however, put their authority for the present quite out of the question. I will neither trouble you with the testimony of Phlegon, nor with the appeal of Tertullian to the public registers of the Romans; but meeting you upon your own ground, and granting you every thing you desire, I will

[11] Est et alia magices *factio*, a Mose *etiamnum* et Lotopea Judæis pendens. Plin. Nat. Hist. Lib. 30. c. 2. Edit. Hardu. Dr. Lardner and others, have made slight mention of this passage, probably from their reading in bad editions *Jamne* for *etiamnum*, a Mose et Jamne et Jotape Judæis pendens.

[12] Tertullian reckons the Sect of the Christians, inter licitas *factiones*. Ap. c.38.

endeavour, from a fair and candid examination of the history of this event, to suggest a doubt, at least, to your mind, whether this was "the greatest phænomenon, to which the mortal eye has been witness, since the creation of the globe."

This darkness is mentioned by three of the four Evangelists; St. Matthew thus expresses himself, - *now from the sixth hour there was darkness over all the land until the ninth hour*; St. Mark says, - *and when the sixth hour was come, there was darkness over the whole land until the ninth hour*; St. Luke, - *and it was about the sixth hour, and there was darkness over all the earth until the ninth hour; and the sun was darkened.* The three Evangelists agree, that there was darkness; - and they agree in the extent of the darkness: for it is the same expression in the original, which our translators have rendered *earth* in Luke, and *land* in the two other accounts; and they agree in the duration of the darkness, it lasted three hours: - Luke adds a particular circumstance, *that the sun was darkened*. I do not know, whether this event be any where else mentioned in scripture, so that our inquiry can neither be extensive nor difficult.

In philosophical propriety of speech, darkness consists in the total absence of light, and admits of no degrees; however, in the more common acceptation of the word, there are degrees of darkness, as well as of light; and as the Evangelists have said nothing, by which the particular degree of darkness can be determined; we have as much reason to suppose it was slight, as you have that it was excessive; but if it was slight, though it had extended itself over the surface of the whole globe, the difficulty of it's not being recorded by Pliny or Seneca vanishes at once.[13] Do you not perceive, Sir, upon what a slender foundation this mighty objection is grounded; when we have only to put you upon proving, that the darkness at the crucifixion was of so unusual a nature, as to have excited the particular attention of all mankind, or even of those who were witnesses to it? But I do not mean to deal so logically with you; rather give me leave to spare you the trouble of your proof, by

[13] The Author of L'Evangile de la Raison, is mistaken in saying, that the Evangelists speak of a *thick darkness*; and that mistake has led him into another, into a disbelief of the event, because it has not been mentioned by the writers of the times - ses historiens (the Evangelists) ont le front de nous dire, qu'a sa mort la terre a ete couverte d' epaisses tenebres en plein midi et en pleine lune; comme si tous les ecrivains de ce tems-la n'auroient pas remarque un si etrange miracle! L'Evan. de la Rais. P. 99.

proving, or shewing the probability at least, of the direct contrary. There is a circumstance mentioned by St. John, which seems to indicate, that the darkness was not so excessive, as is generally supposed; for it is probable, that during the continuance of the darkness, Jesus spoke both to his mother, and to his beloved disciple, whom he *saw* from the cross; they were near the cross; but the soldiers which surrounded it, must have kept them at too great a distance, for Jesus to have *seen* them and *known* them, had the darkness at the crucifixion been excessive, like the preternatural darkness, which God brought upon the land of Egypt; for it is expressly said, that during the continuance of that darkness, *they saw not one another*. The expression in St. Luke, *the sun was darkened*, tends rather to confirm, than to overthrow this reasoning. I am sensible, this expression is generally thought equivalent to another – the sun was eclipsed; – but the Bible is open to us all; and there can be no presumption, in endeavouring to investigate the meaning of scripture for ourselves. Luckily for the present argumentation, the very phrase of the sun's being darkened, occurs, in so many words, in one other place (and in only one) of the new testament; and from that place, you may possibly see reason to imagine, that the darkness might not, perhaps, have been so intense, as to deserve the particular notice of the Roman naturalists: – *And he opened the bottomless pit, and there arose a smoke out of the pit, as the smoke of a great furnace; and the sun was darkened*[14], *and the air, by reason of the smoke of the pit*. If we should say, that the sun at the crucifixion was obnubilated, and darkened by the intervention of clouds, as it is here represented to be by the intervention of a smoke, like the smoke of a furnace, I do not see what you could object to our account; but such a phænomenon has, surely, no right to be esteemed the greatest that mortal eye has ever beheld. I may be mistaken in this interpretation; but I have no design to misrepresent the fact, in order to get rid of a difficulty; the darkness may have been as intense, as many commentators have supposed it; but neither they, nor you can prove it was so; and I am surely under no necessity, upon this occasion, of granting you, out of deference to any commentator, what you can neither prove nor render probable.

---

[14] – και εσκοτιθη ο ηλιος. Αποκ. 9. 2.

But you still, perhaps, may think, that the darkness, by it's extent, made up for this deficiency in point of intenseness. The original word, expressive of it's extent, is sometimes interpreted by the whole earth; more frequently in the new testament, of any little portion of the earth; for we read of the land of Judah, of the land of Israel, of the land of Zabulon, and of the land of Nephthalim; and it may very properly, I conceive, be translated in the place in question by *Region*. But why should all the world take notice of a darkness, which extended itself for a few miles about Jerusalem, and lasted but three hours? The Italians, especially, had no reason to remark the event as singular; since they were accustomed at that time, as they are at present, to see the *neighbouring regions* so darkened for days together by the eruptions of Ætna and Vesuvius, that no man could know his neighbour.[15] We learn from the scripture account, that an earthquake accompanied this darkness; and a dark clouded sky, I apprehend, very frequently precedes an earthquake; but it's extent is not great, nor is it's intenseness excessive, nor is the phænomenon itself so unusual, as not commonly to pass unnoticed in ages of science and history. I fear, I may be liable to misrepresentation in this place; but I beg it may be observed, that however slight in degree, or however confined in extent the darkness at the crucifixion may have been; I am of opinion, that the power of God was as supernaturally exerted in it's production, and in that of the earthquake which accompanied it, as in the opening of the graves, and the resurrection of the saints, which followed the resurrection of Christ.

In another place, you seem not to believe "that Pontius Pilate informed the Emperor of the unjust sentence of death, which he had pronounced against an innocent person:" And the same reason, which made him silent as to the death, ought, one would suppose, to have made him silent as to the miraculous events, which accompanied it: and if Pilate in his dispatches to the Emperor, transmitted no account of the darkness (how great soever you suppose it to have been) which happened in a distant province; I cannot apprehend, that the report of it could

---

[15] – nos autem tenebras cogitemus tantas, quantæ quondam eruptione Etnæorum ignium *finitimas regiones obscuravisse* dicuntur, ut per biduum nemo hominem homo agnosceret. Cic. de Nat. Deo. 1. 2. And Pliny, in describing the eruption of Vesuvius, which suffocated his uncle, says, – Dies alibi, illic nox omnibus noctibus nigrior densiorque.

have ever gained such credit at Rome, as to induce either Pliny or Seneca to mention it as an authentic fact.

I am, &c.

LETTER SIXTH.

SIR,

I mean not to detain you long with my remarks upon your sixteenth Chapter; for in a short apology for Christianity, it cannot be expected, that I should apologize at length, for the indiscretions of the first Christians. Nor have I any disposition to reap a malicious pleasure, from exaggerating, what you have had so much goodnatured pleasure in extenuating, the truculent barbarity of their Roman persecutors.

M. de Voltaire has embraced every opportunity, of contrasting the persecuting temper of the Christians with the mild tolerance of the antient heathens; and I never read a page of his upon this subject, without thinking Christianity materially, if not intentionally, obliged to him, for his endeavour to depress the lofty spirit of religious bigotry. I may with justice pay the same compliment to you; and I do it with sincerity; heartily wishing, that in the prosecution of your work, you may render every species of intolerance universally detestable. There is no reason, why you should abate the asperity of your invective; since no one can suspect you of a design to traduce Christianity, under the guise of a zeal against persecution; or if any one should be so simple, he need but open the gospel to be convinced, that such a scheme is too palpably absurd, to have ever entered the head of any sensible and impartial man.

I wish, for the credit of human nature, that I could find reason to agree with you, in what you have said of the "universal toleration of Polytheism; of the mild indifference of antiquity; of the Roman Princes beholding, without concern, a thousand forms of religion subsisting in peace under their gentle sway." But there are some passages in the Roman History, which make me hesitate at least in this point; and almost induce me to believe, that the Romans were exceedingly jealous of all foreign religions, whether they were accompanied with immoral manners or not.

It was the Roman custom indeed, to invite the tutelary gods of the nations, which they intended to subdue, to abandon their charge; and to promise them the same, or even a more august worship in the city of Rome;[16] and their triumphs were graced as much with the exhibition of their captive gods, as with the less humane one of their captive kings.[17] But this custom, though it filled the city with hundreds of gods of every country, denomination, and quality, cannot be brought as a proof of Roman toleration; it may indicate the excess of their vanity, the extent of their superstition, or the refinement of their policy; but it can never shew, that the religion of individuals, when it differed from public wisdom, was either connived at as a matter of indifference, or tolerated as an inalienable right of human nature.

Upon another occasion, you, Sir, have referred to Livy, as relating the introduction and suppression of the rites of Bacchus; and in that very place we find him confessing, that the prohibiting all foreign religions, and the abolishing every mode of sacrifice which differed from the Roman mode, was a business frequently entrusted by their ancestors to the care of the proper magistrates; and he gives this reason for the procedure, That nothing could contribute more effectually to the ruin of religion, than the sacrificing after an external rite, and not after the manner instituted by their fathers.[18]

Not thirty years before this event, the Prætor, in conformity to a decree of the senate, had issued an edict – that no one should presume to sacrifice in any public place after a new or foreign manner.[19] And in a still more early period, the Ædiles had been commanded to take care, that no gods were worshipped, except the Roman gods; and that the Roman gods

[16] In oppugnationibus, ante omnia solitum a Romanis Sacerdotibus evocari Deum, cujus in tutela id oppidum esset; promittique illi eundem, aut ampliorem apud Romanos cultum. Plin. Nat. Hist. L. 38. C. iv.

[17] Roma triumphantis quotiens Ducis inclita currum
Plausibus excepit, totiens altaria Divûm
Addidit, spoliis sibimet nova numina fecit.   Pruden.

[18] Quoties hoc patrum avorumque ætate negotium est magistratibus datum, ut sacra externa fieri vetarent? sacrificulos vatesque foro, circo, urbe prohiberent? *vaticinos libros conquirerent combureretque?* omnem disciplinam sacrificandi, præterquam more Romano, abolerent? Judicabant enim prudentissimi viri omnis divini humanique juris, nihil æque dissolvendæ religionis esse, quam ubi non patrio, sed externo ritu sacrificaretur. Liv. L. xxxix. C. xvi.

[19] Ut quicumque *libros vaticinos precationesve*, aut artem sacrificandi conscriptam haberet, eos libros omnes litterasque ad se ante Kalendas Apriles deferret: neu quis in publico sacrove loco, novo aut externo ritu sacrificaret. Liv. L. xxv. C. i.

were worshipped after no manner, but the established manner of the country.[20]

But to come nearer to the times, of which you are writing. In Dion Cassius you may meet with a great courtier, one of the interior cabinet, and a polished statesman, in a set speech, upon the most momentous subject, expressing himself to the Emperor, in a manner agreeable enough to the practice of antiquity, but utterly inconsistent with the most remote idea of religious toleration. The speech alluded to, contains, I confess it, nothing more than the advice of an individual; but it ought to be remembered, that *that* individual was Mæcenas, that the advice was given to Augustus, and that the occasion of giving it, was no less important than the settling the form of the Roman government. He recommends it to Cæsar, to worship the gods himself, according to the established form; and to *force* all others to do the same; and to *hate* and to *punish* all those, who should attempt to introduce foreign religions[21]: nay, he bids him in the same place, have an eye upon the philosophers also, so that free thinking, free speaking at least, upon religious matters, was not quite so safe under the gentle sway of the Roman princes; as, thank God, it is under the much more gentle government of our own.

In the Edict of Toleration published by Galerius after six years unremitted persecution of the Christians, we perceive his motive for persecution, to have been the same with that, which had influenced the conduct of the more antient Romans, an abhorrence of all innovations in religion. You have favoured us with the translation of this edict, in which he says – "we were particularly desirous of reclaiming into the way of reason and nature," *ad bonas mentes* (a good pretence this for a Polytheistic persecutor) "the deluded Christians, who had renounced the religion and ceremonies instituted by their fathers" – this is the precise language of Livy, describing a persecution of a foreign religion three hundred years before, *turba erat nec sacrificantium nec precantium Deos patrio more*. And the very expedient of forcing the Christians to deliver up their religious books, which was practised in this

---

[20] Datum inde negotium ædilibus, ut animadverterent, ne qui, nisi Romani Dii, neu quo alio more, quam patrio colerentur. Liv. L. iv. C. 30.

[21] Ταυτα τε ουτω πραττε, και προσετι το μεν θειον παντη παντως αυτος τε σεβου, κατα τα πατρια, και τους αλλους τιμαν αναγκαζε· τους δε δη ξενιζοντας τι περι ουτο και μισει και κολαζε. Dion. Cas. L. 52.

persecution, and which Mosheim attributes to the advice of Hierocles, and you to that of the philosophers of those times, seems clear to me, from the places in Livy, before quoted, to have been nothing but an old piece of state policy, to which the Romans had recourse, as often as they apprehended their established religion to be in any danger.

In the preamble of the letter of toleration, which the emperor Maximin reluctantly wrote to Sabinus about a year after the publication of Galerius' Edict, there is a plain avowal of the reasons, which induced Galerius and Diocletian to commence their persecution; they had seen the temples of the gods forsaken, and were determined by the severity of punishment to reclaim men to their worship.[22]

In short, the system recommended by Mæcenas, of forcing every person to be of the emperor's religion, and of hating and punishing every innovator, contained no new doctrine; it was correspondent to the practice of the Roman senate, in the most illustrious times of the republic; and seems to have been generally adopted by the emperors, in their treatment of Christians, whilst they themselves were Pagans; and in their treatment of Pagans, after they themselves became Christians; and if any one should be willing to derive those laws against Heretics (which are so abhorrent from the mild spirit of the gospel, and so reproachful to the Roman Code) from the blind adherence of the Christian emperors to the intolerant policy of their Pagan predecessors, something, I think, might be produced in support of his conjecture.

But I am sorry to have said so much upon such a subject. – In endeavouring to palliate the severity of the Romans towards the Christians, you have remarked, "it was in vain, that the oppressed believer asserted the inalienable rights of conscience, and private judgment." "Though his situation might excite the pity, his arguments could never reach the understanding, either of the philosophic, or of the believing part of the Pagan world." How is this, Sir? are the arguments for liberty of conscience, so exceedingly inconclusive, that you think them incapable of reaching the understanding, even of philosophers? A captious

---

[22] Συνειδον σχεδον απαντας ανθρωποθς, καταλειφθεισης της των θεων θρησκειας, τω εθνει των χριστιανων εαυτους συμμεμιχοτας. Ορθως διατεταχεναι παντας ανθρωπους τους απο των θεων των αθανατων αναχωρησαντας, προ δηλω κολασει και τιμωρια εις την θρησκειαν των θεον ανακληθηναι. Euseb. Lib. ix. C. 4.

adversary would embrace with avidity, the opportunity this passage affords him, of blotting your character with the odious stain of being a persecutor; a stain, which no learning can wipe out, which no genius or ability can render amiable. I am far from entertaining such an opinion of your principles; but this conclusion seems fairly deducible from what you have said, – that the minds of the Pagans, were so pre-occupied with the notions of forcing, and hating, and punishing those, who differed from them in religion, that arguments for the inalienable rights of conscience, which would have convinced yourself and every philosopher in Europe, and staggered the resolution of an inquisitor, were incapable of reaching their understandings, or making any impression on their hearts; and you might, perhaps, have spared yourself some perplexity, in the investigation of the motives, which induced the Roman emperors to persecute, and the Roman people to hate the Christians, if you had not overlooked the true one, and adopted with too great facility, the erroneous idea of the extreme tolerance of Pagan Rome.

The Christians, you observe, were accused of atheism: – and it must be owned, that they were the greatest of all atheists, in the opinion of the polytheists; for, instead of Hesiod's thirty thousand gods, they could not be brought to acknowledge above one; and even that one they refused, at the hazard of their lives, to blaspheme with the appellation of Jupiter. But is it not somewhat singular, that the pretensions of the Christians to a constant intercourse with superior beings, in the working of miracles, should have been a principal cause of converting to their faith, those who branded them with the imputation of atheism?

They were accused too, of forming dangerous conspiracies against the state: – This accusation, you own, was as unjust as the preceding; but there seems to have been a peculiar hardship in the situation of the Christians; since the very same men, who thought them dangerous to the state, on account of their conspiracies; condemned them, as you have observed, for not interfering in it's concerns; for their criminal disregard to the business of war and government; and for their entertaining doctrines, which were supposed "to prohibit them from assuming the character of soldiers, of magistrates, and of princes:" Men such as these, would have made but poor conspirators.

94 *Religious Scepticism*

They were accused, lastly, of the most horrid crimes: – This accusation, it is confessed, was mere calumny; yet, as calumny is generally more extensive in it's influence, than truth, perhaps this calumny might be more powerful in stopping the progress of Christianity, than the virtues of the Christians were in promoting it: and in truth, Origen observes, that the Christians, on account of the crimes which were maliciously laid to their charge, were held in such abhorrence, that no one would so much as speak to them. It may be worth while to remark from him, that the Jews, in the very beginning of Christianity, were the authors of all those calumnies, which Celsus afterwards took such great delight in urging against the Christians, and which you have mentioned with such great precision.[23]

It is no improbable supposition, that the clandestine manner, in which the persecuting spirit of the Jews and Gentiles, obliged the Christians to celebrate their Eucharist, together with the expressions of eating the body, and drinking the blood of Christ, which were used in it's institution, and the custom of imparting a kiss of charity to each other, and of calling each other by the appellations of brother and sister,[24] gave occasions to their enemies to invent, and induced careless observers to believe, all the odious things which were said against the Christians.

You have displayed at length, in expressive diction, the accusations of the enemies of Christianity; and you have told us, of the imprudent defence, by which the Christians vindicated the purity of their morals; and you have huddled up in a short note, (which many a reader will never see) the testimony of Pliny to their innocence; permit me to do the Christians a little justice, by producing in their cause the whole truth.

---

[23] Videtur mihi fecisse idem Celsus, quod Judæi, qui sub Christianismi initium errorem sparsere, quasi ejus sectæ homines mactati pueri vescerentur carnibus; et quod, quoties eis libeat operam dare occultis libidinibus, extincto lumine constupret, quam quisque nactus fuerit. Quæ falsa et iniqua opinio dudum valde multos a religione nostra alienos tenuit; persuasos, quod tales sint Christiani; et ad hoc temporis nonnullos fallit; quia ea de causa Christianos aversantur, ut nec simplex colloquium cum eis habere velint. Orig. con. Cel. Lib. VI.

[24] The Romans used these expressions in so impure a sense, that Martial calls them, Nomina nequiora. Lib. II. Epig. IV.

Between seventy and eighty years after the death of Christ, Pliny had occasion to consult the emperor Trajan, concerning the manner, in which he should treat the Christians; it seems as if there had been judicial proceedings against them, though Pliny had never happened to attend any of them. He knew, indeed, that men were to be punished for being Christians, or he would not, as a sensible magistrate, have received the accusations of legal, much less of illegal, anonymous informers against them; nor would he, before he wrote to the emperor, have put to death those, whom his threats could not hinder from persevering in their confession, that they were Christians. His harsh manner of proceeding "in an office the most repugnant to his humanity," had made many apostatize from their profession; persons of this complexion, were well fitted to inform him of every thing they knew concerning the Christians; accordingly, he examined them; but not one of them accused the Christians of any other crime, than of praying to Christ, as to some God, and of binding themselves by an oath, not to be guilty of any wickedness. Not contented with this information, he put two maid servants, which were called ministers, to the torture; but even the rack, could not extort from the imbecility of the sex, a confession of any crime, any account different from that which the Apostates had voluntarily given; not a word do we find of their feasting upon murdered infants, or of their mixing in incestuous commerce. After all his pains, Pliny pronounced the meal of the Christians to be *promiscuous* and *innocent:* persons of both sexes, of all ages, and of every condition, assembled promiscuously together: there was nothing for chastity to blush at, or for humanity to shudder at, in these meetings; there was no secret initiation of proselytes by abhorred rites; but they eat a promiscuous meal in Christian charity, and with the most perfect innocence.[25]

Whatever faults then, the Christians may have been guilty of in after times; though you could produce to us a thousand ambitious prelates of Carthage, or sensual ones of Antioch, and blot ten thousand pages with the impurities of the

[25] – affirmabant autem, hanc fuisse summam vel culpæ suæ, vel erroris, quod essent soliti stato die ante lucem convenire: carmenque Christo, quasi Deo, dicere secum invicem: seque sacramento non *in seclus* aliquod obstringere, sed ne furta, ne latrocinia, ne adulteria committerent, ne fidem fallerent, ne depositum appellati abnegarent: quibus peractis, morem sibi discedendi fuisse, rursusque coeundi ad capiendum cibum, *promiscuum* tamen, *et innoxium.* Plin. Epis. XCVII. Lib. x.

Christian clergy; yet at this period, whilst the memory of Christ and his Apostles, was fresh in their minds; or, in the more emphatic language of Jerome, "whilst the blood of our Lord was warm and recent faith was fervent in the believers;" we have the greatest reason to conclude, that they were eminently distinguished for the probity and the purity of their lives. Had there been but a shadow of a crime in their assemblies, it must have been detected by the industrious search of the intelligent Pliny; and it is a matter of real surprise, that no one of the apostates, thought of paying court to the governor, by a false testimony; especially, as the apostacy seems to have been exceeding general; since the temples, which had been almost deserted, began again to be frequented; and the victims, for which a little time before, scarce a purchaser was to be found, began again every where to be bought up. This, Sir, is a valuable testimony in our favour; it is not that of a declaiming apologist, of a deluding priest, or of a deluded martyr, of an orthodox bishop, or of any "of the most pious of men" the Christians; but it is that of a Roman magistrate, philosopher, and lawyer; who cannot be supposed to have wanted inclination to detect the immoralities, or the conspiracies of the Christians; since, in his treatment of them, he had stretched the authority of his office, and violated alike the laws of his country, and of humanity.

With this testimony, I will conclude my remarks; for I have no disposition to blacken the character you have given of Nero; or to lessen the humanity of the Roman magistrates; or to magnify the number of Christians, or of martyrs; or to undertake the defence of a few fanatics, who by their injudicious zeal, brought ruin upon themselves, and disgrace upon their profession. I may not probably have convinced you, that you are wrong in any thing, which you have advanced; or that the authors you have quoted, will not support you in the inferences, you have drawn from their works; or that Christianity ought to be distinguished from it's corruptions; yet I may, perhaps, have had the good fortune to lessen, in the minds of others, some of that dislike to the Christian religion, which the perusal of your book had unhappily excited. I have touched but upon general topics; for I should have wearied out your patience, to say nothing of my readers', or my own, had I enlarged upon every thing in which I dissent from you; and a minute examination of your work would, moreover, have had the appearance of a captious disposition, to descend into illiberal personalities; and might have produced a certain acrimony of sentiment or expression, which may be serviceable in supplying the place of argument, or adding a zest to a dull composition; but has nothing to do with the investigation of truth. Sorry shall I be, if what I have written, should give the least interruption to the prosecution of the great work, in which you are engaged; the world is now possessed of the opinion of us both, upon the subject in question; and it may, perhaps, be proper for us both to leave it in this state; I say not this, from any backwardness to acknowledge my mistakes, when I am convinced that I am in an error; but to express the almost insuperable reluctance, which I feel to the bandying abusive argument, in public controversy: It is not, in good truth, a difficult task, to chastise the froward petulance of those, who mistake personal invective for reasoning, and clumsy banter for ingenuity; but it is a dirty business at best, and should never be undertaken by a man of any temper, except when the interests of truth may suffer by his neglect. Nothing of this nature, I am sensible, is to be expected from you; and if any thing of the kind has happened to escape myself, I hereby disclaim the intention of saying it, and heartily wish it unsaid.

Will you permit me, Sir, through this channel, (I may not, perhaps, have another so good an opportunity of doing it,) to address a few words? not to yourself, but to a set of men, who disturb all serious company with their profane declamation against Christianity; and who having picked up in their travels, or the writings of the deists, a few flimsy objections, infect with their ignorant and irreverent ridicule, the ingenuous minds of the rising generation.

GENTLEMEN,
Suppose the mighty work accomplished, the cross trampled upon, Christianity every where proscribed, and the religion of nature once more become the religion of Europe; what advantage will you have derived to your country, or to yourselves, from the exchange? I know your answer – you will have freed the world from the hypocrisy of Priests, and the tyranny of Superstition. – No; you forget that Lycurgus, and Numa, and Odin, and Mango-Copac, and all the great

legislators of ancient or modern story, have been of opinion, that the affairs of civil society could not well be conducted without *some* religion; you must of necessity introduce a priesthood, with, probably, as much hypocrisy; a religion, with, assuredly, more superstition, than that which you now reprobate with such indecent and ill-grounded contempt. But I will tell you, from what you will have freed the world; you will have freed it from it's abhorrence of vice, and from every powerful incentive to virtue; you will, with the religion, have brought back the depraved morality, of Paganism; you will have robbed mankind of their firm assurance of another life; and thereby you will have despoiled them of their patience, of their humility, of their charity, of their chastity, of all those mild and silent virtues, which (however despicable they may appear in your eyes) are the only ones, which meliorate and sublime our nature; which Paganism never knew, which spring from Christianity alone, which do or might constitute our comfort in this life, and without the possession of which, another life, if after all there should happen to be one, must (unless a miracle be exerted in the alteration of our disposition) be more vicious and more miserable than this is.

Perhaps you will contend, that the universal light of reason, that the truth and fitness of things, are of themselves, sufficient to exalt the nature, and regulate the manners of mankind. Shall we never have done with this groundless commendation of natural law? Look into the first chapter of Paul's Epistle to the Romans, and you will see the extent of it's influence over the Gentiles of those days; or if you dislike Paul's authority, and the manners of antiquity; look into the more admired accounts of modern Voyagers; and examine it's influence over the Pagans of our own times, over the sensual inhabitants of Ottaheitè, over the Cannibals of New Zeland, or the remorseless Savages of America. But these men are Barbarians. – Your law of nature, notwithstanding, extends even to them: – but they have misused their reason; – they have then the more need of, and would be the more thankful for that revelation, which you, with an ignorant and fastidious self-sufficiency deem useless. – But, they might of themselves, if they thought fit, become wise and virtuous. – I answer with Cicero, *ut nihil interest, utrum nemo valeat, an nemo valere possit; sic non intelligo quid intersit, utrum nemo sit sapiens, an nemo esse possit.*

These however, you will think, are extraordinary instances; and that we ought not from these, to take our measure of the excellency of the law of nature; but rather from the civilized states of China and Japan, or from the nations which flourished in learning and in arts, before Christianity was heard of in the world. You mean to say, that by the law of nature, which you are desirous of substituting in the room of the gospel, you do not understand those rules of conduct, which an individual, abstracted from the community, and deprived of the institution of mankind, could excogitate for himself; but such a system of precepts, as the most enlightened men of the most enlightened ages, have recommended to our observance. Where do you find this system? We cannot meet with it in the works of Stobæus, or the Scythian Anacharsis, nor in those of Plato or of Cicero, nor in those of the Emperor Antoninus, or the slave Epictetus; for we are persuaded, that the most animated considerations of the πρεπον, and the *honestum*, of the beauty of virtue, and the fitness of things, are not able to furnish, even a Brutus himself, with permanent principles of action; much less are they able, to purify the polluted recesses of a vitiated heart, to curb the irregularity of appetite, or restrain the impetuosity of passion in common men. If you order us to examine the works of Grotius, or Puffendorf, of Burlamaqui, or Hutchinson, for what you understand by the law of nature; we apprehend that you are in a great error, in taking your notions of natural law, as discoverable by natural reason, from the elegant systems of it, which have been drawn up by Christian Philosophers; since they have all laid their foundations, either tacitly or expressly, upon a principle derived from revelation, A thorough knowledge of the Being and attributes of God: and even those amongst yourselves, who, rejecting Christianity still continue Theists, are indebted to revelation (whether you are either aware of, or disposed to acknowledge the debt, or not) for those sublime speculations concerning the Deity, which you have fondly attributed to the excellency of your own unassisted reason. If you would know the real genius of natural law, and how far it can proceed in the investigation or enforcement of moral duties; you must consult the manners and the writings of those, who have never heard of either the Jewish or the Christian dispensation, or of those other manifestations of himself, which God vouchsafed to Adam and to the Patriarchs, before and after the flood. It would be difficult perhaps any where, to find a people entirely destitute of traditionary notices concerning a Deity, and of traditionary fears or expectations of another life; and the morals of mankind may have, perhaps, been no where quite so abandoned, as they would have been, had they been left wholly to themselves in these points: however, it is a truth, which cannot be denied, how much soever it may be lamented, that though the generality of mankind have always had some faint conceptions of God, and his providence; yet they have been always greatly inefficacious in the production of good morality, and highly derogatory to his nature, amongst all the people of the earth, except the Jews and Christians; and some may perhaps be desirous of excepting the Mahometans, who derive all that is good in their *Koran* from Christianity.

The laws concerning justice, and the reparation of damages, concerning the security of property, and the performance of contracts; concerning, in short, whatever affects the wellbeing of civil society, have been every where understood with sufficient precision; and if you choose to stile Justinian's code, a code of natural law, though you will err against propriety of speech, yet you are so far in the right, that natural reason discovered, and the depravity of human nature compelled human kind, to establish by proper sanctions the laws therein contained; and you will have moreover Carneades, no mean Philosopher, on your side; who knew of no law of nature, different from that which men had instituted for their common utility; and which was various according to the manners of men in different climates, and changeable with a change of times in the same. And in truth, in all countries where Paganism has been the established religion, though a philosopher may now and then have stepped beyond the paltry prescript of civil jurisprudence, in his pursuit of virtue; yet the bulk of mankind have ever been contented with that scanty pittance of morality, which enabled them to escape the lash of civil punishment: I call it a scanty pittance; because a man may be intemperate, iniquitous, impious, a thousand ways a profligate and a villain, and yet elude the cognizance, and avoid the punishment of civil laws.

I am sensible, you will be ready to say, what is all this to the purpose? though the bulk of mankind may never be able to investigate the laws of natural religion, nor disposed to reverence their sanctions when investigated by others, nor solicitous about any other standard of moral rectitude, than civil legislation; yet the inconveniences which may attend the extirpation of Christianity, can be no proof of it's truth. – I have not produced them, as a proof of it's truth; but they are a strong and conclusive proof, if not of it's truth, at least of it's utility; and the consideration of it's utility, may be a motive to yourselves for examining, whether it may not chance to be true; and it ought to be a reason with every good citizen, and with every man of sound judgment, to keep his opinions to himself, if from any particular circumstances in his studies or in his education, he should have the misfortune to think that it is not true. If you can discover to the rising generation, a better religion than the Christian, one that will more effectually animate their hopes, and subdue their passions, make them better men or better members of society, we importune you to publish it for their advantage; but till you can do that, we beg of you, not to give the reins to their passions, by instilling into their unsuspicious minds your pernicious prejudices: even now, men scruple not, by their lawless lust, to ruin the repose of private families, and to fix a stain of infamy upon the noblest: even now, they hesitate not, in lifting up a murderous arm against the life of their friend, or against their own, as often as the fever of intemperance, stimulates their resentment; or the satiety of an useless life excites their despondency: even now, whilst we are persuaded of a resurrection from the dead, and of a *judgement to come*, we find it difficult enough to resist the solicitations of sense, and to escape unspotted from the licentious manners of the world: But what will become of our virtue, what of the consequent peace and happiness of society, if you persuade us, that there are no such things? in two words, – you may ruin yourselves by your attempt, and you will certainly ruin your country by your success.

But the consideration of the inutility of your design, is not the only one, which should induce you to abandon it; the argument *a tuto* ought to be warily managed, or it may tend to the silencing our opposition to any system of superstition, which has had the good forune to be sanctified by public authority; it is, indeed, liable to no objection in the present case; we do not, however, wholly rely upon it's cogency. It is not contended, that Christianity is to be received, merely because it is useful; but because it is true. This you deny, and think your objections well grounded; we conceive them originating in your vanity, your immorality, or your misapprehension. There are many worthless doctrines, many superstitious observances, which the fraud or folly of mankind have every where annexed to Christianity, (especially in the church of Rome,) as essential parts of it; if you take these sorry appendages to Christianity, for Christianity itself, as preached by Christ, and by the Apostles; if you confound the Roman, with the Christian religion, you quite misapprehend it's nature; and are in a state similar to that of men, mentioned by Plutarch, in his treatise of superstition; who flying from superstition, leapt over religion, and sunk into downright Atheism.[26] – Christianity is not a religion very palatable to a voluptuous age; it will not conform it's precepts to the standard of fashion; it will not lessen the deformity of vice by lenient appellations; but calls keeping, whoredom; intrigue, adultery; and duelling, murder; it will not pander the lust, it will not licence the intemperance of mankind; it is a troublesome monitor to a man of pleasure; and your way of life may have made you quarrel with your religion. – As to your vanity, as a cause of your infidelity, suffer me to produce the sentiments of M. Bayle upon that head; if the description does not suit your character, you will not be offended at it; and if you are offended with it's freedom, it will do you good.

> "This inclines me to believe, that Libertines, like Des-Barreaux, are not greatly persuaded of the truth of what they say. They have made no deep examination; they have learned some few objections, which they are perpetually making a noise with; they speak from a principle of ostentation, and give themselves the lie in the time of danger. – Vanity has a greater share in their disputes, than conscience; they imagine, that the singularity and boldness of the opinions which they maintain, will give them the reputation of men of parts: – by degrees, they get a habit of holding impious discourses; and if their vanity be

---

[26] Le Papisme, says Helvetius in a Posthumous Work, n'est aux yeux d'un homme sensè qu'une pure idolatrie – nous sommes étonnès de l'absurditè de la religion païenne. Celle de la religion Papiste étonnera bien d'avantage un jour la posterité. – We trust, that day is not at a great distance, and deism will then be buried in the ruins of the church of Rome; for the taking the superstition, the avarice, the ambition, the intolerance of Antichristianism for Christianity, has been the great error, upon which infidelity has built it's system, both at home and abroad.

accompanied by a voluptuous life, their progress in that road is the swifter."[27]

The main stress of your objections, rests not upon the insufficiency of the external evidence to the truth of Christianity; for few of you, though you may become the future ornaments of the senate, or of the bar, have ever employed an hour in it's examination, but upon the difficulty of the doctrines, contained in the new testament: they exceed, you say, your comprehension, and you felicitate yourselves, that you are not yet arrived at the true standard of orthodox faith, – *credo quia impossibile.* You think, it would be taking a superfluous trouble, to inquire into the nature of the external proofs, by which Christianity is established; since, in your opinion, the book itself carries with it it's own refutation. A gentleman as acute, probably, as any of you; and who once believed, perhaps, as little as any of you, has drawn a quite different conclusion from the perusal of the new Testament; his book (however exceptionable it may be thought in some particular parts) exhibits, not only a distinguished triumph of reason over prejudice, of Christianity over Deism; but it exhibits, what is infinitely more rare, the character of a man, who has had courage and candour enough to acknowledge it.[28]

But what if there should be some incomprehensible doctrines in the Christian religion; some circumstances, which in their causes, or their consequences, surpass the reach of human reason; are they to be rejected upon that account? You are, or would be thought, men of reading, and knowledge, and enlarged understandings; weigh the matter fairly; and consider whether revealed religion be not, in this respect, just upon the same footing, with every other object of your contemplation. Even in mathematics, the science of demonstration itself, though you get over it's first principles, and learn to digest the idea of a point without parts, a line without breadth, and a surface without thickness; yet you will find yourselves at a loss to comprehend the perpetual approximation of lines, which can never meet; the doctrine of incommensurables, and of an infinity of infinites, each infinitely greater, or infinitely less, not only than any finite quantity, but than each other. In physics, you cannot comprehend the primary cause of any thing; not of

[27] Bayle, Hist. Dict. Art. Des-Barreaux.
[28] See A View of the Internal Evidence, &c. by Soame Jenyns.

the light, by which you see; nor of the elasticity of the air, by which you hear; nor of the fire, by which you are warmed. In physiology, you cannot tell, what first gave motion to the heart; nor what continues it; nor why it's motion is less voluntary, than that of the lungs; nor why you are able to move your arm, to the right or left, by a simple volition: you cannot explain the cause of animal heat; nor comprehend the principle, by which your body was at first formed, nor by which it is sustained, nor by which it will be reduced to earth. In natural religion, you cannot comprehend the eternity or omnipresence of the Deity; nor easily understand, how his prescience can be consistent with your freedom, or his immutability with his government of moral agents; nor why he did not make all his creatures equally perfect; nor why he did not create them sooner: In short, you cannot look into any branch of knowledge, but you will meet with subjects above your comprehension. The fall and the redemption of human kind, are not more incomprehensible, than the creation and the conservation of the universe; the infinite Author of the works of providence, and of nature, is equally inscrutable, equally past our finding out in them both. And it is somewhat remarkable, that the deepest inquirers into nature, have ever thought with most reverence, and spoken with most diffidence, concerning those things, which in revealed religion, may seem hard to be understood; they have ever avoided that self-sufficiency of knowledge, which springs from ignorance, produces indifference, and ends in infidelity. Admirable to this purpose, is the reflection of the greatest mathematician of the present age, when he is combating an opinion of Newton's, by an hypothesis of his own, still less defensible than that which he opposes: – Tous les jours que je vois de ces esprits-forts, qui critique les verites de notre religion, et s'en mocquent meme avec la plus impertinente suffisance, je pense, chetifs mortels! combien et combien des choses sur lesquels vous raisonnez si legerement, sont elles plus sublimes, et plus eleves, que celles sur lesquelles le grand Newton s'egare si grossierement.[29]

Plato mentions a set of men, who were very ignorant, and thought themselves supremely wise; and who rejected the argument for the being of a God, derived from the harmony

---

[29] Euler.

and order of the universe, as old and trite;[30] there have been men, it seems, in all ages, who in affecting singularity, have overlooked truth: an argument, however, is not the worse for being old; and surely it would have been a more just mode of reasoning, if you had examined the external evidence for the truth of Christianity, weighed the old arguments from miracles, and from prophecies, before you had rejected the whole account from the difficulties you met with in it. You would laugh at an Indian, who in peeping into a history of England, and meeting with the mention of the Thames being frozen, or of a shower of hail, or of snow, should throw the book aside, as unworthy of his further notice, from his want of ability to comprehend these phænomena.

In considering the argument from miracles, you will soon be convinced, that it is possible for God to work miracles; and you will be convinced, that it is as possible for human testimony, to establish the truth of miraculous, as of physical or historical events; but before you can be convinced, that the miracles in question, are supported by such testimony, as deserves to be credited, you must inquire at what period, and by what persons, the books of the old and new Testament were composed; if you reject the account, without making this examination, you reject it from prejudice, not from reason.

There is, however, a short method of examining this argument, which may, perhaps, make as great an impression on your minds, as any other. Three men of distinguished abilities, rose up at different times, and attacked Christianity with every objection which their malice could suggest, or their learning could devise; but neither Celsus in the second century, nor Porphyry in the third, nor the emperor Julian himself in the fourth century, ever questioned the reality of the miracles related in the Gospels. Do but you grant us, what these men (who were more likely to know the truth of the matter, than you can be) granted to their adversaries, and we will very readily let you make the most of the Magic, to which, as the last wretched shift, they were forced to attribute them. We can find you men, in our days, who from the mixture of two colourless liquors, will produce you a third as red as blood, or of any other colour you desire; *& dicto citius*, by a drop resembling water, will restore the transparency; they will make

---

[30] De Leg. Lib. x.

two fluids coalesce into a solid body; and from the mixture of liquors colder than ice, will instantly raise you a horrid explosion and a tremendous flame: these, and twenty other tricks they will perform, without having been sent with our Saviour to Egypt to learn magic; nay, with a bottle or two of oil, they will compose the undulations of a lake; and by a little art, they will restore the functions of life to a man, who has been an hour or two under water, or a day or two buried in the snow: but in vain will these men, or the greatest Magician that Egypt ever saw, say to a boisterous sea, *Peace, be still*; in vain will they say to a carcase rotting in the grave, *Come forth*; the winds and the sea will not obey them, and the putrid carcase will not hear them. You need not suffer yourselves to be deprived of the weight of this argument, from it's having been observed, that the Fathers have acknowledged the supernatural part of Paganism; since the Fathers were in no condition to detect a cheat, which was supported both by the disposition of the people, and the power of the civil magistrate;[31] and they were from that inability, forced to attribute to infernal agency, what was too cunningly contrived to be detected, and contrived for too impious a purpose, to be credited as the work of God.

With respect to prophecy, you may, perhaps, have accustomed yourselves to consider it, as originating in Asiatic enthusiasm, in Chaldean mystery, or in the subtle strategem of interested Priests; and have given yourselves no more trouble concerning the predictions of sacred, than concerning the oracles of Pagan history. Or if you have ever cast a glance upon this subject, the dissensions of learned men concerning the proper interpretation of the Revelation, and other difficult prophecies, may have made you rashly conclude, that all prophecies were equally unintelligible; and more indebted for their accomplishment, to a fortunate concurrence of events, and the pliant ingenuity of the expositor, than to the inspired foresight of the prophet. In all that the prophets of the old Testament have delivered, concerning the destruction of particular cities, and the desolation of particular kingdoms, you may see nothing but shrewd conjectures, which any one acquainted with the history of the rise and fall of empires, might certainly have made: and as you would not hold him for a prophet, who should now affirm, that London or Paris would

---

[31] See Ld Lyttlet. Obs. on St. Paul. p. 59.

afford to future ages, a spectacle just as melancholy, as that which we now contemplate, with a sigh, in the ruins of Agrigentum or Palmyra; so you cannot persuade yourselves to believe, that the denunciations of the prophets against the haughty cities of Tyre or Babylon, for instance, proceeded from the inspiration of the Deity. There is no doubt, that by some such general kind of reasoning, many are influenced to pay no attention to an argument, which, if properly considered, carries with it the strongest conviction.

Spinoza said, That he would have broken his atheistic system to pieces, and embraced without repugnance, the ordinary faith of Christians, if he could have persuaded himself of the resurrection of Lazarus from the dead; and I question not, that there are many disbelievers, who would relinquish their Deistic tenets, and receive the gospel, if they could persuade themselves, that God had ever so far interfered in the moral government of the world, as to illumine the mind of any one man with the knowledge of future events. A miracle strikes the senses of the persons who see it, a prophecy addresses itself to the understandings of those who behold it's completion; and it requires, in many cases some learning, in all some attention, to judge of the correspondence of events with the predictions concerning them. No one can be convinced, that what Jeremiah and the other prophets foretold of the fate of Babylon, that it should be besieged by the Medes; that it should be taken, when her mighty men were drunken, when her springs were dried up; and that it should become a pool of water, and should remain desolate for ever; no one, I say, can be convinced, that all these, and other parts of the prophetic denunciation, have been minutely fulfilled, without spending some time in reading the accounts, which profane Historians have delivered down to us concerning it's being taken by Cyrus; and which modern travellers have given us of it's present situation.

Porphyry was so persuaded of the coincidence between the prophecies of Daniel and the events, that he was forced to affirm, the prophecies were written, after the things prophesied of had happened; another Porphyry has, in our days, been so astonished at the correspondence between the prophecy concerning the destruction of Jerusalem, as related by St. Matthew, and the history of that event, as recorded by Josephus; that rather than embrace Christianity, he has ventured (contrary to the faith of all ecclesiastical history, the opinion of the learned of all ages, and all the rules of good criticism) to assert, that St. Matthew wrote his Gospel after Jerusalem had been taken and destroyed by the Romans. You may from these instances perceive the strength of the argument from prophecy; it has not been able indeed to vanquish the prejudices of either the antient or the modern Porphyry; but it has been able to compel them both, to be guilty of obvious falsehoods, which have nothing but impudent assertions to support them.

Some over-zealous interpreters of scripture have found prophecies in simple narrations, extended real predictions beyond the times and circumstances to which they naturally were applied, and perplexed their readers with a thousand quaint allusions and allegorical conceits; this proceeding has made men of sense pay less regard to prophecy in general; there are some predictions however, such as those concerning the present state of the Jewish people, and the corruption of Christianity, which are now fulfilling in the world; and which, if you will take the trouble to examine them, you will find of such an extraordinary nature, that you will not perhaps hesitate to refer them to God as their author; and if you once become persuaded of the truth of any one miracle, or of the completion of any one prophecy, you will resolve all your difficulties (concerning the manner of God's interposition, in the moral government of our species, and the nature of the doctrines contained in revelation) into your own inability fully to comprehend the whole scheme of divine providence.

We are told however, that the strangeness of the narration, and the difficulty of the doctrines contained in the new Testament, are not the only circumstances which induce you to reject it; you have discovered, you think, so many contradictions, in the accounts which the Evangelists have given of the life of Christ, that you are compelled to consider the whole as an ill-digested and improbable story. You would not reason thus, upon any other occasion; you would not reject as fabulous the accounts given by Livy and Polybius of Hannibal and the Carthaginians, though you should discover a difference betwixt them in several points of little importance. You cannot compare the history of the same events as delivered by any two historians, but you will meet with many circumstances; which, though mentioned by one, are either wholly omitted or differently related by the other; and this observation is peculiarly applicable to biographical writings: But no one ever thought of disbelieving the leading circumstances of the lives of Vitellius or Vespasian, because Tacitus and Suetonius did not in every thing correspond in their accounts of these emperors; and if the memoirs of the life and doctrines of M. de Voltaire himself, were some twenty or thirty years after his death, to be delivered to the world by four of his most intimate acquaintance; I do not apprehend that we should discredit the whole account of such an extraordinary man, by reason of some slight inconsistences and contradictions, which the avowed enemies of his name might chance to discover in the several narrations. Though we should grant you then, that the Evangelists had fallen into some trivial contradictions, in what they have related concerning the life of Christ; yet you ought not to draw any other inference from our concession, than that they had not plotted together, as cheats would have done, in order to give an unexceptionable consistency to their fraud. We are not however disposed to make you any such concession; we will rather shew you the futility of your general argument, by touching upon a few of the places, which you think are most liable to your censure.

You observe, that neither Luke, nor Mark, nor John have mentioned the cruelty of Herod in murdering the infants of Bethleem; and that no account is to be found of this matter in Josephus, who wrote the life of Herod; and therefore the fact recorded by Matthew is not true. – The concurrent testimony of many independent writers concerning a matter of fact, unquestionably adds to it's probability; but if nothing is to be received as true, upon the testimony of a single Author, we must give up some of the best writers, and disbelieve some of the most interesting facts of ancient history.

According to Matthew, Mark, and Luke, there was only an interval of three months, you say, between the baptism and crucifixion of Jesus; from which time taking away the forty days of the temptation, there will only remain about six weeks for the whole period of his public ministry; which lasted however according to St. John, at the least above three years. – Your objection fairly stated stands thus, Matthew, Mark, and Luke, in writing the history of Jesus Christ, mention the several events of his life, as following one another in continued succession, without taking notice of the times in which they happened; but is it a just conclusion from their silence, to infer that there really were no intervals of time between the transactions which they seem to have connected? many instances might be produced from the most admired Biographers of Antiquity, in which events are related, as immediately consequent to each other, which did not happen but at very distant periods: we have an obvious example of this manner of writing in St. Matthew; who connects the preaching of John the Baptist with the return of Joseph from Egypt, though we are certain, that the latter event preceded the former by a great many years.

John has said nothing of the institution of the Lord's supper; the other Evangelists have said nothing of the washing of the disciples' feet: – What then? are you not ashamed to produce these facts, as instances of contradiction? if omissions are contradictions, look into the history of the age of Louis the fourteenth, or into the general history of M. de Voltaire, and you will meet with a great abundance of contradictions.

John, in mentioning the discourse which Jesus had with his mother and his beloved disciple, at the time of his crucifixion, says, that she with Mary Magdalene, stood near the cross; Matthew, on the other hand, says, that Mary Magdalene and the other women were there, beholding afar off: this you think a manifest contradiction; and scoffingly inquire, whether the women and the beloved disciple, which were near the cross, could be the same with those, who stood far from the cross? – It is difficult not to transgress the bounds of moderation and good manners, in answering such sophistry; what! have you to learn, that though the Evangelists speak of the crucifixion, as of one event, it was not accomplished in one instant, but lasted several hours? And why the women, who were at a distance from the cross, might not during it's continuance, draw near the cross; or from being near the cross, might not move from the cross, is more than you can explain to either us, or yourselves. And we take from you your only refuge, by denying expressly, that the different Evangelists, in their mention of the women, speak of the same point of time.

The Evangelists, you affirm, are fallen into gross contradictions, in their accounts of the appearances, by which Jesus manifested himself to his disciples, after his resurrection from the dead; for Matthew speaks of two, Mark of three, Luke of two, and John of four. That contradictory propositions cannot be true, is readily granted; and if you will produce the place, in which Matthew says, that Jesus Christ appeared twice and *no oftener*, it will be further granted, that he is contradicted by John, in a very material part of his narration; but till you do that, you must excuse me, if I cannot grant, that the Evangelists have contradicted each other in this point; for to common understandings it is pretty evident, that if Christ appeared four times, according to John's account, he must have appeared twice, according to that of Matthew and Luke, and thrice, according to that of Mark.

The different Evangelists are not only accused of contradicting each other, but Luke is said to have contradicted himself; for in his Gospel he tells us, that Jesus ascended into heaven from Bethany; and in the Acts of the Apostles, of which he is the reputed author, he informs us, that he ascended from Mount Olivet. – Your objection proceeds either from your ignorance of geography, or your illwill to Christianity; and upon either supposition, deserves our contempt: be pleased, however, to remember for the future, that Bethany was not only the name of a town, but of a district of Mount Olivet adjoining to the town.

From this specimen of the contradictions, ascribed to the historians of the life of Christ, you may judge for yourselves, what little reason there is to reject Christianity upon their account; and how sadly you will be imposed upon (in a matter of more consequence to you than any other) if you take every thing for a contradiction, which the uncandid adversaries of Christianity think proper to call one.

Before I put an end to this address, I cannot help taking notice of an argument, by which some philosophers have of late endeavoured to overturn the whole system of revelation: And it is the more necessary to give an answer to their objection, as it is become a common subject of philosophical conversation, especially amongst those, who have visited the continent. The objection tends to invalidate, as is supposed, the authority of Moses; by shewing, that the earth is much older, than it can be proved to be from his account of the creation, and the scripture chronology. We contend, that six thousand years have not yet elapsed, since the creation; and these philosophers contend, that they have indubitable proof of the earth's being at the least fourteen thousand years old; and they complain, that Moses hangs as a dead weight upon them, and blunts all their zeal for inquiry.[32]

The Canonico Recupero, who, it seems, is engaged in writing the history of mount Etna, has discovered a stratum of Lava, which flowed from that mountain, according to his opinion, in the time of the second Punic war, or about two thousand years ago; this stratum is not yet covered with soil, sufficient for the production of either corn or vines; it requires then, says the Canon, two thousand years, at least, to convert a stratum of lava into a fertile field. In sinking a pit near *Jaci*, in the neighbourhood of Etna, they have discovered evident marks of seven distinct lavas, one under the other; the surfaces of which are parallel, and most of them covered with a thick bed of rich earth; now, the eruption, which formed the lowest of these lavas, (if we may be allowed to reason, says the Canon, from analogy,) flowed from the mountain at least fourteen thousand years ago. – It might be briefly answered to this objection, by denying, that there is any thing in the history of Moses repugnant to this opinion concerning the great antiquity of the earth; for though the rise and progress of arts and sciences, and the small multiplication of the human species, render it almost to a demonstration probable, that man has not existed longer upon the surface of this earth, than according to the Mosaic account; yet, that the earth itself was then created out of nothing, when man was placed upon it, is not, according to the sentiments of some philosophers, to be proved from the original text of sacred scripture; we might, I say, reply, with these philosophers, to this formidable objection of the Canon, by granting it in it's full extent; we are under no necessity, however, of adopting their opinion, in order to shew the weakness of the Canon's reasoning. For in the first place, the Canon has not satisfactorily established his main fact, that the lava in question, is the identical lava, which Diodorus Siculus mentions to have flowed from Etna, in the second Carthaginian war; and in the second place, it may be observed, that the time necessary for converting lavas into fertile fields, must be very different, according to the different consistencies of the lavas, and their different situations, with respect to elevation or depression; to their being exposed to winds, rains, and to other circumstances; just as the time, in which the heaps of iron slag

---

[32] Brydone's Travels.

(which resembles lava) are covered with verdure, is different at different furnaces, according to the nature of the slag, and situation of the furnace; and something of this kind is deducible from the account of the Canon himself; since the crevices of this famous stratum are really full of rich, good soil, and have pretty large trees growing in them.

But if all this should be thought not sufficient to remove the objection, I will produce the Canon an analogy in opposition to his analogy, and which is grounded on more certain facts. Etna and Vesuvius resemble each other, in the causes which produce their eruptions, and in the nature of their lavas, and in the time necessary to mellow them into soil fit for vegetation; or if there be any slight difference in this respect, it is probably not greater than what subsists between different lavas of the same mountain. This being admitted, which no philosopher will deny, the Canon's analogy will prove just nothing at all, if we can produce an instance of seven different lavas (with interjacent strata of vegetable earth) which have flowed from mount Vesuvius, within the space, not of fourteen thousand, but of somewhat less than seventeen hundred years; for then, according to our analogy, a stratum of lava may be covered with vegetable soil, in about two hundred and fifty years, instead of requiring two thousand for the purpose. The eruption of Vesuvius, which destroyed Herculaneum and Pompeii, is rendered still more famous by the death of Pliny, recorded by his nephew, in his letter to Tacitus; this event happened in the year 79; it is not yet then quite seventeen hundred years, since Herculaneum was swallowed up: but we are informed by unquestionable authority, that "the matter which covers the ancient town of Herculaneum, is not the produce of one eruption only; for there are evident marks, that the matter of six eruptions has taken its course over that which lies immediately above the town, and was the cause of it's destruction. These strata are either of lava or burnt matter, *with veins of good soil betwixt them.*"[33] – I will not add another word upon this subject; except that the bishop of the diocese, was not much out in his advice to Canonico Recupero – to take care, not to make his mountain older than Moses; though it would have been full as well, to have shut his mouth with a

---

[33] See sir William Hamilton's Remarks upon the Nature of the Soil of Naples and it's Neighbourhood, in the Philos. Trans. Vol. lxi. p. 7.

reason, as to have stopped it with the dread of an ecclesiastical censure.

You perceive, with what ease a little attention will remove a great difficulty; but had we been able to say nothing, in explanation of this phænomenon, we should not have acted a very rational part, in making our ignorance the foundation of our infidelity, or suffering a minute philosopher to rob us of our religion.

Your objections to revelation, may be numerous; you may find fault with the account, which Moses has given of the creation and the fall; you may not be able to get water enough for an universal deluge; nor room enough in the ark of Noah, for all the different kinds of aerial and terrestrial animals; you may be dissatisfied with the command for sacrificing of Isaac, for plundering the Egyptians, and for extirpating the Canaanites; you may find fault with the Jewish œconomy, for it's ceremonies, it's sacrifices, and it's multiplicity of priests; you may object to the imprecations in the psalms, and think the immoralities of David, a fit subject for dramatic ridicule;[34] you may look upon the partial promulgation of Christianity, as an insuperable objection to it's truth; and waywardly reject the goodness of God towards yourselves, because you do not comprehend, how you have deserved it more than others; you may know nothing of the entrance of sin and death into the world, by one man's transgression; nor be able to comprehend the doctrine of the cross and of redemption by Jesus Christ; in short, if your mind is so disposed, you may find food for your scepticism in every page of the Bible, as well as in every appearance of nature; and it is not in the power of any person, but yourselves, to clear up your doubts; you must read, and you must think for yourselves; and you must do both with temper, with candour, and with care. Infidelity is a rank weed; it is nurtured by our vices, and cannot be plucked up as easily as it may be planted: your difficulties, with respect to revelation, may have first arisen, from your own reflection on the religious indifference of those, whom from your earliest infancy, you have been accustomed to revere and imitate; domestic irreligion may have made you a willing hearer of

---

[34] See, Saül et David Hyperdrame.
   Whatever censure the author of this composition may deserve for his intention, the work itself deserves none; it's ridicule is too gross, to mislead even the ignorant.

libertine conversation; and the uniform prejudices of the world, may have finished the business at a very early age; and left you to wander through life, without a principle to direct your conduct, and to die without hope. We are far from wishing you to trust the word of the Clergy for the truth of your religion; we beg of you to examine it to the bottom, to try it, to prove it, and not to hold it fast unless you find it good. Till you are disposed to undertake this task, it becomes you to consider with great seriousness and attention, whether it can be for your interest to esteem a few witty sarcasms, or metaphysic subtleties, or ignorant misrepresentations, or unwarranted assertions, as unanswerable arguments against revelation; and a very slight reflection will convince you, that it will certainly be for your reputation, to employ the flippancy of your rhetoric, and the poignancy of your ridicule, upon any subject, rather than upon the subject of Religion.

I take my leave with recommending to your notice, the advice which Mr. Locke gave to a young man, who was desirous of becoming acquainted with the doctrines of the Christian religion. "Study the holy scripture, especially the new Testament: Therein are contained the words of eternal life. It has God for it's author; Salvation for it's end; and Truth without any mixture of error for it's matter[35]."

I am, &c.

---

[35] Locke's Posth. Works.

A REPLY TO THE REASONINGS OF MR. GIBBON, IN HIS HISTORY OF THE DECLINE AND FALL OF THE ROMAN EMPIRE
by Smyth Loftus

CHAPTER I.

My firm belief of that religion which distinguishes its author and itself by a commandment to "love one another," and consequently to promote, to the utmost of our power, the happiness of all mankind, and more especially of all our fellow-christians, hath induced me to attempt a defence of it against the attacks of the more ingenious than candid Mr. Gibbon, who, in his History of the Decline of the Roman Empire, has endeavoured totally to destroy it, and to introduce I know not what, it is more than probable he himself knows not what, in the place of it; but this I can tell him, he would introduce such a profligacy of principle and manners, as must totally disqualify the reader, with whom he has any success, for any happiness either in this or the next world; and that, whether considered as an individual, or a member of society, the providence of God, and the nature of man, both of them unite to bear me out in this assertion.

I look upon it as a fortunate incident for Ireland, that Dr. Watson's Answer came out here almost as soon as Mr. Gibbon's book; for it confutes the most difficult and pernicious parts of it. But as this gentleman hath studied conciseness so much as to omit many things which to the less knowing reader may want an explanation, I have endeavoured to remedy this defect, by writing these observations, which will give a tolerable view of the whole controversy, and extend to those objections against christianity, which are the great foundations of our modern unbelief.

One should imagine, that deistical writers, who all declare for a religion of Nature, and this so perfect, that nothing can be added to or diminished from it, and the whole of it likewise so certain and manifest that no instruction can be wanted or given in it even by God himself: – one should imagine, at least, that these gentlemen would confer some honour upon christianity, not only for teaching a much more perfect and beneficial morality, and enforcing it by infinitely more powerful motives, than had ever been known by mankind before; but likewise for its furnishing us with a perfect knowledge of God, his laws, nature, government, and true religion, and the pure worship with which he is to be served; which knowledge must be most advantageous to virtue and the happiness of mankind, and thereby preserve them from that abominable superstition of the heathens which must prove so pernicious to both: – one should imagine that this absurd and idolatrous paganism should be as severely, as it would be most justly, condemned by those setters-up of religion, and christianity in the same manner approved of and commended by them. But nothing like this, nay, the very reverse of this, is to be found in all our infidel writings.

The great genius and learning of Mr. Gibbon, and his acquaintance with the heathen and primitive christian writers, must have informed him, that the grossest immorality was not only permitted but required by the Gentile religion; that their gods, nay the very chief of them, were made up of the undutiful and incestuous, of the abusers of themselves with mankind, of the savage and murderer, of the thief and cheat. He cannot be ignorant that they confessedly worshipped evil beings to prevent their doing them mischief; that human sacrifices were universal among them; that they were practised even in their most civilized nations, and frequently offered up with an excess of cruelty and torture. He must know that many of their religious services did require drunkenness, lewdness, pollution, blood, murder, even to their burning to ashes their own living children, and sometimes in great numbers, of their most noble and best families, to their horrible and malicious idols and devils: for nothing but such accursed spirits could have inspired or been pleased with such a service as this.

With all these things must Mr. Gibbon be well acquainted, and must likewise know that all their wise philosophers were so ignorant or timorous in these matters, that they all, outwardly, conformed to the religions of their several countries, and advised all others to do the same; and when christianity arose, instead of abandoning this detestable superstition, did, generally, endeavour to defend it; and, therefore, with equal falsehood and malice, did misrepresent christianity, and abuse it as the basest and most abominable of all false and bad religions. He cannot be, he is not, ignorant of their absurd notions of a future life, and the retributions of it; but makes their very honest philosophers, and the priests themselves, deride the whole of their religious services, whilst they officiated in them. What a charming religion of nature was this, and what worthy guides in it were their philosophers and great men, upon whose integrity Mr. Gibbon, in other places, can himself repose, and would have others likewise repose, such an unlimited confidence.

Thus abominably false was the pagan religion; and what a sad effect must this have had upon the morals of the people, when they were, even by their religion, initiated into wickedness; and must, besides, be naturally led to imitate the actions of these gods whom they worshipped and thought it their duty to please? These were their gods, and such their worship, whilst the one true God was totally abandoned by them; and yet Mr. Gibbon, in page 553 of his first volume, instead of condemning, seems rather to praise this perversion of all religion. The folly and falsehood of it are, indeed, acknowledged; but its uncleanness, madness, violence, cruelty, are all kept out of sight, and this monstrous superstition treated by him rather as an innocent and useful, than a most criminal and pernicious deceit; and an occasion taken to commend it for its mildness and toleration; although it would bear no religion but such as was founded upon its own bottom, nor sometimes all of this neither; and though it shewed itself so cruel and bloody to the best of mankind for professing christianity, and refusing to join in this their abominable idolatry.

CHAP. II.
Having, with the primitive christian apologists, concisely shewn what that heathenism was which Mr. Gibbon so undeservedly spares, or rather commends, let us with them turn to christianity, and see, likewise, what this religion is which he so unmeritedly condemns, and is endeavouring to destroy.

Christianity informs us that there is one infinite, eternal, all-powerful, omniscient Spirit, whom we call God; who, as he is absolutely perfect in his being, and the producer of all other beings, so likewise in morality or holiness; for he is infinitely pure, just, merciful, good, and true, and therefore the greatest lover possible of virtue, and hater of vice. It tells us that the heavens and the earth, and all things in them, were created, do subsist, and are governed by him: – that he was too good to make man for this insignificant life alone, but hath formed him for an endless and perfect existence in a new life, and an everlasting and inconceivable glory and happiness in it, provided he will, by proper behaviour in this world, qualify or make himself capable of them: – that the qualification required, is for him so to act in this present life as shall render him the most lovely and happy being in himself, most beneficial to every creature with whom he is connected, and to whom his influence can extend, and as shall fill him with those affections which will assimilate him to the all-perfect God, and train his heart to the enjoyment of that Being in whom alone the perfect happiness of all intelligent creatures is to be found, and upon a likeness to whom it must for ever depend.

Christianity tells us, that weak, fallen, and sinful as all men are, and perfectly holy and just as their God, yet he is not man's enemy, but his most affectionate and beneficent friend; for even to us sinners God is love: – that he does not desert us as soon as he has made us, but watches continually over us to do us good, and this with such a particular providence, that a hair falls not from our heads but with his knowledge and by his permission: – that we may, in every case, address ourselves to him in prayer, for protection, deliverance, guidance, blessing, and be sure of obtaining them all, so far as they are good for us; provided we intreat them with fit dispositions, and in the proper manner which he hath prescribed to us; and from hence shews us we have a certainty, that, with our own honest endeavours, he will carry us safe through all our dangers here, whether of life or death, and never quit our protection till he has lodged us for ever safe in heaven and its inconceivable bliss. What glorious and happy privileges are these for men! But christianity tells us, that this is a blessed condition, to which we are not of ourselves entitled, but which has been most dearly purchased for us by our redemption in Christ.

For inasmuch as all men are sinners, and the great Creator and Governor of the universe is of such a nature as to hold all sinners in abhorrence, and he must likewise, as he values the happiness of his whole creation, dissuade by the most powerful motives possible from all sin, and persuade to virtue; therefore has the most perfectly just and holy, but most merciful and loving God, contrived a way to save man, which shall the best answer to both these purposes, at the same time that it procures pardon, favour, and happiness for man, the sinner. For to save mankind from the destructive nature and horrible effect of sin, did that Son of God, who is himself that efficient and final cause and sustainer of all things, become man, with all the innocent weakness and infirmities of this low nature, that, by therein performing for us the whole will of God, without any sin, he might cloath us with his own righteousness; and, by dying in all the tortures of the cross for us, he might expiate our sins, and reconcile us to his all-holy father, and our offended God. By all these providences have we the greatest detestation possible shewn to sin, and yet love to his creatures though sinners: and nothing could ever so affectingly prove the dreadfully odious and pernicious nature of vice, and the absolute necessity of virtue in order to our future happiness, as does this christian scheme of salvation. And, to encrease this conviction, we are not yet, with all this excess of kindness manifested to us, permitted to put up a petition to him but through the mediation of this infinitely-deserving Redeemer; nor are we capable of any acceptance from him, but through the sanctification of his all-powerful and Holy Spirit, who shall new create our fallen and corrupted nature, and thereby render us capable of that divine favour and happiness for which we were at first created. And thus is the whole of our salvation from our God, who himself atones, sanctifies, pardons, blesses, and is all in all to the true christian. Besides, to give us an undoubted assurance of his having obtained all these blessings for us, he rises from the grave and conquers death, the penalty of sin, ascends into heaven, the place of our happiness, to take possession before-hand for us; he is invested with all power, both in heaven and earth; he visibly sends down from thence the gifts of his Holy Spirit upon men: and because he loved us to such an inconceivable degree, therefore is he appointed the judge of all creatures, and he himself it is who is to award them all to their proper fate, whether of happiness or misery, for ever; and our salvation put entirely into his power.

By these means have we the most certain and comfortable assurance of our being all saved upon the easy terms of the Gospel, and made partakers of endless life and inconceivable happiness. And shall any man wilfully cast away these blessings from him? It is true that they are most wonderful;

and, where a wrong biass of mind hath been contracted, that they will appear hard of belief, or utterly incredible. But, to take off this incredibility, let it be considered, that God is an infinite being, and must therefore be exalted as much above men in his workings, as in his incomprehensible nature; and as every person acquainted with his material creation, must acknowledge, that he is here inscrutable where yet there can be no opposition made to his will, so must he be much more inscrutable in the formation and government of his moral creatures, who to be moral must be free, and therefore governed according to their freedom; but who, if they be free, will many of them, for present gratification, be ever flying off from that rule of right to which all happiness is, and must be, annexed, and thereby introducing evil, instead of the Creator's intended good, into his good creation. Where this happens to be the case, a remedy will be manifestly wanted; and certainly it is so in this our world: and we find that the divine power, wisdom, goodness, are greatly, I had almost said principally, here displayed, by the very many and various remedies which he hath provided for the numberless evils which immorality and wickedness have introduced into our world, and to which we are here so miserably subjected.

Besides, the divine Being must ever be distinguished and glorified by his workings, and chiefly, no doubt, by his workings to do good; and, if so, it must be by providences of mercy and kindness which shall be expressive of his infinity, and therefore stupendous and wonderful beyond all created conception. And if it be considered, that a love to virtue and his creatures must ever be the highest affections in the divine mind, and must, by the manifestations which he shall herein make of his nature, do the most honour to himself and benefit to all moral beings; (for this will beget in them the greatest love to, and happiness in him, and fill them with these affections which are of all others the most lovely and blissful;) we shall then see abundant reason for this providence of Christianity, and in fullness of conviction acknowledge, that he hath hereby deservedly gotten himself a name which is above every name that ever was or shall be named, whether in heaven or earth, whether in this world or in the world to come; and does most peculiarly merit the most thankful and high adoration and praise of every creature, upon account of this wonderful work of our redemption in Christ.

But it will be asked, Is this, indeed, the whole of Christianity? I answer that it is not; for this religion is made up of threatenings as well as of promises; and denounces a Hell of never-ending torments to the wicked, as well as it engages a Heaven of the like happiness to the virtuous person: – a declaration this, truly affecting and awful to the most virtuous of men; but, to the many wicked among us, so horrible, that it must make them wish, and eagerly too, that death may be to them, what it is now frequently styled, the end of all existence. But who are they with whom this must be the case? Why only with those men who will sacrifice the boasted dignity of rational and moral man, to the low appetites and passions of irrational and immoral brute. And where this is the cause of infidelity to any, how very base and detestable must the infidel be? Every animal is made to desire enjoyment; and man, by knowing that there can be no enjoyment without existence, is made to desire existence, and this without end: and herein his animal nature joins in with his reason; for it makes him abhor, and, to the utmost of his power, to resist and strive against death and an extinction of being. And what is it, then, which can cause these people to wish for this extinction? Why it is, that they may here wallow in all sensuality without any thought or care of religion or futurity, and yet avoid that wounded conscience which would make them justly apprehend, that, if there should be another life, they must be miserable in it; for it is manifestly better not to be at all, than to subsist in misery.

And does, then, their perfect and boasted religion of Nature bring them at last to this unnatural pass, that they will, upon the basest of motives, and contrary to their own nature and to the intention of their all-beneficent God, who has made them for an infinitely better existence than that of this life, and such glorious enjoyments in it, will they pin themselves down to the transitory, insignificant gratifications of this present world, and wish for nothing more, nay, that there might be no more, but all end with this life? Let there be but a place of any considerable profit or honour offered to any of them, and how will he rejoice in it, and what difficulties will he not go through to obtain or preserve it? And how is it, then, that this man shall spurn away from him the infinitely more valuable offer of an endless possession of inconceivable glory and happiness? This person may, in this, certainly see his own baseness, unreasonableness, and demerit: but, as we made not ourselves, nor can alter that constitution of things which the divine will hath established, it is our chief business, in effect our only business, most carefully and impartially to enquire whether these most important matters be not so as Christianity has represented them; and, if they be, to conform ourselves to them; for otherwise we may, and deservedly shall, undo ourselves by this most unreasonable and criminal neglect.

CHAP. III.
Christianity tells us, that there is to be another life after this, and that it shall be a state of retribution; and the natures both of God and man tell us the same. The Heathen philosophers, through their ignorance of the divine Being, and his moral and particular government of the world, could make nothing of this argument. Seneca, as well as Mr. Gibbon, tells us, that although they had promised, yet they had not proved, this future existence: but it is not so with them whom Christianity has enlightened.

Man is a moral creature; and to be moral, is to deserve love and reward, or hatred and punishment, for his good or evil behaviour: he feels that it is so. The divine Being is likewise moral, moral in the highest possible degree; and must, therefore, have these affections to the man, and see that he merits the one or the other of these retributions. And shall he not deal with him in a manner comformable to them? This would be a direct contradiction to both their natures; and, therefore, he must, as certainly as he is moral himself, and much more as he is the moral governor of the world, reward the one, and punish the other. And as this retribution is not always, perhaps never, adequately administered in this world, it must be so in another; and that constitution of Nature, which the Creator of the world hath established, demonstrates that it shall be so.

All happiness depends upon virtue; and, to be complete in happiness, we must be entire in virtue: for wherever vice is admitted, misery must be there. If, then, the all-gracious God hath designed us for any happiness hereafter, and much more for a happiness which is to be complete and certain, he must breed us up to virtue here; for we are made every-thing, we are even made reasoners, by exercise and habit: and if we shall accustom ourselves to contradict and despise the obligations of virtue for the love of sensuality and vice, we must, by a natural necessity, render ourselves incapable of happiness hereafter, and plunge ourselves into misery and ruin; and remain in this misery till we have changed our nature, and made that virtuous and good which was before vicious and bad. Religion and virtue are, then, the most important of all matters; and the infidel neglect of them the most irrational and destructive that can be. We must in this life take care to habituate ourselves to love and to chuse the things which are good, and to abominate and cast from us the things which are evil. And man's own nature shews him that this was the very end of his creation, and the cause of his being introduced into the present world.

That man is detestable and vicious who is not governed by virtue; and virtue always requires, that, in the things concerning itself, we act above this world; and, where any competition comes between the interests of the two, that we act in direct contradiction to the latter, and sacrifice all the enjoyments of life, nay, and life itself, to the obligations of virtue; and this too, although it should be by the most painful of deaths. And so certainly as man's nature requires this of him, so certainly does it prove that he was made for a future life, and a just retribution in it: for, otherwise, his moral and all-gracious Creator and Governor must have caused him to lose all enjoyment, nay, and his existence too, for the doing of that which he wills and requires him to do, must love him for having done, and for which he must see that he deserves a reward; and the higher reward, the more he acts in this manner. These things cannot be, it is impossible that they should be; and therefore a future life, and a just retribution in it, are as certain to those who truly know their God, as that there is such a Being, and that he made and governs the world. And, in fact, a notion of this kind is so natural to man, that it has generally prevailed over the whole earth; and we can hardly find any nation, however barbarous, in which this has not been their belief; but so obscured and perverted, where Christianity did not enlighten them, that it became useless, and even ridiculous, to the thinking part of mankind.

How just and beneficial, then, is Christianity, which hath opened and ascertained all these most important matters to us, and assured us all of everlasting life, glory, happiness, upon the easy terms of the Gospel? And what shall we think of that person, who, by destroying Christianity, would strip us of that hope so glorious in itself, and always so necessary to cheer us in the many misfortunes of this present life, and which would, at the same time, nearly reduce this world to a hell of wickedness and misery; for the taking away all expectation of a future life, or retribution in it, must produce all these horrible effects: it must give to our animal and brutish appetites and passions, the entire dominion over the man, and thereby annihilate every thing which is worthy of esteem, or productive of happiness, and throw him into every vice which is most debasing and hurtful; and this not only to others, but even to himself. And thus having opened and vindicated the truth and benefit of Christianity in the foregoing most important particulars, upon the mistaking of which the greater part of our modern infidelity is founded, I shall proceed to examine Mr. Gibbon's objections against this religion, and return, as I hope, a satisfactory reply to them.

CHAP. IV.
It is certain, from Mr. Gibbon's declaring the polytheistick worship of the Heathens to be all foolish and false, and yet avoiding to give any commendation to that of the Christians, which is all confined to the one true God, and is a spiritual service befitting his spiritual and infinite nature; but, on the contrary, blaming them for refusing all communication with the heathens, in their religious offices; – it is certain that he must totally condemn all adoration of God as a piece of superstition and folly. But, as Christianity and Judaism, upon which it is founded, have laid the greatest stress upon this matter, and made divine worship the first of all duties, it is become absolutely requisite that we enquire into the necessity and reasonableness of this worship; and this is not only for the confutation of unbelievers, but also for the conviction of many of those who call themselves Christians, but, by the sophisms of our infidels, have been drawn into such a neglect and contempt of this great duty, as a total rejection of Christianity, and indeed of all religion, can alone vindicate.

  I will not suppose my antagonist to be an atheist, but a theist and a believer of God and his attributes; and upon this foundation will I argue the case with him. It is the office of reason to make us enquire and know, and principally in those things which are most excellent in themselves, and important to us. And as the being and nature of God, his government of the world, our dependence upon and obligations to him, and the returns which it is proper we should make for them, are of all other subjects the most noble and interesting, so must it be the principal end for which reason was given us, the chief of its offices, and our most important business to enquire into, and make ourselves knowing in, all these matters. And upon any proper enquiry, we must find our God to be the Creator of all things, that they all do subsist but by his will, and every one of them depend upon him for its being, and all the blessings which any creature possesses. And we shall likewise find that he is so perfectly excellent in himself, and so infinitely good to men, as to deserve all the esteem, reverence, love, thankfulness, which our hearts can contain: and when a sensibility of these things has been acquired, we must see it to be our duty, and the first of all duties, to entertain such affections for him, as are suitable to his all-perfect nature and our obligations, and from hence know, that we ought to take all proper means to entertain, preserve, invigorate, and express these sentiments to him; and as soon as the soul has contracted these dispositions, we shall prostrate ourselves before him in the most humble adoration of dependence, love, trust, gratitude, praise.

Neither is this grateful homage our duty only, but also our highest interest. Although man be at the head of our world, there is not any animal in it which has so many wants, and is of himself so little able to supply them. He is, indeed, that great beggar who subsists upon the joint alms of the whole creation. There is no other animal who feels such want of enjoyment, that is subject to so many evils, and suffers so often and grievously, as he; none of them which are so insecure in their blessings, nor troubled with those reasonable fears and anxieties which so often fill and torture the human breast: and if every man experiences these wantings in the affairs of this life, how much more does the religionist feel them in those of his eternal concerns! This is unquestionably his case; and by these wants, as well as his own natural inclinations, is he urged on, is he almost compelled to look out for some superior being, upon whose goodness and power he may depend for protection and for succour, suitable to his many dangers, and all his craving wants. And to his greatest possible advantage, he may have all this in his almighty and most loving and kind God; for he himself has assured him, that he will, upon his properly asking them in prayer, save him from every evil, and bless him with every good, so far as these shall be really beneficial to him. What an inestimable benefit, then, is this Christian worship to men! when we, who must care for all these things, know that we can thus lay all our care upon one who careth for us, and is always as willing and ready, as he is powerful and mighty, to protect and save us.

But this is not all: the divine Being stands in another relation to man, which is of all others the most important, and to which he ought most carefully to attend; namely, that he is the moral governor and judge of the world; which relationship, besides adding another reason for divine worship, will introduce a new and different species of it.

We know that the heaven of heavens cannot contain him, that he fills the whole of creation, and all space, which is infinitely beyond it, and is more intimately present to every creature than any creature can be to itself, and understands much better whatsoever it thinks or acts; and with this absolutely perfect knowledge of them all, we know that he must, both from the nature of himself and his government, reward or punish men for their good or evil behaviour here. As man is, then, a sinner, and obnoxious to the divine vengeance, so must he, in his adoration, address his God with those sentiments and expressions which are suitable to his sinful condition. He must, if he will hope for the so exceedingly wanted mercy and pardon from his offended God, who cannot be deceived, and is of too pure eyes to behold, or bear with, iniquity, – he must conceive and declare his sense of, and sorrow for, his sins, confess them all to him, humble himself for them, resolve to amend them, and implore the forgiveness of them, and the divine assistance to enable him to conquer them hereafter, and live a more virtuous life. That sinner, and every man is a sinner, who does not thus humble himself before his God for his manifold transgressions, has no knowledge of himself or the great Governor of the world, nor any sense of, nor repentance for, sin; and neither deserves nor is capable of mercy or happiness whilst he continues such: for, without a reformation of soul, he is disqualified for both of these; and he can have no reformation till he is filled with those dispositions and sentiments which I have now described.

And here it is to be observed, that, as the great end of all true religion and religious worship, is to qualify men for the favour and happiness of God, and neither of these is possible to be obtained but by virtue, so must all true religion tend to make us virtuous: – and as no means can be so powerful for this purpose as those which shall beget in us an unfailing and most lively sense of the being of a God, and his constant inspection of, and regard to, our behaviour, as our just governor and judge, – and prayer is the best means possible to preserve and enliven this sense, as also to breed in our hearts all those affections which are most virtuous and inciting to virtue, – so is it from hence manifest, that prayer is not only the first but the most important of all duties; for to love that incomprehensible Being who is all perfection, loveliness, goodness, and bliss, with all our heart, with all our soul, with all our mind, and with all our strength, is, both from reason and revelation, the greatest of all the commandments; and prayer is the breeding, exercising, and improving all these affections in us.

It is from hence now equally plain and certain, that it must prove a direct contradiction to the whole reason and nature of religious worship, to offer it up to any other than the one true God? And could, then, the primitive Christians join with the Heathens in their religious services? No! To have given this to the highest and purest of angels would have been idolatry; and how much more so when these were performed to such abominable creatures, and in such abominable rites as the Heathen worship consisted of!

Besides, as the innocent and necessary business, refreshments, and amusements of this life must totally engross the man, if there were not some proper means appointed by which to take off his attention from them, and fix it upon his infinitely more important concerns of futurity, so is prayer of all others the most forcible to work this effect upon him. And now let my reader think what an invaluable privilege it is to have the Almighty Governor of the world ever open to our petitions, and ready to grant them; and what a benefit Christianity has conferred upon us in preserving and making acceptable our proper worship; and what an infinite prejudice it must do to the world, to have both this religion and religious adoration totally destroyed! In this have we a signal instance of the uncertainty and great imperfection of that religion of nature, as it is called, which our infidels would set up, and are used so mightily to extol, when the great genius and learning of Mr. Gibbon could not yet discover that religious worship was at all a duty, or appropriated to the one true God; but he holds it all to be a piece of superstition and folly. It is not, however, a duty to be admitted by any deist; for this concession would necessarily imply, that the divine Being had a regard to the behaviour of men, and was governor of the world: and this implication would so mightily disturb the quiet of those gentlemen who think, with Lord Bolingbroke, that they can have no reason to fear God, though there should be a future life, for he can never do any of his creatures any harm, that this was by all means to be rejected from their belief. And here, too, we have a signal instance of what the generosity and boasted dignity of these gentlemen amount to; who, instead of being moved to virtue by this unbounded goodness of their God, do, from hence, take occasion not only to neglect him and his particular duty, but to run into the most shameful and pernicious wickedness that the fashion of the world, or a regard to their own reputation, will allow of.

And having now seen what Heathenism was, and Christianity is, and how exceedingly absurd and abominable the former, even in the most polished, inquisitive, and knowing nations; and how entirely true, useful, consistent, and important the latter; it will be easy to observe, that he must have a mind deeply prejudiced, who does not here discern the certainty and truth of the Christian religion, and that founded not only on reason, but in its goodness and happy effects; and see that it must come from that infinitely beneficent Being, who loves and would make happy all his creatures, not willing that any should perish, but that all should come to everlasting life.

CHAP. V.
Mr. Gibbon, in page 536, accounts for the prevalence of the Christian religion in these words: *It was owing to the convincing evidence of the doctrine itself, and the ruling providence of its great Author.* What a pity it is that this gentleman does not always write in the same manner! – but afterwards, with a manifest inconsistency, applies all his endeavours to extirpate this religion, which in this place he so justly commends for its usefulness and truth. But leaving this to his own heart, whether for ridicule or seriousness, I am to observe, that one most material proof for our religion is here totally suppressed; namely, the very numerous and stupendous miracles which Christ and his Apostles worked for the confirmation of their divine mission; and which, as Dr. Watson observes, are in the Scriptures so interwoven with their doctrines, that it is impossible to separate them the one from the other; and which, although they had all ceased with the lives of the Apostles, were yet so authentically set forth by them in a most undoubted history, that all men might be

as certain of them as if they had been the objects of their own senses. Never men gave such proofs of their integrity as the writers of them did; and all that they delivered was from their own certain knowledge, for they had seen and heard them. Nor were these miracles wrought in a dark corner, or in the presence of friends, to cover up or promote an imposture, or to prove things pleasing to the world, or where the great of it could be flattered by them; but it was to introduce a new and abominated religion, and in the presence of adversaries, the most eager and spiteful against them, and in a most knowing nation, who had all power in their hands, and were, by the strongest ties both of interest and inclination, driven on to discover and expose the cheat, if any thing of that kind could be found in them; but who, by authentic proofs drawn from their own writings, are shewn to have acknowledged them: only by ascribing them to magick, they destroyed their effects, and even made them the subjects of ridicule to their own people. Let us, however, go on to consider some of the internal evidences which our author himself allows to be in Christianity.

For a proper representation of this matter, in many of the most striking instances, I am happy in being able to refer the reader to Mr. Jenyns's late book upon this subject, who was once as much prejudiced, and wrote as perniciously, against Christ's religion, as Mr. Gibbon himself; but to whom a thoughtful hour, when the vanities of this world ceased to have an undue influence upon his mind, brought conviction along with it; and this upon such just and forcible reasons, that, if Mr. Gibbon will as justly consider them, as they are justly set forth, they will make a believer of him as they did of Mr. Jenyns. This being, however, a most important subject, I will add something both to its internal and external proofs.

The latter gentleman, with the greatest truth, observes, that before Christianity there existed nothing like true religion upon the face of the earth, except only among the Jews, who were enlightened by Christianity's precursor; for all of the Heathens, as held by their greatest reasoners and wisest philosophers, was falsehood, superstition, idolatry. But Christ was a carpenter, and the reputed son of a carpenter; and his Apostles, all of them, illiterate, and the most of them poor ignorant fishermen: and yet these low people have given to the world such a compleat rule of duty both to God and man, that there is neither super-abundance nor deficiency in it; but where the sharp eyes of a Shaftesbury condemns, and would have it amended, he would have but perverted and spoiled the whole by the proposed change. These men, too, set forth in their writings a scheme of providence so very high and wonderful, and so well adapted to, and explanative of, the ancient and previous revelation of the Jews, that we may safely pronounce the invention of it to be far beyond all human wisdom, and much more the wisdom of these ignorant, poor Apostles.

These illiterate men also give us the history of the life, actions, teaching, of a man who assumed a character great beyond imagination, and to which nothing in this world was equal, or had any likeness to it; namely, of his being both God and Man. And have they, indeed, made him act up to this claim? Let the reader know, to his astonishment, they really have; that they have done it in every instance, and where the things were most stupendous and difficult; where they were to fill up this seemingly contradictory character, long before described in many prophecies, and to be manifested by a series of miraculous works, which were totally beyond all human powers, and in which the greater part of this character was directly repugnant to their own expectations, their deepest prejudices, and all their hopes and comfort in this world; and the whole of these transactions described in the most plain and artless narration that ever was penned: and all this with a discovery of their own great faults, their worldly-mindedness, stupidity, and perverseness; and their master's reprehensions for them. Here have we internal evidence indeed; and I will, besides, add to it an external proof likewise.

It was impossible that the Apostles could be deceived, or deceivers; and therefore their testimony is true. They must have known whether Christ taught such doctrines, worked such miracles, died upon the cross, was buried, rose again from the dead, and proved himself to be alive again by many infallible tokens; they must have known whether he did, according to the promise made them whilst he was alive, send down upon them, after his death, the gifts of his Holy Spirit, whereby to make them know and receive his true religion, against which they were before most inveterately prejudiced; – to understand and speak a variety of languages, with which they were before totally unacquainted; to enable them, in consequence of his previous promise, to perform the same miracles which he had done in confirmation of their divine mission, and to give to these former worldlings and cowards such a contempt for this world, such a regard for the truth, the salvation of men, and the rewards of virtue in a future life; and such an undaunted daring spirit in doing the thing which was right, as caused them, though before well warned of the fatal consequences of the thing, to go about and preach Christ's religion to every nation under heaven; and to persevere in this work against all the persecutions which malice, power, cruelty, could inflict upon them, even to the most torturous of deaths. These things they must have all known; it was impossible for them to be deceived in any of them; and yet their Master, in sending them out, puts their mission upon such a bottom, as renders it impossible for them to be deceivers.

For as he did, contrary to all the ends of imposture, fix the truth of his own office upon his undergoing the most ignominious treatment, and cruel death; so did he send out his Apostles upon the same footing. His own words are, Behold I send you forth as sheep among wolves: – ye shall be betrayed by fathers, mothers, sisters, brethren; ye shall be called before kings for my sake, scourged in their synagogues, put to death, and so hated of all men, that he who killeth you will think he doth God service. Very strange it is, that such a religion as theirs should produce such an effect; but he fore-saw and predicted it to them: these predictions they every where published wherever they preached, and these miseries they were therefore as certainly to meet with, as their preaching was true: and they also told to their converts, that they should experience the same, and it proved so; and yet they not only undertook, but persevered in, this most difficult, dangerous, and unpromising work, and endured, in the prosecution of it, such opposition, hatred, inflictions, as it is hard to think how human nature could risque, or any resolution enable them to bear them. Let the reader turn to 2 Cor. 11 chap. where St. Paul is forced to give an account of his own sufferings for the preaching the Gospel, and he will find this thoroughly exemplified. And all this done by them, not to obtain any worldly advantage, but an excess of misery, and for the sole purpose of turning men away from every vice to every kind of virtue, and to the practice of every duty which can adorn and perfect human nature, and render men fit for the favour of their all-holy God, and that everlasting and inconceivable happiness which he hath created them for: – a proceeding this, which never could have flowed from any other source than such an uprightness of soul as made them incapable of any deceit.

These are but a very few of our evidences for Christianity; and had the ingenious and learned Mr. Gibbon given a proper attention to them, few as they are, we never had been hurt, nor his country neither, by the infidel part of his book.

CHAP. VI.
Numberless passages in the History shew that the author of it intended it to destroy Christianity entirely; and yet p. 535, it is with him a pure, humble, and commended religion. This is very surprising, but possibly it may be accounted for: possibly he may suppose Christianity to be what Dr. Tindal would seem to make of it, a republication of the religion of Nature; which, although Christ and his Apostles were a set of deceivers and profligate liars, yet have they given to the world in a much more perfect manner than any others ever did; only they have mixed with it a great many falsehoods, and incredible facts; and, what is worst of all, have given men occasion to fear, as well as to hope, by the declarations of it.

Page 537, the religion and worship of the Jews are manifestly condemned, and Herodotus's account of their circumcision preferred before that of the Scriptures, which tell us, that Abraham received it from God, and upon a particular occasion, and not from the Egyptians: but to which of them we ought to give credit, to them or an author confessedly fabulous in many instances, it is easy to see. There is nothing else worthy notice in that page; only that the abuse of the Jewish religion is taken from Heathen malice and ignorance, and not from the truth. Page 538, the miracles which he would have ascribed to the convenience of the Israelites, should have been set down for the good of mankind, for the manifesting the true God, and his true religion and worship, which were then most miserably mistaken by the whole world; those only excepted whom he had enlightened by his own law. The pretended incredulity of the Jews has been shewn by Dr. Watson to be a mistake; Christians, without abandoning their faith, are often tempted to distrust, and murmur against, Providence. But, besides the Israelites, those great miracles of Moses, &c. must have been known to all the nations around them, and have had a very powerful effect to bring them back to the true religion, and the knowledge and worship of the one true God, from which they were all then most horribly estranged.

Page 539, the Jewish establishment was justly appointed by a good God, not for conquest, but for the people's safety. The end of all true religion is virtue, and virtue is never promoted, but always destroyed, by conquests and large dominion; and, therefore, the Jews, although a very numerous and powerful nation, were never able to obtain a territory of any considerable extent; and this was peculiarly the case whilst they were under God's more immediate government, by his Judges. That they worshipped the one true God, and him only, and with a service suitable to his spiritual and infinite nature, although here represented in an indifferent light, was to them, in reality, the highest honour and the greatest advantage. Page 541, Christianity is here confessed to be founded upon, and armed with, the Jewish law, and yet this law is all along condemned by Mr. Gibbon; and from hence we can easily discern what he thinks of this religion. The eternal life of glory, assured to every virtuous person by the Gospel, warranted the most ardent zeal for it; and Christ's command to his Apostles to go out and preach this religion to all the world, and throughout such difficulties and sufferings, proved that it came from the almighty and beneficent God, who can govern all creatures as he pleases, and make the meanest instruments effect the greatest purposes; who would do every thing possible to benefit his creatures, and would most amply reward his faithful servants for any thing they had suffered upon his account; that is, for doing good to his world.

Page 542, Mr. Gibbon's words are: *Every privilege that could raise the proselyte from earth to heaven, that could exalt his devotion, secure his happiness, or even gratify that secret pride which, under the semblance of devotion, insinuates itself into the human heart, was still reserved for the members of the Christian church.* Was it a fault in Christianity, that it prepared men, by a Christian and pure life here, for a heaven of perfect happiness hereafter; and assured those who were so prepared, of obtaining this inconceivable blessing? And is it a fit epithet for Christian devotion, because it brings us into an intercourse with the Divine Being, and makes us certain of being accepted by him, to call it a gratification of pride? Or can, indeed, that religion render us proud, which tells us that our only worth arises from another, and that we are in ourselves incapable of any access to God, even in our very best services? What can this gentleman's notion of religion be? If we are at all to pray, must it not be in hopes of being favourably heard; and if we can be sure that we are so, must it not give us delight? Christianity has shewn us that we are made for everlasting happiness, and that the means to obtain this happiness is virtue, and Christianity is abundantly proved; and, therefore, as it must be most virtuous to receive, so must it be criminal to reject, such a religion, and such a conviction as this.

The enfranchisement of the Christian church from the Jewish ceremonial law, was to the Jews a matter of great difficulty, and therefore of some length of time. And no wonder, when it had the riveted prejudices and the excessive pride of the Israelites, in being the chosen and peculiar people of God, to contend with and master before it could be received. The arguments here offered against Christianity, are acknowledged to have met with a confutation: but this in such a manner as, in my opinion, to make them require a particular reply.

The immutability of the God of the Jews is no argument for the immutability of their law. The divine constitutions must be changed as the mutability and exigencies of that inconstant creature man shall require. The religion of the patriarchs, before Moses, was a divine law, as much as that which Moses himself gave; and yet his law made great alterations in it. All that could be wanted was a sufficiency for salvation, and this sufficiency might be obtained by various institutions, and different degrees of light. The great point of all was, along with this, properly to fore-shew and prepare men for the reception of a Redeemer to come; and it might have been, it must have been, most prejudicial to have the whole of the design at once opened; it must have prevented the completion of it. God's providence is his infinite power, justice, wisdom, goodness, put into action; and it is most wickedly presumptuous for any man to find fault with it, when, to have any proper understanding of the matter, the whole of the case, with all the reasons upon which he acts, must be made known to us. But man can never see any thing like this; a most inconsiderable part only can possibly be discovered by him; probably not one link of the chain in a thousand; and it is a signal instance of the divine contrivance, that he has enabled us men, at all, to account for his workings, and vindicate them in so many instances as we really can.

The repeal of the ritual law was more manifest than the establishment of it. The miracles wrought by Christ and his Apostles, were as great, and out of all comparison more numerous, than those of Moses and all the Prophets put together; and the law itself, besides all its typical services which pointed to Christianity, and received the whole of their value from this future dispensation, did, in many places, expressly declare, that it was to give way to, and be superseded by, a new and better covenant. Great caution was, however, necessarily to be used in this matter, lest it should give occasion to the Jews to despise and cast off this law before its time, (to which they were for a great while strangely inclined,) which was, in time, to bring them to Christ, and the rest of mankind along with them: – the principal design, and the very end, of the law.

That Christ and his Apostles observed it, is no proof of its perpetuity. These were all Jews, and therefore, in conscience, obliged to keep it as long as it lasted; and this was till our Saviour's dying, rising again, ascending into heaven, the immediate presence of the Father, and sending down from thence the gifts of his Holy Spirit upon men, had fulfilled and abrogated the whole ritual part of the law. Modern discoveries in the Hebrew have made it plain, that the most material of its rites were appointed to shadow forth our redemption in Christ.

A full knowledge of Christianity was not at once given to the Apostles; they were not, for some time, *able to bear it:* and if it had been given, they might, without incurring the charge of ambiguity, which is here laid upon them, have acted as they did. They might yield to men's weaknesses in innocent matters, rather than, by insisting upon them, to cut off many well-meaning, but deceived men, from all hope of salvation. This was the known practice of St. Paul. He conformed to the Jewish prejudices in some lesser matters, to take away their offence against Christianity; but when the necessity of these was insisted upon, he refused to conform, and utterly condemned and rejected them all. This was also the decision of the great council of Jerusalem, so soon after Christ that some of the Apostles assisted in it: and as certainly as Christ sent out his Apostles to preach his religion, so certainly was the opinion of the Judaising Christians false, that it was still necessary to be circumcised, and to keep the law. Christ Jesus came into the world to save the whole of it, and not one family only, or his own family more than any other: father, mother, sisters, and brethen, were they who kept his commandments.

CHAP. VII.
The four next pages I think of no consequence, but the 547th is a laboured attempt, by the means of the antient Gnosticks, to destroy the Jewish law; as, by the means of this law, Mr. G. had before endeavoured to destroy Christianity. And as these arguments are not replied to by Dr. Watson, but a reference made to others for the confutation of them, I shall, to save the reader's trouble, myself give a particular answer to them.

Polygamy was permitted, but not enjoined, by the Jewish law; and our Saviour's argument that only one woman was at first made for one man, when the world most needed population, was an unquestionable proof that God so intended it, and that it always ought to be so. David and Solomon were men, and therefore sinners; but the former of these an excellent man, though still a sinner. Men are made for a future life; it is the great end of their being: and when the religion and practice of any people become incurably wicked, and destructive of that end, it then becomes the Divine Goodness utterly to destroy them; that so he may hinder others from being by them corrupted to their destruction, and by this past vengeance deter them from following their wicked example. And these reasons are over and over again declared by Moses to be the causes of the Canaanites extirpation. The great Governor of the world is not found fault with for sending plagues, famines, and the most destructive wars among men, to punish them for their wickedness; and how much better must it serve to this purpose, to make, professedly, another people the executioners of his vengeance, whom he hath warned against those abominable crimes, and caused to inflict this punishment upon them? – A most necessary caution this to the people of our countries, and especially to the propagators of infidelity among us: for whenever the rejection of Christianity, and a wickedness without fear, becomes prevalent among us, it will then be the case with us, as it was with the Canaanites, and at last with the Jews themselves; we shall be totally destroyed.

The Gnosticks had the whole world against them as to bloody sacrifices, and were as certainly wrong in condemning them before Christianity, as Christianity itself is true, which yet they pretended to believe. These sacrifices clearly shewed, that some expiation, besides the sinner's repentance, was necessary to take away sin; and that sin was so excessively odious to the Divine Being, that it could not be expiated but by the greatest possible punishment to the oblation, even the death of it. And the Jewish law, besides, by making this sacrifice an expiation for sin, and so to save the life of the sinner, did manifest, that a vicarious punishment should be accepted for him; and thus pointed out and prepared the world for the receiving that stupendous atonement, which was to be made, in due time, for the sins of all mankind, by the death of the Son of God; and thereby fitted men for the embracing that religion, which was to be founded upon it, when it should be preached to the world, and which, without this previous preparation, we may certainly conclude, would never have been embraced by it. These were certainly the ends of bloody sacrifices; although, it must be confessed, that all the Gentiles, and the generality of the Jews, had, for a long time before, lost all just notion of them.

It is true, that the Mosaic law was built upon temporal promises, the promises of the land of Canaan, and prosperity in it; but these were understood, by the virtuous, as intended to shew forth an infinitely better life in the world to come. And if these retributions, abstracted from this latter expectation, be insufficient to combat with the outrageous appetites and passions of men, when administered by human weakness and ignorance, as they confessedly are, yet must they have a much more powerful effect, when they are dispensed by the hands of him who can neither be resisted or deceived; and more especially, as he had by many, the most severe punishments, manifested his great displeasure to sin and vengeance against it; and had, besides, in his law, given so many hints of a future life, and a just retribution in it. By these means must the temporal sanctions of the law have had a very powerful effect upon the Jews; certainly, a much more powerful effect than that system which our infidels are all endeavouring to introduce, who neither allow any future life, nor a moral governor of the world, nor any regard in him to the behaviour of any man: – an important matter this, well worthy of those gentlemen's most serious consideration, who yet blame the Jewish law for its deficiency in this matter, when they themselves are endeavouring to reduce the world to an infinitely worse pass.

It is also to be added, that the most merciful Judge of the world will certainly treat these comparatively ignorant men with a greater lenity, and upon easier terms of acceptance, than the others to whom he has communicated a greater degree of knowledge, and more powerful motives of obedience. And so the Gospel tells us it shall be. The times of this ignorance God winked at. If nothing, however, of better information had been given to the Jews, they would not have been left in a worse condition than the rest of mankind, who were to be saved as well as they: but even we can, in our weakness, discover some probable reasons why a future life of just retribution was not yet thoroughly opened and ascertained to mankind; namely, that, till Christ had, by his death, made atonement for the sins of the world, and, by his resurrection and ascension into heaven, and the merits of his entire obedience on our account, had procured us an entrance into this place of everlasting bliss, it might carry with it too great an extenuation of the evil of sin (the heinousness of which it is the great business of all true religion to manifest and aggravate) to make the blood of a beast expiate sin, and procure pardon and salvation to the sinner, and this in the favour, mansion, and happiness of an all-holy and just God. Besides, to have declared that any possible obedience of sinful man should entitle him to this perfect happiness, would be at once to destroy that whole scheme of redemption which the divine wisdom, holiness, goodness, had planned for the salvation of the world, and all true religion consequent of Adam's fall: and to have openly foretold, that this should be brought to pass by the obedience and death of the Son of God, must certainly have prevented the completion of the design; for, then, neither would the Jews have crucified Christ, nor the devils have tempted them to it.

It is not true, that eternal damnation came upon all men by the fall of Adam. The atonement made by Christ (he is the lamb slain from the foundation of the world) extends to all mankind, whether living before or after him; and will certainly save all those who acted up to the best light they could have. If God at all speaks to men, it must be in a manner intelligible to them; and, therefore, in giving an account of his creating the world, he must express himself as working, as finishing his work in six days, as ceasing from it, as resting, and being refreshed on the seventh. But both Scripture and reason tell us, that we are to remove all imperfection from these words when applied to him; and it is well known, that Moses's description of this matter is so just and noble, as to have gained him an universal admiration; and it is also to be observed, that, at the very time he uses these expressions of resting, being refreshed, &c. he tells us, God only speaks, and the thing is created and done. The formation of Eve out of Adam's rib, was necessary to make them both, and all mankind, who were to descend from them, one flesh; and to manifest to them and all others, how man and wife ought to love and be joined to each other. And as the want of this rib in Adam was a perpetual memorial of this transaction as long as Adam lived; so was the want of a navel in them both an undoubted conviction that they were the first man and woman, and that they and the world were created by God, and received at such a time their existence from him.

The placing this pair at first in a garden, wherein was made to grow every plant which was good for food, sight, or smell, was a proper means to make them, at once, acquainted with every production of nature, and thereby render them more sensible of, and thankful for, the divine goodness: as was likewise the bringing all the animals before Adam, that he might view and name them; who, by being able to do this with such justice, that their Creator himself approved of his names, clearly manifests the wonderful perfection of man before his fall, and the excessive degradation to which this fall has reduced him. The prohibiting them only the fruit of one tree, out of the prodigious profusion which abounds throughout all the world, namely, of the tree of the knowledge of good and evil, was a positive command, and such only could be given them in their state of innocence and virtue: but this was entirely proper to keep them ever mindful of their God, and his government over them, and their absolute dependence upon him; as also, we may be sure, to give them, in that state, the probation which was most necessary and proper for the breeding them up to virtue, and thereby securing to them, at the last, that perfect happiness which their good God intended and created them for. And here it may not be amiss to mention another instance of the Creator's care to impress a deep sense of his dependence upon Adam's mind. Eve was not formed till after he had viewed every animal, and seen them in pairs, and in company; and how must he have been affected to have found himself, who the most of all wanted, and was the best fitted for, society, totally destitute of it? The whole world must then have appeared a desert to him, and have made him desire, long for, and eagerly pray to his God to give him this so much wanted companion; and this with such a pining after it, as might well throw him into that slumber or trance, wherein the rib was taken out of him, Eve formed, and all the rights of marriage revealed to him. And when, by this instance, as well as many others, he was made duly sensible of his dependence upon God, behold his wife is presented to his view, all-perfect, out of the hands of their gracious God, and, to be sure, more lovely and beautiful, both in body and soul, than any of that most beautiful sex has since been. Here had he an equal cause given him both for humility and thankfulness. The Devil, who was a liar and a murderer from the beginning, spoke in the body of the serpent, but pretended that he both reasoned and talked by the virtue of this forbidden fruit, which he eat before the woman, and thereby ensnared her and Adam; and it would have been to their everlasting ruin, had not the mercy of God interposed to save them. Numberless possessions of this kind, and even of men, to shew how man at first fell, are recorded in the Gospel, by whose organs the devils spoke and conversed.

The fall of Adam, which comprehended in it the fall of all mankind, is, indeed, a very difficult subject to speak of; but in a matter of such exceeding height and difficulty, it ought not to be any argument against it, that we could not at all account for this providence, because it is one of the most stupendous, – in truth, it is in itself the most stupendous of all the workings of the one infinite Being who is higher than the heavens above us; and must infinitely transcend the reach of the wisest of his creatures, till he himself shall be pleased more fully to open and declare the matter. But something he hath opened to us, and, with a proper consideration of that, we may possibly come to some knowledge of this providence.

The end of all God's creating and working is, most assuredly, to communicate happiness. This end must principally be obtained by his making himself more known, who is perfect excellence, and must ever be glorified by all his works, and fill all the highest faculties of his highest creatures with the greatest delight; and those works shall best answer this purpose, which are made with such a variety as shall, in their formation, shew more of his power, wisdom, goodness; and truly wonderful is that variety of every kind, which we experience in this our little world: and, as in our world, so, certainly, in others, as well as in ours; and the different colours and sizes of the several planets in our system make it plain that he has done so in them. We are, then, to look for a wonderful peculiarity in his several worlds; and as in the worlds, so in the creatures; and as in the creatures, so in the providences by which they shall be governed and conducted to their happiness. It was the eternal purpose of God to redeem man by Jesus Christ: man's fall was therefore foreseen, and permitted to be brought about by the malice of the Devil; and, certainly, because the divine wisdom and goodness had determined to provide a remedy for the mischiefs of it, which should at once do the most honour to himself, and benefit to all his creatures, because it should open his nature and beneficence in the most astonishing instances, and make this beneficence be productive of the greatest good.

Reason and revelation equally shew, that to be happy we must be virtuous; and to be complete in happiness, we must be entire in virtue: and experience along with these equally manifests, that we cannot have this unfailing virtue, but through the exercise and habit of a previous probation. The most strengthening of all probations must undoubtedly be the experiencing the misery of sin, without being undone by the evil of it: and, therefore, has the infinite wisdom of the Divine Being, and his goodness to his creatures, contrived a way to give man this most necessary and useful probation; and this by the most astonishing providence that his infinity has ever afforded, or ever will afford.

As all men were permitted to fall by the weakness and fault of one man, so was it fitting, and, indeed, absolutely necessary, that they should be redeemed by the strength and virtue of another: and therefore were mankind suffered to come into such a condition by the sin of Adam, as did necessarily require that the goodness, nay, the justice of the Creator should interpose, and remedy this evil by some extraordinary providence. And we find, by Christianity, that he has done so; and has, at the same time, most benefited his creatures, and done the highest honour to himself: for he has thereby given them the most advantageous probation, and shewn himself in the most lovely and glorious light. I am confident that these reasonings are well founded and just; and, if they be, what a monster is our Deism for its presumption, ingratitude, folly!

To the charge of the God of the Jews being liable to passion and error, capricious in his favour, implacable in his resentments, meanly jealous of his own superstitious worship, and confining his partial providence to a single people, and this transitory life, I need only, after what has been already said, observe, that, whenever his moral creatures change in their behaviour to him, their great Governor must, in his affections to them; and his abhorrence of vice is the greatest that can be, because most contrary to his own nature, and destructive of all happiness; and that the welfare of the whole world requires him to manifest the most dreadful detestation of it; that he is jealous of his own worship, because it is the first and most important of all duties; and that it is a most palpable and strange mistake, to make him confine his providence to the Jews, when the Scriptures, by so many and severe instances, shew that he extended it also to the Gentiles. And as to the last charge, that of his chusing the Jews for his own people, and leaving the Heathens to themselves, I reply, that, when we have a history of God's moral government of the world so well authenticated as that of the Old Testament, it must be most presumptuous and criminal in any man, to find fault with this dispensation upon his own foolish conjecture. The one all-wise Being may have many and the best reasons for acting in such a manner, although every one of them should be undiscoverable by us, and they should, in our weak eyes, all of them seem contrary to wisdom and goodness, and even to justice itself. But this is not the case here; we can discern many reasons for his leaving the Heathens to themselves, and taking the Jews into his peculiar protection and government, and revealing himself and their duty to them.

    The former of these providences might be necessary to shew the sad and ruinous condition of man when left to himself; and to manifest the absolute necessity both of a Redeemer and of a Revelation, whereby not only to atone for sin, but to instruct in righteousness, and the virtuous means necessary to our future salvation: which necessity Mr. Gibbon knows to be even now denied by many people. And then, by God's winking at, and making proper allowances for, their almost invincible ignorance, this ignorance might be as profitable, or more so, to their salvation, than a greater degree of light and knowledge. But, as the leaving the whole earth in such excessive darkness might cause them to degenerate so far as would be destructive of all virtue and happiness, and as the chusing one people to himself, and instructing them in his true religion and virtue, and making it known that he did himself govern all things, and would not only reward the virtuous, but also punish the wicked, as by these means he should do the more good to them, keep the others to more knowledge and better obedience, and give himself an opportunity of reclaiming the rest whenever he should think fit; and as this would require such providences, not otherwise to be introduced, as would be peculiarly honourable to himself, and beneficial to his creatures; and, more especially, as this particular law should foreshew and keep up the expectation of that wonderful Redeemer, who was not immediately, but in the fullness of time, to come into and save the world; so, for these reasons, and, to be sure, infinite others unknown to us, was it equally wise and good in the Creator and Governor of all things to leave the Heathens thus far to themselves, and take to himself the Jews for his peculiar people. And here we can certainly see, that the very stubbornness and rebellions of this nation were of peculiar service to the world; as, by God's so severely punishing them for their wickedness, he demonstrated the falsehood of that antient destructive opinion of all the philosophers, and this modern one of all our unbelievers, that the God of the world cannot hurt or make miserable any of his creatures. But I might have cut short this defence; for, let the deists say what they will, they must either acknowledge polytheism to be a true religion, or confess that God did reveal himself to the Jews, and to the Jews only.

And now the reader may see that we can effectually defend the holy scriptures of the Old Testament against these self-sufficient hereticks, without having recourse to any allegory, whose particular tenets were so unreasonable and ill-founded, that, were I to repeat them, they would appear rather to deserve the name of madmen, than that of *knowers*, which they most arrogantly assumed to themselves. And if the primitive Christians did give a little into allegory, this is certainly to be excused by Mr. Gibbon, who knows that the philosophers were compelled to allegorize the whole of the Heathen religion, in order to make any defence at all for it, and this with such a force and absurdity, that it made them a ridicule to some of their own people.

What credit their assertion of the church's corrupting the Scriptures deserves, is manifest from hence, that Christianity is as certainly founded upon Judaism, as Christianity is true; and yet all these Gnosticks condemned and rejected that religion.

Tertullian tells us, that the hereticks of his time were wont to make the same false charge against the church; but he confutes them, by appealing to all the great churches founded and taught by the Apostles, which, by all agreeing in one doctrine, and this doctrine conformable to that of the Scriptures, demonstrated that this was the true faith, and not that which those people set up in opposition to it. And it is manifest, that the many dissentions which were among the Christians themselves, and which made them a continual watch upon each other; the numberless copies taken, and every where spread abroad, of the Scriptures; and the many translations made of, and quotations taken from them, must have rendered all wilful and material corruption of them utterly impossible.

Mr. Gibbon thinks, that, although these people disturbed the peace of the church, they did not retard, but furthered, the progress of it: but our Saviour was of a different opinion, and so was another person too, not at all deficient in cunning. Christ tells us, it was the Devil who sowed tares among his good seed of the word: and did he this, indeed, to serve Christianity? Does not Mr. Gibbon know, that the people of his principles, as well as the Papists, make the uncertainty of the Scriptures sense, and the Christian dissentions about it, an argument against our religion? Can it be denied, that the Papists did, by these means, put a stop to the reformation, which otherwise threatened to annihilate the Romish church; and that they have ever since been endeavouring to destroy ours by the same means, and did, for a time, accomplish its ruin, in the reign of Charles I? And is it any adequate advantage, that a dissenter is now and then gained over to this church, as was the case with Augustine?

CHAP. VIII.
Page 552. We have here a keen ridicule upon the primitive Christians, for their notion of evil spirits, and their supposing them to be the authors of idolatry; but, if they believed the Scriptures, they must have believed this: for what thinks he of these passages, and numberless others which might be produced? "He was a liar and a murderer from the beginning; the Devil entered into Judas; the Gentiles sacrificed to devils, and not unto God; all these will I give thee, if thou wilt fall down and worship me" – and of the numberless possessions recorded in the New Testament? It may seem strange and unaccountable to us, as it did to Lord Bolingbroke, that such evil beings should be suffered

in the world by a good God; but this only shews us how little able we are to judge of the divine ways. Nothing but the malice of these impure spirits could have inspired the impure, cruel, and murderous idolatry practised by the Heathens: and we find many of that cast still among men – many powerful tyrants, who desolate whole nations by all the rapines and cruelty of bloody and unjust wars; and many who are more pernicious than they – many who employ the whole of their great abilities to destroy all religion, and consequently all happiness either here or hereafter, and reduce, even this world, to a hell of misery. But this disbelief of devils is a necessary part of the deistical negative creed: for, if angels, so much superior to men, could yet, by their wickedness, be so lost to all virtue and happiness, it might be, it must be so with men likewise; and then there would be room for those fears in the hearts of profligates, which it is the great end of our infidelity totally to expel. And here it is to be observed, that our modern deists all go against their own scriptures; namely, the opinions of the philosophers in this matter; for they, with the Christians, all acknowledged the reality of these evil beings, which our modern infidels do all deny and ridicule.

As to the great caution of the Christians, not to join in any of the Heathen idolatries, they had abundant reasons for it. "Thou shalt worship the Lord thy God, and him only shalt thou serve," was to them the first and greatest of all commandments, and therefore ought to be the most strictly observed. But here I cannot help expressing my astonishment at Mr. Gibbon's making the want of intercourse between them and the Heathens, which this must necessarily occasion, the first of his causes for the growth of Christianity, when it was so manifestly fitted to obstruct the same. That it contributed to its preservation, cannot, I think, be denied; for had the Christians joined themselves to the Heathen worship, it must, in my opinion, have hurt or annihilated their religion: but, although this was a necessary means of preserving Christianity, it cannot be set down for the furthering its growth, but by such a far-fetched and indirect inference, that, I am confident, Mr. Gibbon will not insist upon it.

The second of his secondary causes is, the doctrine of the soul's immortality. He seems, a few pages before, to believe this future immortality, and a just retribution in it; yet, here he attributes the reception of them in the eastern countries to an established priesthood, which employed the motives of virtue as an instrument of ambition. But certainly he might have discovered a better reason for this most important belief: he might have founded it upon a notion so natural to man, that it has generally prevailed over the whole world, and even in the most barbarous nations; and upon an intercourse in the East with the patriarchs and Jews, who all expected this future existence, who had many hints for it in the writings of Moses, and open declarations of it in the Psalms and the Prophets; and in the book of Job (at least as ancient as any of the Scriptures) a probable reason was given why it was not entrusted to the hereditary priesthood of Aaron. But this is only an objection against Providence, which ought never to be made; because we can never judge of this matter with any propriety, till we can, and do, see all the reasons upon which the Divine Being acted; which is utterly impossible to men, or, indeed, to any creature.

Page 560, he asserts, that all the Jews, from Moses to their return from the captivity of Babylon, did not believe the soul's immortality, although he had before acknowledged that many expressions in the Prophets did indicate such. And here I will return an answer to that objection against the Jewish law, that it was founded upon temporal promises, and gave no notion of a future life; which, that I might take in the whole of the matter at one view, I did reserve to this place.

It is true that Moses did found his law upon temporal promises; but these were intended to reach beyond this present world; and he has therefore, in his writings, given us many hints which are decisive for a future life: that Adam was not to die if he did not transgress; when he did transgress, and must experience a temporal death, that yet his seed was totally to conquer his enemy, which would neither have been done, nor prove a comfort to him, unless death was to be conquered likewise; that he was certainly to die for his sin, and yet an atonement made by sacrifice for it, and accepted by God; and that he called his wife's name Eve, in Hebrew Life, because she was to be the mother of all living, rather of all life, or of him who was life; that righteous Abel was killed because he was righteous, and his sacrifice accepted by God; that Enoch was taken away because he walked with God and pleased God, who also left a prophecy, preserved to the Apostles times, of God's coming in another life to judge the wicked; that God styled himself the God of Abraham, Isaac, and Jacob, some hundred years after the death of them, which phrase shewed them to be still in being, and him the greatest good to them; and this, too, by the name of Elahim, which is, convenanters by an oath or curse, and this oath certainly to redeem man. These things did abundantly prove a future existence, and that of retribution, from the writings of Moses alone. And, besides the many declarations for this future hope, in the Psalms and Prophets, we have Elijah and Elisha raising the dead, and the former of these visibly ascending into heaven, to confirm this hope. And we know, likewise, from the Epistle to the Hebrews, that it was the very intention of the Jewish tabernacle and temple, and the most solemn service of them, to shadow forth our entrance into a heaven of the highest happiness, by the atonement which our Great High Priest and Redeemer was to make of himself for the sins of the whole world.

We may expect, then, to find the belief of the Jews directly contrary to Mr. Gibbon's assertion; and so it is undeniably proved to every Christian, by St. Paul, Heb. xi. 13. "And confessed that they were strangers and pilgrims upon earth." 14. "For they that say such things, confess plainly that they seek another country." 16. "A better country, that is, an heavenly." 32. "For the time would fail me to tell of Gideon and Barach, and Sampson and Jeptha, David, Samuel, and the Prophets." 39. "And these all having obtained a good report by faith, received not the promise."

Page 561. He has my thanks for saying that the doctrine of life and immortality is dictated by nature, approved by reason, and confirmed by the example and authority of Christ; for if any truth be in any of these matters, and more especially in the latter of them, Christianity is truth: and whether it were or not, if such a future life be received, it is manifest, that wickedness must disqualify for the happiness of it; and then there must be in every way an end of infidelity: for the certain knowledge which Christianity gives us of this future life, and our salvation in it, will take away all prejudice against this pure religion; and then it shall be as universally, as it will be reasonably, embraced.

That the expectation of Christ's immediate coming to judgment was not justly founded upon Scripture, has been made certain by Dr. Watson; I will, however, add, for the farther clearing of this matter, that every one acquainted with the exposition of the prophecies, knows that there is a figurative, as well as a literal, meaning intended in them. Sir

Isaac Newton has a particular treatise upon this head, shewing that sun, moon, stars, heavens, earth, seas, &c. signify kings, rulers, nations, peoples, civil policies; and that in this sense, our Saviour's prophecy of the destruction of Jerusalem, was all fulfilled in that generation; although, in the literal sense, it shall not be till the end of this world. St. Paul has convinced us, as well as 17 centuries, that it was not to be in his time. 2 Thess. ii. 2.

Page 562. The doctrine of the millennium is so thoroughly cleared by Dr. Watson, that I shall say no more to it, than that it is very strange in Mr. Gibbon to make the joys of a future earthly habitation have greater force to promote Christianity than the joys of God's own habitation, and an heaven of unutterable bliss; and this too, when none but martyrs were to partake of them. It is also surprising to make the Christians threatening damnation to the Heathens a principle motive of their conversion, when these could hardly have any intercourse with the others; when they and their religion were so hated and despised by them; when all retribution was denied by all their philosophers; and when it was by this conversion absolutely required that they should abandon every vice, and live the most careful and virtuous lives in every instance afterwards; and this too under a more severe and certain ruin for their being Christians, if they did not; and when, too, we experience that these are the very things, these threatenings and these severe lives, which make so many Heathens among us Christians at this day. The double sense of the prophecies explains all those expressions of the precious stones with which the new Jerusalem was to be built, upon which this gentleman plays with so great an *impartiality*.

As to the conflagration of Rome, and the world, and his attributing our sense of the former to our prejudices against Popery, I must say, that either he has not read the late Protestant writers upon this subject, or else he has a most unjust partiality to that corrupted, idolatrous, and bloody church. But this is not the only instance in which I have found the Deists favourable to Popery.

Page 567. His 3d cause of Christianity's growth, is the miraculous powers of the primitive Christians.

He says, with a sneer, the Deity suspended the laws of Nature for the benefit of religion. Be it so, then; but it was because religion is the happiness of those creatures for whose benefit these laws were instituted. He quotes Irenæus for saying, the knowledge of foreign languages, although communicated to others, was not so to him when he preached the Gospel to the natives of Spain: but he ought to have known, that this is an imposition put upon the reader and him by Dr. Middleton; for Irenæus says no such thing. Theophilus was right in not undertaking to raise a dead man for the conviction of a noble Greek. It was the Divine Being who was to work the miracle, and he might find cause to refuse it, although to men it might seem ever so proper. The Apostles themselves could only work miracles when the all-knowing Spirit of God urged them to it. Christ Jesus would not gratify Herod with the sight of one miracle, although it might have saved his life. His account of the Christian inspiration is so certainly false, that the only thing to be said in his vindication is, that he never examined the matter, but trusted to Dr. Middleton, without reading the answers given to his book; which, to speak the truth of it, is written with a prejudice and disingenuity the most disgraceful to any cause, or to any author. Let any one but read over 1 Cor. xiv. chap. and he will see that the Christian inspiration was the farthest in the world from being an unreasonable furor or madness; for, ver. 32, "the spirits of the prophets were subject to the prophets."

If this Doctor were treated in the same way that he has treated the primitive Fathers, whom he so severely condemns for some erroneous reasonings, and, as he will have it, misrepresentation of facts, that they are not to be credited in any thing about religion, his own character would suffer a great deal more than theirs has done by this kind of treatment. This gentleman makes use of great artifice and disingenuity to discredit the miracles of the primitive Christians, and has inserted some passages in his book which equally discredit all miracles in general; which passages, though often called upon, he would never retract. This gentleman did, also, publish a book against prophecy, by which he would have rendered that proof of our religion equally nugatory and ridiculous, and thereby destroyed the two great foundations of Christianity; and yet this author held to his death an ecclesiastical preferment in our Christian church, and was very angry, to the last, that he could not get in it a more ample provision: and ought we to give him any credit in these matters?

Tertullian's Apology was written to the Roman magistrates, upon their persecution of the Christians; and it is hard to think that he would put the defence of his cause upon a certain imposture. His words are, *I come now to things, and give you a demonstration, from facts, that your gods and the dæmons are the same. Let a dæmoniac be brought into court, and the spirit which possesses him be demanded by any Christian to declare what he is, and he shall as truly confess himself to be a devil, as he did before falsely pretend to be a god. If all these do not declare themselves in court to be devils, not daring to lie in the presence of a Christian, that Christian is willing to be taken for a cheat, and to answer for it in his own blood.* It is to be observed, that all this was to be done in a Heathen court, and upon a person produced by themselves, and therefore certainly known by them, and liable to the most careful inspection, and where, too, all power was in their hands; and there could therefore be no possibility of a Christian juggle. And now let any one judge whether that person could be right in his senses who would place his religion, comfort, life, and the lives of all his professions, upon such a defence, if this defence were really false and an imposture. But lest this proof should be thrown off by a reference to Dr. Middleton's Free Enquiry, I shall, for this once, subjoin an examination of his reasoning upon this head.

To say that the Christians were then too poor to have a sufficient number of their Apologies transcribed, when so very few of them would have served this purpose; when they were so numerous in Bithynia long before this, as almost to annihilate the Heathen worship, by Pliny's confession; when Tertullian himself asserts, the senate, the army, &c. to be all full of them; and Cyprian did, not long after this, and in this very place, raise above 800 pounds at once, for the redemption of Christian captives; and Mr. Gibbon owns, they did then make up a tenth part of the city of Carthage: – to say that the Heathen magisrates did not think it worth their while to enquire into these matters, when Pliny did put two women to the rack for this purpose, and these magistrates were every day examining, imprisoning, torturing, banishing, confiscating the goods of Christians, and putting them to the most cruel deaths, for their faith – to say that the Christians had then a particular order of men to take care of, and instruct and cure these possessed people, providing lodgings in their churches for them, when they were just now so poor as not to get a few books transcribed for the saving their lives and fortunes; when he has not any authority for such a supposition at that time, but many against it, as may be seen in Mr. Bingham's Christian antiquities; and we may be sure the Heathen magistrates would never suffer any of those to be brought into examination, nor could the Christians be able to collect and support them all – to say such things in confutation of Tertullian's challenge, and of almost all the other Christian writers before and after him – and Dr. Middleton says them all – speaks not any fairness of mind, but the deepest and most rancorous prejudice. And here I will advise Mr. Gibbon not to follow Mr. Voltaire, as he here has the Doctor, in his future history, when he comes to the worship of images in the Christian church; because this great genius's account of this matter is totally copied from Baronius, and where the interest of the Roman church is concerned, there cannot be a more partial and unjust historian than this very great and learned cardinal.

Page 570. It will readily be acknowledged, that the pretended miracles of the church of Rome have much hurt our religion with many people; but it ought not to be so. Real miracles will probably introduce a pretence to feigned ones. And if it is considered that the Popish miracles are only propagated and believed where their religion entirely prevails, and no examination can be made of them, it must appear that this is no just argument against those of the primitive Christians, where every thing was the reverse with them; and yet they boldly required an examination of them by their most powerful, obstinate, and cruel enemies: – a distinction this so manifest, that it is wonderful how Mr. Gibbon could overlook it, and so confound times together, as to make it impossible to say when miracles did cease, because always reported to continue in the church, when, both from this and the settlement of Christianity, we can see, how they gradually became unnecessary, and the certain falsehood of these contemptible late reports.

We find, from the replies given to Dr. Middleton, that several Christian writers of the 3d and 4th centuries did acknowledge miracles to be then very rare among them, and nearly to have ceased from the church; and we can easily discern the fitness of this proceeding. As Christianity was the power of God to salvation, it was absolutely necessary for him, if he intended us this salvation, to support it by his own miraculous power so long as this extraordinary interposition was requisite: and, considering the nature of his religion, that it had nothing in the world to recommend it, but all the pleasures, interests, prejudices of it, to obstruct and destroy its progress – and considering that these miraculous powers were scarcely less necessary after, than before, the death of the Apostles, and that many others, besides the Apostles, were, in their own times, endowed with these gifts – these things considered, we have the justest reason to believe they still continued in the church, and that the testimony given of them by so many writers is well founded and true. But so soon as Christianity was able to stand upon its own legs, so soon as men's prejudices against it were pretty well worn off, and the powers of this world were no longer its enemies, but became its friends and supporters, and it could, by the common course of nature, maintain and increase itself, then was it fit that this extraordinary interposition should be gradually lessened, and, at last, totally taken away. This reasoning is manifestly just, and I can confirm it by an instance, which, I am confident, Mr. Gibbon will not controvert.

In the middle of the fourth century, when Julian, the apostate Emperor, in order to invalidate our Saviour's prophecy about the destruction of Jerusalem and the temple, did call home the Jews to their own country, and employ both the power of this zealous people, and all the strength of his own mighty dominions, to execute this purpose; and when there were no human means, which could possibly defeat it, the hand of God did itself visibly interpose, and, by shakings of the earth, which threw up the foundations, and fire bursting out, which consumed the workmen and their work, compel them to desist from and abandon the undertaking: and this miraculous fact is acknowledged in the history of Ammianus Marcellinus, who, as a Heathen writer, may be believed, and who, as writing against his own principles, must be believed, in his account of this matter. And thus are the suppositions of Dr. Middleton, and of Mr. Gibbon, both of them destroyed by a Heathen attestation, and mine as undoubtedly confirmed.

Page 572. Fourth Cause of the growth of Christianity, the good lives of the Christians.

It is certain, that all the primitive apologists did boast of the virtue of the Christians, and it is here acknowledged to be a fact: – the purity of their practice was conformable to the purity of their faith, and this in a world of a totally different cast: – which virtue effectually proved the truth of their religion, by the beneficial effects which flowed from the profession of it. And no wonder, when no other religion in the world ever taught such pure morality, and enforced it by the like powerful motives of an infinitely holy and just God observing every action, and rewarding or punishing it with an eternity of the greatest happiness or misery, as the moral creature's behaviour should deserve. In this had they such motives as were fitted to produce this virtuous life, and, in justice to Christianity, he ought to have mentioned them; and, to be sure, along with these, in this most dangerous and difficult time, they had an extraordinary assistance of the Holy Spirit of God, to influence their minds, and govern their practice. These things, in justice to Christianity, he ought to have produced: but instead of that, the reader's attention is turned off to two other causes, which could be of little or no benefit to this religion; indeed, the first of them, a considerable prejudice to it, namely, repentance for past sins, and a laudable desire of supporting the society into which they were entered. He here retails the malicious falsehoods which the Heathens cast upon the Christians, of alluring into their party the most atrocious criminals; and adds, *Those persons who in the world had followed, though in an imperfect manner, the dictates of benevolence and propriety, derived such a calm satisfaction from the opinion of their own rectitude, as rendered them much less susceptible of the sudden emotions of shame, of grief, and of terror, which have given birth to so many wonderful conversions.* – Will not hope have some effect upon a generous mind? And must not, then, the Christian assurance, given to every virtuous person, of an endless life, of inconceivable glory and happiness for ever in it, be more powerful to persuade the good man to the embracing this religion, who had no alteration to make in his practice, and must have this self-satisfaction so prodigiously increased, by knowing, that he hereby had acquired the favour of his God, and was certain of his protection and blessing here, and his eternal reward hereafter – must not these be more likely to work upon a virtuous and generous mind, than to be left totally destitute of them; and be, indeed, more powerful to convert him, than the fear of future punishment could be to any profligate Heathens, which punishment they expected not, and were all taught to despise, and who, to become Christians, must change the whole course of their lives, get the better of long and established habits of vice, and ever after live in direct opposition to all their beloved lusts, passions, interests? Has he, indeed, known many of these conversions in a Christian country, where the motives to them are so much more powerful? If he has, his experience is very different from that of all the rest of mankind; and yet, upon this very false supposition, he goes on to vilify and abuse even our Saviour himself.

Page 573. *After the example of their Divine Master, the missionaries of the Gospel disdained not the society of men, and especially of women, oppressed by the consciousness, and very often by the effects, of their vices.* – It is impossible that a man should be a believer in Christ, or of any moderation in his infidel principles, who writes in this malevolent manner of the most holy, but compassionate Jesus: for, was it not his custom to preach in their synagogues every Sabbath-day, and in all places of the most public resort, at their great festivals, and in their temple, and to the Scribes and Pharisees, and Jewish rulers; *so that in secret he did nothing?* And was not this also the practice of the Apostles? What is it, then, which gives a pretence for this infamous scandal? (Not to be warm upon such an occasion would be a foolish and criminal apathy.) Why, Christ had some women to attend him, one of whom had been a great sinner; and he also tells the Pharisees, that he came "not to call the righteous but sinners to repentance:" – a severe sarcasm this upon these hypocritical men, who were all abominably wicked, and yet gloried in their outward righteousness; and a dreadful denunciation likewise against all those, who, as men, must be sinners, and, as infidels, almost always the greater sinners, but who will yet refuse to receive any atonement for sin, or divine assistance against it, and will mostly insolently stand upon their own strength and rectitude for acceptance and happiness with the all-holy and just Governor and Judge of the world.

Most palpably mistaken and unjust is Mr. Gibbon, then, in this part of his cause of Christianity's progress; and as to the care of the sect's reputation, this is such a poor motive to virtue, that I should never have thought it worthy of notice, if this gentleman had not made it so. Every sect has this motive, but every sect is not made virtuous by it; nay, we know ourselves the very reverse to happen. Our infidels, as to number, are nothing, I thank God, in comparison of our Christians; and do they therefore excel in righteousness? We have also among us many sects of believers, and none of them are remarkable for their superior virtue, and some of them are infamous for a very different character: and if we will believe the primitive Christian writers, it was so in their time. But as Mr. Gibbon will hardly allow them any credit, I will produce him two, which no Christian can deny, Rev. ii. 6. *But this thou hast, that thou hatest the deeds of the Nicolaitanes, which I also hate*; and 2 Thess. ii. 10, *Whose coming is with all deceivableness of unrighteousness*; and one that he will not deny, namely, the bad character which these writers give of the Gnosticks, which, as these were Christians in name, and the scandal injured the Christians themselves, we may be sure that they would not have so openly confessed, was it a thing to be doubted of, or with truth to be denied. This charge against them Mr. Gibbon himself acknowledges; but it is here worthy of notice, that he gives from them the same retort upon the church, and hereby contradicts himself, and effectually destroys that very cause of Christianity's growth, which he is here insisting upon.

The severity of the then Christian morals, set forth in so many pages, is a still farther proof of the insufficiency, and even falseness, of this his pretended cause. The state of persecution to which the Christians were then continually liable, and by which they frequently suffered, to the loss of every thing dear to them, and the being afflicted with every thing that is miserable in this life, made it most necessary for them to disengage, as far as it was possible, their affections from this dangerous world; and more especially from the endearments of marriage, which must have proved a most violent temptation, and a dangerous snare to them; so violent indeed, that St. Paul advises the Christians in these seasons to abstain from marriage: and the many idolatries practised by the Heathens upon almost every occasion, rendered it equally requisite that they should keep themselves at a distance from those offices which would entangle them in this great and justly-abominated crime. These, however, were not so many as to render the Christians useless to the commonwealth; for we find many of them employed in many departments of it, which Mr. Gibbon seems to think inconsistent with their religion, though, notwithstanding all their then strictness, it is certain that they did not. The first Heathen convert to Christianity was, we know, a proselyte to the Jewish religion, who must necessarily abhor and avoid all idolatry; and yet he was a centurion in the Roman army.

Page 581. The fifth cause of the growth of Christianity, the active government of the church.

He here attributes a great deal of the safety and aggrandizing of it to the Christian's ambition of raising themselves to the offices of the church: but the weakness, nay, the injustice, of this cause, must appear, when it is considered that all these offices were for life, and could not be frequently filled; that not one in a thousand could obtain any one of them, nor in ten thousand the highest of them all; that, when obtained, they did but subject the possessor to an excess of trouble and danger, danger both of body and soul, and, if there be any truth in Christian history, were, till near the close of the third century, much more eagerly shunned, than sought for, by the Christian people.

As to the church government established by the Apostles, it is nothing to our present purpose; and so I pass on to page 586, where he makes the union of the church one great cause of its growth: but had he given the real cause here, he would have set it down, the divisions and contests of the church; and of these he himself has furnished us with a good many instances. This would have been the just representation of the matter, but to do this would have been to turn the cause directly against his purpose; and, therefore, the very reverse is asserted by him.

CHAP. IX.

Page 591. A community of goods was not adopted by the first Christians in the manner he has stated it. The zeal of some drew them into this practice; but it was not required of any, it was voluntary in them all. St. Peter's words are, *While it remained with thee, was it not thine own, and after it was sold, was it not in thine own power?* And even Mr. Gibbon's words are, "The converts were permitted to retain the possession of their patrimony." It was, therefore, for the lie, and intended deceit, that Ananias and his wife were struck dead; and thus the Scriptures declare it. He might, therefore, have spared the following innuendo, *that in hands less pure than those of the Apostles it might soon have been corrupted.* Never men shewed such an honest disregard to this world and all its interests as the Apostles did, their great Master excepted; and even in this instance, we find them immediately casting away the care of this money from themselves, and putting it into other hands. But a reflection of this kind would be pleasing to many people, and beget a smile against the Apostles; which was an advantage not to be lost.

It may, perhaps, be proper, also, to mention another instance which may seem to countenance Mr. Gibbon, although not noticed by him. Our Saviour required the young rich man to sell all that he had, and give to the poor, that he might become his disciple, and have treasure in heaven: but this was then necessary, because his religion was to be for a long time in a most dangerous and persecuted condition; and if the man could not beforehand resolve to abandon his possessions, he could not remain a follower of Christ, but must afterwards apostatize, to his greater condemnation and ruin.

That the charity of the Christians, in not only relieving their own poor, but many of the Heathen besides, and also in saving, and carefully breeding up, many of their children, whom their horrible and brutish ignorance had exposed to destruction, must have had a very beneficial effect for the Christian religion, cannot be denied: but this belongs to, and ought to have been inserted in, his account of the fourth cause, the good lives of the Christians. Yet there it is not; and why so? Why it would, in that place, have done honour and service to their religion; it is in this so introduced, as to be made a reproach and detriment to it. And here it ought to be noticed, that the then Christians, who were made so poor by Dr. Middleton, as to be unable to purchase a few copies of a small Apology, in defence of their lives, properties, and religion too, are found to be so rich in Mr. Gibbon, as to bribe over the Heathens to their party. – But I must mention another species of their charity, practised in Cyprian's time, which is not noticed by Mr. Gibbon: that when, in a great plague which raged in Africa and Carthage, the nearest relations fled from infected persons, and left them to perish for want of assistance, many of the Christians went to, and took care of, those people, and saved their lives; though, to be sure, often with the loss of their own.

Page 597. Public pennance. Excommunication was ordered and practised by St. Paul; and with excommunicated persons the Christians were not so much as to eat. It was the delivering the unhappy person to Satan; who, according to the evil, malicious nature of apostate spirits, was used most horribly to torment the poor criminal, till, by his being again restored to Christ, he was delivered from Satan's power, and made happy in the favour and protection of his Saviour and his God, and in an assurance of pardon and everlasting happiness in heaven: - a demonstration this of the necessity, truth, benefit, of the Christian religion; and no wonder, then, that an exclusion from it was so excessively dreaded, and so much endured by the penitent to have it taken off. But, certainly, this severity of discipline was more likely to hinder, than promote, a conversion to this faith. It laid those people under a most violent temptation to abandon such a harsh religion as this; and, in case they had done it, we may be sure that the Heathens would have received them with the greatest cordiality; and they could have nothing to dread from the resentment of their former friends. It cannot be doubted, that the liberal alms of the Christians must have occasioned some conversions among the poor; but that merciful and loving temper, which was enjoined even to enemies, by this religion, must have made a great many more, and those of the most virtuous and happy dispositions. This is, indeed, an argument strong in Christianity's favour, and we do accept it from Mr. Gibbon with all thankfulness, whatever his design was in confessing it.

Page 602. We have, in this place, such expressions as only befit a Christian; but it is impossible this author should be such. The whole bent of his soul appears to be set against Christianity, and he sees nothing in it, but with that jaundiced eye which turns every thing to its own blackness and horror. And here he thinks his five causes so powerful, that, instead of being surprised at the rapid progress of Christianity, his wonder is, that it was not still more universal and rapid. Let us, then, more carefully examine this matter; for to me this appears an easiness of belief greater than that with which modern Deists are wont to reproach us Christians, and sadly shews, to what an unreasonable length a deep prejudice can carry a bright and penetrating genius. I remember a learned man, of these principles, to have doubted whether there ever had been such a person as Christ. But something of this kind was necessary to be done, in order to take off, if possible, one of our arguments, thoroughly enforced by Mr. Jenyns, for the truth of Christianity, namely, the greatness of its growth, when the cause, and the propagators of it, were naturally so unfit to produce such a wonderful effect.

CHAP. X.
When Christ Jesus was going to die for the salvation of the world, he tells his Apostles, that before the destruction of Jerusalem, not then 40 years distant, *this Gospel of the kingdom shalt be preached in all the world*; (and St. Paul tells us it was so within 30 years;) and, from the parable of the leaven, and the grain of mustard-seed, foreshews the prodigious encrease of it: – strangely, but most surely prophetic this denunciation, when his religion, and the means to effect it, were both of them of such an unpromising nature; when there was nothing to propagate it, but the preachings of twelve illiterate fishermen, who were equally destitute of learning, address, or eloquence; and who were to wander about the world with this seemingly silly tale in their mouths, that one Jesus, who was by his countrymen, the Jews, put to the most cruel death, for being the vilest of malefactors, was risen from the dead, and become the Saviour of the world; that he had commissioned, and sent them out to tell all mankind, that they must believe in him and the one true God, repent of all their sins, abandon every vice, and practise every virtue; that they must resist and abhor the religions of the several countries in which they had been educated, and to which they were most deeply prejudiced; give up all the goods of this life, and endure every thing miserable in it, even to the most torturous of deaths, which they must surely expect; and all for the sake of this new religion, and the happiness which it promised in a future life. These were the men our Saviour sent out to propagate his religion, and this was the work he had given them to do: and very strange it is, that he should know them so thoroughly, as to think, nay, be sure of it too, that they would meddle in such an undertaking, and, much more, persevere in it; and stranger still, that these missionaries should be able to convert the most powerful, knowing, and polished nation that ever was in the world, convert them from that ancient religion of theirs, which had all their lusts, prejudices, passions, gratifications, and worldly interests, to attach them to it; which had all the wit of their philosophers, all the learning and power of the world to defend it; to which religion they attributed the growth and prosperity of their mighty empire, and to the abandoning of which, by the Christians, they imputed every calamity which

befel them after the rise of the new religion; and *that*, therefore, they treated with all the abuse, hatred, persecution, which malice so powerfully urged on could inspire, and which Christ so justly and particularly foretold to his Apostles when he was sending them out.

By these means, and in this manner, and against such an opposition, was Christianity to be propagated; and let any man of the least impartiality say, whether it was possible for the Apostles to have any success in this work, unless favoured with that high and miraculous interposition of God which the New Testament gives an account of, and which it is Mr. Gibbon's intention to deny, and his endeavour totally to destroy; and, along with this, an inspiration and divine influence of the Holy Ghost, to work upon the minds of the hearers, and give them that ingenuousness of heart which should cause them to attend to, and be convinced by, their preaching and miracles. This most important period, upon which all future proceedings of the Christians did entirely depend, is passed over without notice by Mr. Gibbon: and if truth was to be thrown out of the case, and he had nothing more to regard than the credit of his understanding, he would have been very wise in this proceeding: for although it be certain that he no more believes the miracles of Christ and his Apostles than those of the after-Christians, yet to have at once condemned the former would have given such disgust to many, would so clearly have shewn the impossibility of the Apostles succeeding in this work, and have exposed him to such a certain confutation, that it was not a thing to be undertaken. He would have been disproved by the very existence of such a book as the New Testament. He was, therefore, necessitated to take up Christianity at a later date, when, from its being very generally propagated and well established in many places, he could, with the greater plausibility, ascribe its wonderful growth to the five causes he has assigned for it. But then, it is to be observed, that, as these will not at all relate to the first planting of Christianity, they are indeed totally beside his purpose, and prove nothing at all for him. Let us, however, go on to consider them as he has been pleased to state them; and here we shall not find him to succeed, but to be palpably defeated in his attempt, although he has, by the most partial calculations, endeavoured to lessen the progress of this religion. That they would, if justly set down, be of considerable effect, is not to be denied; but, as in this light they would all of them have given most convincing proofs of Christianity's truth, he has been compelled, in order to avoid this consequence, so to pervert them, as in all of them to lessen, and most of them to annihilate their whole force, and, in some instances, to turn them to the destruction of his own intended proof.

If he had said, that Christianity, by ascertaining and opening the being and nature of God, and shewing him to be the Creator, Sustainer, and Moral Governor of the world, who had a regard to the behaviour of his moral creatures, and would reward or punish them as they should deserve, and by these means merited from all rational creatures, capable of knowing him, such a high homage of adoration, suitable to his holiness, justice, goodness, and infinite power, as made it peculiar to him; and that this religion, by prescribing and making known such a spiritual devotion as was fitting for man to give, and the Divine Being to receive, and by procuring for us sinners, and our imperfect and worthless services, an acceptance from his infinite purity and justice – if he had said, that Christianity by these means did render itself so exceedingly reasonable, amiable, and beneficial, that it ought to have drawn over every sensible person to the embracing of it, and more especially so when set in opposition to the impure, abominable, superstition of the Heathens – (and in so saying he would have done no more than justice to our religion) – if he had said this, he then, indeed, had given a cause which must have been of great force for the promotion of Christianity. But as this would have been so convincing an argument of its goodness and truth, he was compelled to evade it; and he has, by making nothing of divine worship, and by blaming the primitive Christians for their refusal to give any to the Heathen gods, not only destroyed the force of his own cause, but manifestly turned it against himself: for such an unreasonable, obstinate denial in the Christians to do what was innocent in his eyes, and meritorious in that of the Pagans, could not fail of breeding in the latter such an hatred to the Christians, and such a wide separation between them, as must have proved a very great detriment, instead of any advantage, to the Christian cause. Every one at all acquainted with mankind, knows that it is not an unreasonable, perverse opposition to their wills, but an easy compliance with them as far as we can, which will best gain upon the understanding, and so win over their hearts as to render them most susceptible of conviction.

A Reply to the Reasonings of Mr. Gibbon 163

The same, also, is to be observed of his second cause: The immortality of the soul, and the retributions of a future life. – If he had said, and in justice to Christianity he ought to have said, that the nature of God and man was such as to make man deserve and expect a future life of retribution; that Christianity did, by giving us a certainty of this future life in an infinitely more perfect existence, and for ever enjoying in it an inconceivable degree of glory and happiness, which happiness every man must wish for, and this religion has ensured to every virtuous person upon the reasonable and easy terms of the Gospel, but which had been banished from the Heathen world by their absurd notions of this future life, and retributions of it, as also by the false reasonings of their philosophers upon this most important subject; if he had said, that these Christian discoveries contributed to the growth of this religion, he would have offered a cause which had real weight in it, and must be very powerful for his purpose. But as a most material proof would have from hence resulted to Christianity, he was necessitated to turn off the reader's attention from it, and fix his mind upon other matters; namely, the false expectation of a judgment immediately to come, of an early millennium, of the conflagration of Rome and this world; and to an excess of threatening and fear, which the wisest of the Heathens all despised, and which must render this cause of very little, if indeed of any effect at all, to the promoting Christianity: and to compleat the destruction of it, he ridicules the prophetic language in the Scriptures, of the gold and precious stones wherewith the New Jerusalem was to be built; and thus destroying the credit of those writings, which, by his own confession, do alone insure this immortality to us, he annihilates his second cause.

Third cause: The miracles of the primitive Christians – Had he declared, that, although all miracles had ceased with the lives of the Apostles, yet was there so authentic a testimony left of them in the Scripture, that there could be no reasonable doubt entertained of them, he then would have given a cause most powerful indeed for the promotion of Christianity: and, besides, had he farther confessed, that there were some remains of the same miraculous powers continued in the church to the 2d and 3d centuries, to testify for Christ's religion, he would have added force to his cause, and demonstrated its truth and tendency to propagate and encrease that religion. But as this was a thing not to be done by him, he has artfully turned off the whole into an inspiration false and ridiculous, said many things subversive of all miracles, and made plausible impostures of all those which the primitive Christians asserted of themselves; and he has hereby not only ruined his design, but turned his own cause against himself: for this false pretence to miracles would only have put them upon a level with the Heathens, who frequently ascribed the same power to their Gods; so that little good could have arisen from this pretence to the Christians: but if their imposture had been discovered, as certainly it must have been in a Heathen government, and with such a majority of the people, and they all so eager, against them, it must have torn up Christianity by the roots, and entirely extirpated it. Those people, who were such bitter enemies to the Christians, as to load their religion and them with the horrid and unjust calumnies of worshipping an ass's head, killing and devouring children, and using promiscuous copulations, would have blazed this matter abroad, to their total subversion. But so palpably different was the case here, that those miraculous powers which Mr. Gibbon so strenuously denies, were then acknowledged by the Heathens themselves, though under the name of magick, by which they rendered them not only useless, but even pernicious, to Christianity.

Fourth cause: The virtue of the primitive Christians. – We have an odd contrast here: the imposture and villainy of these people were Mr. Gibbon's 3d cause; their integrity and virtue are, in this instance, to constitute his 4th cause. But passing this over, I am to observe, that, if he had, as in justice to Christianity he ought to have done, set down, as a cause, the manifest truth and purity of the Christian morality, and the strong motives it held out to virtue, which were infinitely more powerful than the world ever before knew, and these suitably acknowledged by a superior purity and goodness of life in the Christians, which must have drawn upon them and their religion the esteem of every virtuous and sensible person, (and sometimes he finds occasion to speak of Christianity in this manner,) he then would have produced a cause most justly and greatly operating in Christianity's growth. But as a representation of this kind would have been too favourable for this religion, he is forced to suppress it, and to substitute in its place that excessive severity of life and doctrine into which those miserable times of persecution had driven the oppressed

Christians; and has thereby destroyed the intended effect of his own cause, and turned it against himself: for that rigidness and severity of living which was then required of every believer in Christ, must have been very discouraging, and greatly obstructed, instead of promoting a conversion to this faith. It is not a very easy matter to persuade a great number of people to embrace such a severe and miserable austerity of life as he has here spoken of.

As to his 5th cause, that, if justly given, would have been of some advantage to Christianity; but it is surprising how he could fall into such a palpable mistake, as to make the union of the church any help to its spreading, when there was nothing but dissention, and the most rancorous divisions, among them. The apostolical writings shew us, that this was the case with them even in the first century, whilst the Apostles were alive, and miraculous power and divine inspiration were common in the church; (so unwilling are men to give up their own prejudices to any conviction whatsoever!) and the Christian writers, afterwards, shew that this was the case with them in the 2d and 3d centuries: but in the 4th, when Paganism was brought to its expiring gasp, the controversy between the Trinitarians and the followers of Arius, raised such a flame in the church, and bred such animosities between the contending parties, as made them the derision and sport even of the Heathens themselves. These are incontestible facts, and will hereafter be fully proved even by Mr. Gibbon himself; and therefore this most learned writer was strangely mistaken when he made the union of the church one cause of its prodigious encrease. Let us not, however, at the present, give up this dispute; but, for the reader's more perfect satisfaction, let us go on to examine the heads of this cause, as he is pleased to set them down in his book.

The active government of the church, the primitive freedom and equality, the institutions of bishops and presbyters and of provincial councils, the progress of the episcopal authority, the metropolitans, the ambition of the Roman Pontiff, the distinction of laity and clergy, these are (to stop for a while) made by him a principal means of Christianity's wonderful growth; but how either one, or all of these put together, should have any considerable effect in the conversion of the Heathens, I see not, nor do I believe that any impartial, considerate person will see. If such a government as this had been peculiar to the Christians, it must have proved of some benefit to their religion; but where is the civilized nation that is destitute of it? It is certain that the Romans were not, and that they had all the advantages which could possibly arise from any of these institutions in the greatest perfection; truly in much greater perfection than the Christians did, or could possibly, possess. It is easy to discern that some policy of this kind was absolutely necessary to the existence of Christianity; but how this little weak government of the little weak church, without any other support than what conscience could give it, should enable these few religionists not only to resist, but prevail against, that policy which was so firmly established, and had all the encouragement that law, power, learning, prejudice, wickedness, the most dreadful punishments, and the most ample rewards, could give it, I cannot discover, although I have given it the most careful consideration. Hitherto, then, his own cause militates against himself: but he also adds, the oblations and revenues of the churches, and the distribution of them, excommunication, public pennance, and the dignity of the episcopal government. To these I answer, That to make excommunication and pennance, which were so excessively severe against all apostacy from the faith, or any wickedness in it after its reception, a cause of Christianity's growth, is strange indeed; he should have set them down as a great obstruction to it. The dignity of the bishops, and the revenues of the churches, were certainly as nothing in comparison of the Roman magistracy, wealth, and power; and the very frequent and miserable persecutions by which the Christians often suffered, and to which they were continually exposed, must have rendered these advantages of still less efficacy to Mr. Gibbon's purpose, – must, in fact, have turned them entirely against it. That love of the world, which alone could have given them any force with the Christians, must have cast them off from Christianity, and made Heathens of them all.

Upon the whole of this matter, then, we find this ingenious writer to be very unfortunate in the causes he has assigned for the growth of such a religion as Christianity. They are all wrongly stated; they are all ineffectual for his purpose; and in many instances directly make against it.

CHAP. XI.
There are some other reasons afterwards offered by him, which, it must be confessed, would have been of advantage to this religion, if properly stated; namely, the philosophers seeing

the folly of Heathenism, the incredulity and ridicule of the learned, and of the priests themselves who officiated in their religious services, and the great scepticism which these things produced among many of their people. It is certain that there is strength in these causes, and that in such a state of things they must have been very considerable helps to Christianity; so considerable, indeed, that they seem to have affected Mr. Gibbon himself, and for a while to have made a convert of him. His words are, *Some deities of a more fashionable cast, might have occupied the deserted temples of Jupiter and Apollo, if, in the decisive moment, the wisdom of Providence had not interposed a genuine revelation, fitted to inspire the most rational esteem and conviction, whilst, at the same time, it was adorned with all that could attract the curiosity, the wonder, the veneration, of the people.*

How to reconcile this to the whole tenour of his book, and many of his direct expressions, I know not. Must not both Christ and his Apostles have been, according to him, a set of the most profligate deceivers? And are these the people who brought down this genuine and amiable revelation from heaven? This is strange indeed! Nor can I see how he can reconcile it to the character of his most highly esteemed and commended historian Tacitus, who, in his own translation, uses these words of the Christians and their religion : *Branded with deserved infamy, a dire superstition was even introduced to Rome itself, which receives and protects whatever is atrocious; they were all convicted, not so much for the crime of setting fire to the city, as for their hatred of mankind*: – in which words, besides the manifest and spiteful falsity of them, and the direct contradiction given to Mr. Gibbon himself in the above-cited passage, it might easily be shewn, were it worth insisting upon, that he has made his translation worse than the original, in order to throw an odium upon Christianity. And as to its being fitted to attract the curiosity, wonder, and veneration of the people, this will not, I suppose, be accounted a reproach to it: and how, indeed, could it be otherwise, when it was to open to us the nature of the One Infinite Being, and the most stupendous of all his wonderful providences; – providences, which the angels desire to look into, and which were to be the most expressive of, and honourable to, his infinite nature, that he would ever shew for the good of his creatures.

But it is proper that we should enquire into those particulars which have given him such a high notion of the easiness of Christianity's success. They are set down, pages 601-2: *The fashion of incredulity was communicated from the philosopher to the man of pleasure or business, from the noble to the plebeian, and from the master to the menial slave who waited at his table, and who eagerly listened to the freedom of his conversation. On public occasions the philosophical part of mankind affected to treat with respect and decency the religious institutions of their country; but their secret contempt penetrated through the thin and awkward disguise: and even the people, when they discovered that their deities were rejected and derided by those whose rank and understanding they were accustomed to reverence, were filled with doubts and apprehensions concerning the truth of those doctrines to which they had yielded a most implicit belief. The decline of ancient prejudice exposed a very numerous portion of human-kind to the danger of a painful and comfortless situation. A state of scepticism and suspence may amuse a few inquisitive minds. But the practice of superstition is so congenial to the multitude, that, if they are forcibly awakened, they still regret the loss of their pleasing vision. Their love of the marvellous and supernatural, their curiosity with regard to future events, and their strong propensity to extend their hopes and fears beyond the limits of the visible world, were the principal causes which favoured the establishment of polytheism. So urgent on the vulgar is the necessity of believing, that the fall of any system of mythology will most probably be succeeded by the introduction of some other mode of superstition.* And so he goes on, in the words already quoted, to wonder that the progress of Christianity was not, in these circumstances, still more rapid and universal. We must, then, examine this matter, as laid down by him.

Mr. Gibbon dates this scepticism from the rise of Christianity to the extinction of Heathenism; but, upon enquiry, we shall not find this assertion verified, but falsified, by stubborn facts. The philosophers, indeed, denied all futurity, and derided the Heathen notion of retribution there; but we do not find them in any readiness, nor the people either, to give up their old religion, but, on the contrary, tenacious, persevering, obstinate, in the defence of it, and doing all that power, malice, falsehood, genius, learning, could do, for the support of it.

Thus we have seen it to be with his favourite historian Tacitus; and this is abundantly proved by Christianity's not being able to prevail for a hundred years together, and till Heathen Rome had become Christian, under the authority of Constantine the Great: it is, besides, proved, by the many and cruel persecutions inflicted upon the Christians during this time; by the cries of the people, upon every occasion, to have the Christians given to the lions; and by the defence acknowledged by Mr. Gibbon to be made for Heathenism by the philosophers of the second and third centuries. He is, therefore, most shamefully mistaken in that state of the case which he has given, and upon which he hath so confidently founded Christianity's success. And if any one be desirous to see this fact undoubtedly confirmed, I refer him to Vol. I. chap. 16, of the late Dr. Leland's Advantages and Necessity of the Christian Revelation, where he will receive entire satisfaction on this point: only, as this truly learned and great man hath not mentioned Plutarch among his Heathen authorities, I will observe, that this philosopher, in accounting for the cessation of oracles among the Heathens by the supposed death of the dæmons who gave them, and who, though very long lived, might not be immortal, and by his endeavouring to explain away, and account for, the monstrous idolatry of the Egyptians, gives me a strong suspicion that he knew of Christianity, and took these methods to preserve that most absurd and bloody superstition from being destroyed by the reasonableness, purity, and truth, of the Christian religion. And I must, also, for the same purpose, mention that great genius, and learned philosopher, Longinus, who shews himself to be well acquainted, both with Judaism and Christianity; and yet, what concern does he express at Homer's battle of the Heathen gods! And what care does he take to hinder it from hurting their religion!

It is true, that there was a Lucian in the second century, who did most severely ridicule the Heathen superstition; but then he did so to Christianity as well as to that, and, indeed, to all religion along with them; and is, therefore, nothing to Mr. Gibbon's purpose. And it is also true, that Seneca, in the first century, spoke very harshly of the Heathen worship; but then it is equally true, that he advises the people to conform to it. But although erroneous in this his state of the case, Mr. Gibbon is not so as to the consequences which must follow from such a freedom of conversation, and much more from such an infidel freedom of writing as he has assumed.

It is his opinion, and certainly the truth, that the people will have some religion or other. Man's nature requires it; and this natural inclination, as well as the reason of the thing, is a demonstration, that it is natural to man, and ought to be received by every one of this nature, and must be, and will be so, if he be not debased to the lowest degree of wickedness and wrong judgment. And now, from his own mouth, I beseech Mr. Gibbon to consider what he has been doing in this his attempt to destroy Christianity; and whether the world will owe him any thanks for it, even if there was not to be a future life after the present, or any retribution in it. Can he find any other religion upon earth so good for us as that of Christ, which he has but just now justly described to be "a genuine revelation, fitted to inspire the most rational esteem and conviction?" Can he find any so good as this, and that as it is taught in his own national church, for the reasonableness, purity, and usefulness of its precepts, and for its most powerful enforcements of virtue? – And can he avoid seeing the dreadful consequences which must follow from its being destroyed? for which he has, however, so heartily laboured, and which will not be without its effect (I pray God, that it may be but little) upon a now luxurious, careless, and very profligate people. Possibly he may need to be told, but the reader certainly ought to be told, the dreadful consequences of it.

These writings of his will propagate scepticism and infidelity, by a great deal already too rife among us; these a total disrelish to, and breach of every virtue; these a hatred of all the sanctions, which enforce virtue and restrain from vice; these the keenest hatred of the Gospel, and every thing enjoined by it; and these an increase and inundation of wickedness, till it produces a total disregard to the welfare of the state, great mischief to it, and to all the individuals of it, and till it shall at last throw it into slavery, and all the absurdities, superstition, and idolatry of the church of Rome, from which we have, by our Reformation, been so long and so happily emancipated: for then the baseness of the people's minds will make them require the iron hand of arbitrary power to controul their perniciousness, will render their remains of liberty but a curse to them, and themselves, therefore, not only unwilling to defend, but eager to give it up; and this baseness will make their minds so connatural to the baseness and superstition of Popery, that they will be ready to abandon their own true and holy belief, and eager to accept of the outward services, the conjurations, and the absolutions of the church of Rome. And thus shall our true and spiritual religion, the boast of Christianity, and our free and happy constitution, the admiration and envy of every sensible and virtuous man, be totally destroyed from among us; and this, not only by the just judgment of an offended God, but by the natural effects of the things themselves: – an event so certain to follow from the increase of infidelity, that he must either wish for it, or be judicially blinded, who does not discern it, and from hence see the encreasing danger of our countries at this time.

Mr. Gibbon ought, therefore, out of love to the truth, to the welfare of mankind, and the good of his own country, to have struck out those parts of his book which are so hurtful to Christianity. Dr. Watson, in my opinion, yields a great deal too much to our Deists, when he allows that the usefulness and benefits of Christianity are no sure evidence of the truth of this religion: for as the Divine Being is infinitely good, and this his goodness was the cause of all creation; so it can never be, that the thing which is absolutely and entirely good, can be false – it must proceed from Him who is entire goodness and truth. And although we may, in other instances, be easily mistaken, yet not so in this of Christianity: it is so highly necessary to our welfare, both here and hereafter, indeed absolutely so, and so perfective of our nature, and surely productive of happiness, both in this and in the other world, that it must be true.

CHAP. XII.
Page 602. It is said, that the conquests of Rome paved the way for the conquests of Christianity. The assertion is true, and most highly honourable to this religion; because, as Rome civilized, and made its people thoughtful and intelligent, it shewed that Christianity is of such a nature, as to prevail where the people are most fitted to reason, to enquire, and to understand: and for want of this among the savages of America, our religion, to this hour, has not been able to make any considerable progress there.

That the Jews were so incredulous to the miracles of the divine prophet, as to render it unnecessary to publish any Hebrew Gospel, is a great mistake; but shews plainly what this gentleman thinks, and would have his readers think, of the miracles of

Christ and his Apostles. Acts ii. 41, we find 3000 converted by one preaching and the miracle preceding it. Acts iv. 5000 converted by another preaching. Acts v. 14, it is, "And believers were the more added to the Lord, multitudes both of men and women." Acts vi. 7, it is, "And the word of God increased, and the number of the disciples multiplied in Jerusalem greatly, and a great company of the priests were obedient to the faith." And Acts xxi. 20, James, who then presided over and governed the church of Jerusalem, declares, "Thou seest, brother, how many thousands of Jews there are who believe:" – the original is, myriads or ten thousands. It is, then, a mistake in this learned man to make the Jews so incredulous to the Christian miracles: and he must, consequently be mistaken in the reason he has assigned for there never having been a Hebrew Gospel; which, although the thing be doubtful, I do not believe there really ever was. The cause of this is, however, easily discerned. There was one or more of the Apostles always residing at Jerusalem (to which place the necessity of a Hebrew Gospel was confined), till they were all killed, or had fled from it at the approach of that Roman war which destroyed Jerusalem, the temple and public worship, and all the Jewish legal rites; and from his mouth, and the teachers authorized by him, the Jews must have had such a full information of every thing in Christianity, as rendered it unnecessary for them to have any Gospel in writing. And here I must observe, that, as the Jewish teachers then did, as the church of Rome now does, assume to themselves an infallibility in interpreting their Scriptures, and had, in fact, to make good this claim, texts by a great many more numerous and forcible than Rome can produce for herself; as their people were so long used to allow them this high prerogative; and as these rulers did almost all of them, in their conjunct body, deny and reject Christ; – considering these things, it is really wonderful how Christianity could make any progress at all among them; and it is hence fully shewn, that the miracles wrought for confirmation of it, must have been stupendous and convincing indeed. It is observed by Dr. Middleton's antagonists, that, according to his own Introduction, he ought to have begun his Enquiry with an examination of the miracles of the first century, as set forth in the New Testament, and have shewn why and when the power of working them ceased in the church; but, instead of this fair proceeding, he begins his Enquiry with those of the fourth century, when the necessity of them was nearly superseded; when the morals of the Christians were exceedingly corrupted by the outward peace and prosperity of the church, and more especially by the animosities and violent contentions raised by the Arians against the Trinitarians, which made some of each side ready to forge miracles for the support of their different tenets, and the willing and credulous people too ready to receive them; when, too, their love of monkery, and the saints and their rotten relicks, greatly hurt the purity of their faith even in that century, but in the next threw them into downright superstition and idolatry. This is the time in which Dr. Middleton chose to begin his Enquiry, ascending afterwards to the third and second centuries; and in this he has been very nearly followed by Mr. Gibbon. The miracles of the third and second centuries are first condemned by the latter; and when he thinks he has brought those into contempt, the miracles of Christ and his Apostles are likewise attacked by him; and although in a covert, yet in a most pointed manner. To have begun with those of Christ and his immediate followers, would have been an enterprize too dangerous and offensive. It was, therefore, his most successful method, at first, to dispute those of a later time, which could not be so certainly proved, and would not give so great an offence; and then, as soon as the reader's mind was sufficiently prejudiced, he might deny them all in general, when such condemnation would be the more easily swallowed, and any hints taken which might destroy the belief of them.

I do not say that this was the real design of Mr. Gibbon; but I must affirm, that his proceeding thus was so well fitted to produce these effects, that he, who would defend the truth, ought not to let it pass without notice. Self-deceit is the easiest of all others, and where there is any prejudice in the mind, it is the most difficult to be avoided: and if ever man was prejudiced against any thing, Mr. Gibbon is, and most deeply so, against Christianity; for he sees nothing belonging to it in a just, but distorted light, and this has drawn him here into palpable self-contradiction. He repeatedly allows a strong internal evidence to be in Christianity, and yet in this place he effectually destroys it. He will not allow the primitive Christian writers to have offered any reason for their religion which was fitted to move a sensible man; and yet their principal defence of it was, the strong internal evidence with which it abounded. They not only exposed the absurdity, falsehood, wickedness, of Heathenism; but they dwelt, and chiefly too, upon the infinite benefit which Scripture instruction had done, in opening and ascertaining the being and nature of God, his creation of the world, his moral government and providence over it, the pure worship by which he is to be served, his observance of, and regard to, the moral behaviour of every man, and his having appointed a day in which he will judge the whole world in righteousness, and reward or punish every man with an eternity of the greatest happiness or misery, according to his good or evil behaviour in this life; by his giving us a perfect rule of duty, which forbids even the least vice, and enjoins the most perfect virtue and purity of life; purity, not only in our outward words and actions, but inwardly in our most secret thoughts and inclinations: and all this, as we hope to escape this most horrid and threatened misery, and obtain this promised and most glorious happiness. And is there, indeed, nothing which can convince in all these things; and this, too, when they are set in opposition to the monstrous corruptions and errors of Heathenism? Mr. Gibbon does, in effect, affirm that there is not; but at the same time he equally contradicts reason, and his own previous declaration. And here it must be observed, that, as he makes nothing at all of prophecy, utterly denies all miracles, and in this place destroys all internal evidence of Christianity, he does, indeed, hereby effectually render it, as he here would have it, unworthy the reception of any sensible man: but then we have shewn him to be mistaken in every one of these instances, and even to contradict himself.

As to the proportion of the Christians to that of the Heathens, it is of but small consequence; and therefore I pass it over, and proceed to page 613, where it is said, that *the new sect of Christians was almost entirely composed of the dregs of the populace, of peasants and mechanics, of boys and women, of beggars and slaves, the last of whom might sometimes introduce the missionaries into the rich and noble families to which they belonged. These obscure teachers . . . whilst they cautiously avoid the dangerous encounter of philosophers, mingle with the rude and illiterate crowd, and insinuate themselves into those minds, whom their age, their sex, or their education, has the best disposed to receive the impression of superstitious terrors:* and this picture, although confessed to be an enemy's exaggeration, is yet declared not to be void of a faint resemblance. – That the majority of every religion must be made up of the populace, is unquestionable; but that the Christians were not entirely composed of them, but had many of station and learning among them, is certain from Pliny's letter to Trajan, as well as from all the Christian apologists. Had it, however, been as it is here represented, are we to be governed by the fashion of the world, or the reasonableness of the thing? Can Mr. Gibbon think that the writing in this manner will do honour either to himself or to his cause? As to the Christians avoiding to encounter with the Heathen philosophers, what can Mr. Gibbon intend by such an expression? Were not many of the then Christians philosophers, and men of deep learning; and were they not spoken to, and converted by, the Christians? Is Heathenism, indeed, the religion which the philosophers professed, and endeavoured to defend, to be in reason preferred before Christianity? And is the latter found to be unable to defend itself in the opinion of rational people? It cannot be affirmed: the very reverse is but now asserted by Mr. Gibbon himself; and he must know that the most learned and worthy men of our nation, men who have done the highest honour to it by their genius, knowledge, virtue, have been staunch believers; and of how different a character from them the heads of our unbelievers have been, the world need not be told from me.

Page 614. – It is a most certain fact, that almost all heresies have arisen in the church of Christ from men's giving too much deference to their own weak reason, and too little to the revelation of an all-knowing and infinite God; and never was any fault more rife in the world, than this at present is among our people.

Page 614, 615. – It is acknowledged, but with restrictions, that there were many persons of rank and learning at that time professing Christianity, though these too few to take off entirely the imputation of ignorance and obscurity: – but this, he allows, does, after all, give us the more reason to admire the merit and success of the Christians. – He also says, that, while Christianity promises a heaven to the poor in spirit, and the afflicted chearfully listen to it, the fortunate are satisfied with the happiness of this world. – That they are ever endeavouring to make themselves so, is allowed; but that they are able to accomplish their purpose, I absolutely deny: and the continued, various, and ruinous pursuits of those who are highest in the world, confirm this to be the truth, as well as the confessions at last made by themselves, and by the great Solomon. And, indeed, the clearest reasons, as well as the constant experience of all mankind, shews us it ever must be so.

Man can never be gratified by the pleasures of sense; because sense is but one, and the lowest, part of him. His highest faculties are those of reason and morality, from which must man's chief happiness ever arise; but whereof he has such an imperfect use in this world, that they can never satisfy him: and, to aggravate his misfortune, man is ever found to sacrifice the pleasures of these to the lower and baser pleasures of sense. Besides, Mr. Gibbon allows that man is made for a future life; and if he be, what shall we say to the folly and baseness of him, who, in opposition to this most exalted prerogative, the end of his own nature, and the intention of his most beneficent Creator, shall endeavour to pin himself down, and give up all his affection and care, to this insignificant world; and this, to the total neglect of that infinitely important futurity, wherein such neglect must prove his certain and everlasting destruction? – Is it any reproach to Christianity, that men of this stamp are not to be gained over to it?

Page 616. The great philosophers, by *their language or their silence, equally discover their contempt for the growing sect* of Christianity, which could not *produce a single argument that could engage the attention of men of sense and learning.* – What! Has Mr. Gibbon, indeed, found our religion deserving of such a censure as this! Has not he himself made the purity and power of its precepts, one great cause of its success? And is not this, too, that genuine, divine revelation, which, in his own words, deserves all esteem and veneration? And has he not but now confessed, that there were some men of sense and learning among the Christians? And how, then, can he talk with such condemnation of them, and praise of those philosophers, who, in opposition to this religion, persevered in, and defended, such a one as their Paganism was?

Very deep, indeed, must this gentleman's prejudice be, when it could hinder him from seeing that he must expose himself by such an attack: for when we have the Gospel and its proofs before us, it is of no consequence to us what others have thought of these matters. Will Mr. Gibbon, indeed, set up authority above reason and truth? – But what were those philosophers, upon whose conduct Mr. Gibbon, in thus severely condemning the Christian writers, lays such an extraordinary stress? I shall, shortly, but with the greatest integrity and justice, shew. Till Christianity had made a considerable progress, they, for the most part, rejected a future life, but all of them denied any retribution in it. Their religion was only regarded in order to obtain the good things of this world, and had nothing in it of morality or virtue, but abundance of immorality and wickedness. The end of man, and his chief happiness, was totally mistaken by them all: and, besides a most unreasonable attachment to their several and contradictory sects, which they thought themselves bound to follow and maintain, the principles of almost all of them were founded upon dogmas, not only unfavourable, but most adverse to Christianity; and we know, that every one of them allowed of several vices which true religion abhors and rejects. I need not enlarge upon this matter; Mr. Gibbon must be conscious of it; I will only hint at a few particulars.

Plato, in his Republic, recommends a community of wives, and would have those men, who had done most service to the public, allowed a greater liberty in this way. Socrates himself was infamous for that vice which drew down fire from heaven upon Sodom and Gomorrah; and the philosophers were so commonly addicted to it, that no man, who had a regard to the purity of his son, dared to commit him to their tuition. How just, therefore, is the character given of them by St. Paul, Rom. first chap. that *pretending to be wise, they became fools*, and abandoned themselves to the most shameful and abominable vices! It was a known matter among themselves, that their practice, and their reasoning about virtue, were totally different. – Are these, then, the men, upon whose opinion we are to reject Christianity! – reject the purest religion which the world ever saw, and throw ourselves back, it may be, into Heathenism, with all its abominations; – destroy the most perfect system of morality, take away all incitements to virtue, and discouragement from vice? – leave no hope of futurity, or, if there should be such, no possibility of our being happy in it! Are these the men, upon whose virtue and integrity we are so entirely to depend, as, upon their account, to do ourselves all these destructive and irreparable mischiefs!

Besides, I am to observe, that these men could relish nothing but reason, the very pride of silly reason; and that it was one main end of the Gospel to destroy this very foolish and criminal presumption, when applied to religion. It was (besides the teaching us such a purity of life, as might fit us for the happiness of heaven) to open the One Infinite Nature to man, and to do the highest honour to it; and therefore consisted, not of a revelation which could be reasoned on by man, or any creature, but of such as could only be made known by the Creator himself, and proved by the display of his own almighty power; that is, by controuling that course of nature which he has established, and which could be done by his own hand alone; as, also, by his predicting, some hundreds, I might have said thousands, of years, before the completion, many contingent events, which should, in their due time, come to pass: – a knowledge this, which no creature could have, and which some of our *reasoners* will not allow to be possible even to God himself. This revelation was to be the power of God, and the wisdom of God; that is, the exertion of these attributes in the highest degree: and was to regard the whole world, and the government of it, in a manner most conducive to its happiness, even from the creation to the consummation of all things; and must, therefore, be as superior to the faculties of men or angels, as the heavens are above the earth. No wonder, then, that it should be despised by those self-opinionated men, who imagined all reason confined to themselves, but, in truth, never had any proper ideas about religious matters. It neither came, nor was proved, in the way that they wished; and, therefore, it was foolishness to them. But St. Paul's assertion will ever remain true, that the foolishness of God is wiser than men; and so it has remarkably proved in this instance. As to the understanding and knowledge of the primitive Christian writers, let their works, still extant, speak for them. The general opinion of the world has hitherto been most highly in their favour; and whoever will read them with any impartiality, will, I believe, entertain the same sentiments.

Page 617. Mr. Gibbon doubts whether the philosophers perused the Apologies of the Christians for themselves and their religion. Possibly, they did not; but this should not be said by any man who has a regard for their character: for what reasoners, or respecters of religion, must they be, who could be so well satisfied with Heathenism, as to refuse even to hear any thing that could be said in opposition to it! He laments, also, that the Christian *cause was not defended by abler advocates; they expose, with superfluous wit and eloquence, the extravagance of polytheism, and interest our compassion by displaying the innocence and sufferings of their injured brethren.* – But how was this superfluous, when the philosophers still persevered in the defence of this religion, and the people still went on in the cruel persecution of the Christians?

But they insist much more strongly on the predictions which announced, than on the miracles which accompanied, the appearance of the Messiah. – We ought, at this great distance of time, to be very cautious how we condemn the method of defence used by the primitive Christians. We have Origen's book against Celsus, who, in regard to his own reputation, to his religion, and to the authority by which he is so often controuled, and hindered from running into allegory, we may be sure, has given us a just state of this philosopher's controversy: and now I ask Mr. Gibbon, who has certainly read this work, whether he thinks the arguments of Celsus strong or well-chosen? I will answer for him, that he does not. And yet the Christians, if they would at all reply, must answer such reasonings as these. They, who had been bred up Heathens themselves, and lived among them, and were intimately acquainted with their religion and philosophy, must be much better judges than any of us can be, what the best methods were with which to defend themselves, and to persuade others; and it might have been folly in them to have recourse to such as may now seem to us most fitting and powerful for their purpose. In this instance, however, we can effectually vindicate them.

Those philosophers had the Scriptures before them, which contained an authentic account of many and most stupendous miracles having been wrought by Christ and his Apostles, which account, it appears, the Heathens themselves did not contradict; and, if these could not convince them, how much less the fewer and lesser that were performed in the church afterwards. But as all these were by the Heathens attributed to magick, and their own gods were presumed to perform the like, it was manifestly improper for the Christians to rest their principal defence upon a proof of this kind. There was, however, one of them, which was proper, and this I find insisted upon by Athenagoras, Theophilus, Tertullian, Minutius, Felix, Cyprian, and Origen, and, probably, by many others; and this is the power, which Tertullian so strongly insisted upon, of the Christians making the dæmons confess whom the Heathens worshipped – that they were dæmons, and not gods. And this very reason is given by Origen, in his defence of Christianity. He affirms, that some remarkable footsteps of this miraculous power, for the confirmation of the truth of Christianity, did remain to his days; that the church was appointed to destroy the power of infernal dæmons; that it was absurd to suppose the Apostles did no miracles at all, but relied on their doctrines only; and that there were some remnants of this power to dispossess dæmons still preserved among them – If he should relate miracles of his own knowledge, it would furnish the infidels with a subject of laughter, who would be ready to suspect the Christians, as the Christians did them, of inventing fictions to support a bad cause; but he calls God to witness, that in him it was only, by a proper evidence, to maintain Chrsitianity's divine origin. – Thus speaks the great Origen.

But prophecies were much more convincing to the Heathens. The particulars of our Saviour's life and actions are strongly insisted upon by the Christian advocates; and the exact eventual completion of the predictions thereof, so many hundred years after they had been made, was so full a proof in behalf of Christianity, as left no way to evade it, but by a denial of their antiquity, which, as maintained by Christ's greatest enemies, the Jews, could not be discredited without a most manifest absurdity; yet even this absurdity, great as it was, we find some of them driven to, affirming the prophecies to be written after the accomplishment of the facts.

What the books of Orpheus, Hermes, and the Sibyls were, neither I nor Mr. Gibbon know; but that the latter (which only is here of importance) were not a Christian forgery, is unquestionably certain, because they were quoted by Virgil, and formed a material part of Christ's character, some years before he was born: and Athenagoras shews, that Plato cited them more than 300 years before Christ, to prove their gods to be deified men. The learned Prideaux has a long dissertation upon this matter, and concludes, not that they were Christian forgeries, but that there were some interpolations made in them by the Christians; which was very foolishly done by them, for they thereby rendered these books useless to the cause they were intended to support. But even this cannot be allowed to that very learned and honest man, whose desire of impartiality has, in this instance, carried him a great deal too far.

There were too many of the Sibylline books, and in too many hands, to have been all corrupted by the Christians; nor was it possible, when the Heathens had all power in their hands, for the Christians to quote these interpolations, without being confuted and exposed by their enemies, and this to the ruin of their religion. And that the reader may have entire satisfaction in this matter, I will here subjoin Mr. Reeves's note upon it, in his translation of Justin Martyr's first Apology.

"The great objection against the Sibylline oracles, is, that they so plainly and expressly foretel Christ to the Heathen world; as plainly as (or more so than) the prophets to the Jews. But was not Christ as manifestly foretold by Balaam the Aramitick Sorcerer, as by the prophet Isaiah? Did not Job, who was not of Israel, speak of the great article of the resurrection? Did not Daniel, in his captivity, communicate his prophecies to the Gentiles, as well as to the Jews? And was not a prophet sent to Jeroboam, an Israelite indeed by birth, but a Pagan by religion. All which evidently prove, that God never delivered himself more plainly by his prophets, than when the occasion respected the Gentiles, and not the Jews. And this likewise proves what Clemens Alexandrinus tells us, 6 Stro. p. 270, That, as God raised up prophets among the Jews, to bring them to salvation, "sic & selectissimum quemque a Paganis servare voluisse, prophetas ipsis proprios propria ipsorum dialecto excitando;" and to these Sibyls, Justin Martyr, Clemens, Origen, Eusebius, Lactantius, sent the Heathens for the truth of Christianity, and laid so great a stress upon them as to be called Sibyllists. But now, had all these been forgeries, (not to mention the baseness of a pious fraud, abominated by the first Christians,) they never would have been so sillily impudent, as to have appealed to them before the Emperors, and before the world; and Origen never could have challenged Celsus, or any of the Heathens, to give a considerable instance where these books were interpolated by the Christians, which, no doubt, they would have triumphantly done, had there been such interpolation to produce. Moreover, it is certain, that, in Cicero's time, the Sibylline prophecies were so interpreted by some in favour of Cæsar, as to predict a monarchy. Divi. lib. 2, "Eum quemque revera Regem," &c. *That, if we would be safe, we should acknowledge him for a king who really was so*; which interpretation, Cicero, after Cæsar's death, was so much offended with, that he quarrels with the oracles and their interpreters: "Quamobrem Sibyllam quidem sepositam," &c.

Wherefore, let us shut up the Sibyl, and keep her close, that, according to the decree of our ancestors, her verses may not be read without the express command of the Senate. And then he adds, "Cum Antistitibus," &c. *Let us also deal with the Quindecemviri, and the interpreters of these Sibylline books, that they would rather produce any thing out of them than a king.* And in the eclogue of Virgil, "Ultima Cumæi venit," &c. written about the beginning of the reign of Herod the Great, and flatteringly applied to Pollio's son, Salonius, such a golden age, and renovation of all things, are spoken of, as cannot be fulfilled in the reign of any earthly king, and in a strain prophetick. The same year that Pompey took Jersualem, one of the Sibyl oracles made a great noise, that Nature was about to bring forth a king to the Romans: and Suetonius, in the Life of Augustus, saith, that this so terrified the Senate, that they made a decree, that none born that year should be educated; and that those, whose wives were with child, applied the prophecy to themselves. And Appian, Plutarch, Sallust, and Cicero, all concur in saying, that it was this prophecy of the Sibyls which stirred up Cornelius Lentulus at that time, upon the false hope that he was the man designed for the king of the Romans. The words of Suetonius in the Life of Vespasian are very remarkable: "Percrebuerat Oriente toto vetus & constans opinio, esse in Fatis, ut eo tempore Judea profecti rerum potirentur." And to the same purpose are those of Tacitus: Hist. lib. 5, "Pluribus persuasio inerat, antiquis Sacerdotum libris contineri, eo ipso tempore fore, ut valeret Oriens, profectique Judea rerum potirentur."

"Now, what I look upon as the most probable account of these express prophecies concerning Christ, I mean, as to the manner of their becoming so rife among the Heathens, is this: – The Jews, in their dispersions, took all occasions to speak the most magnificent things of their expected Messiah; and the prophecies concerning his glory, by the more than ordinary grace of God, shone brighter and clearer upon their minds during their captivity, and afforded the greatest support to them under their exile; and on these occasions it was, I believe, that the Jewish oracles came to be admitted into the Sibylline books laid up in the Capitol. The books of the Sibyls were of two kinds; those bought by Tarquin, and burnt with the Capitol in the time of Sylla, we find from Livy, were full of nothing but idolatry and superstition: but after the re-building of the Capitol, there were others brought from Erythræ, by the three ambassadors deputed for that purpose; and afterwards others were sent by Augustus upon the same design, as we are informed by Tacitus, Ann. c. 6; "Quæsitus Samo, Ilio, Erythris, per Africam etiam & Siciliam & Italicas colonias, Carminibus Sibyllæ, datum Sacerdotibus negotium, quantum humana ope potuissent vera discernere." And to the same purpose Suetonius, Aug. cap. 31. Now, who can doubt but in this search after the Sibylline oracles many of the Jewish prophecies were picked up (especially those famous ones concerning their new king), and carried with the rest to Rome: for, after the first were burnt with the Capitol, who could possibly distinguish the one from the other? And, therefore, Tacitus cautiously adds, in the fore-cited passage, "quantum humana ope potuissent."

Thus argues the learned Mr. Reeves; and now, Dean Prideaux's mistake, and Mr. Gibbon's too great readiness to abuse the Christians, must be manifest to every reader.

The assertion of inattention paid by the Heathens to the miracles of Christ and his Apostles, is founded upon a great mistake. All the miracles of our Saviour were performed among the Jews, a very few in the adjoining Heathen nations excepted; and what were done among the Heathens in general by the Apostles, we know not, except a small number performed by St. Paul to confirm his preaching. Neither Seneca nor Pliny might ever have seen one of them; nor is it probable that they did. To people prejudiced beyond conviction they were never shewn; and that All-wise Being who was to work them, knew before-hand when they would be useless. Or these very people might have seen and neglected them, or not have chosen to speak any thing of them; and unless they had been converted by them, it is certain that they would not. We are now too well acquainted with the character of *philosophers*, to expect such a self-denying fairness and candour from any of them. The spiteful misrepresentations which they give of Christianity, when they at all speak of it, warrants this assertion. But the defenders of the primitive Christian miracles, against Dr. Middleton, have shewn that there was not that dead silence of the Heathens about them which Mr. Gibbon asserts: they are often mentioned by them, though only to be ridiculed and condemned as magick.

The darkness of our Saviour's crucifixion might have been confined to the land of Judea, and it is now generally thought to have been so. But that Phlegon's testimony is by us wisely given up, I know not: Dr. Chapman's dissertation upon this subject, at least, shews the probability to be on the other side; and, from Origen's quoting it, it is plain to be of a very ancient standing. – The answer given in Dr. Watson's book, to the representation here made of Pliny, shews it to be a great mistake.

As to Mr. Gibbon's 16th Chapter, it contains matter so much less affecting Christianity, and what is offensive in it is so particularly confuted by much abler pens than mine, that I shall say nothing to it. But here I will congratulate my Christian reader upon the certainty and strength of his holy faith; for very certain and well-founded must it indeed be, when it can withstand, and without any the least injury to itself, the fiercest attacks that Mr. Gibbon, with all his genius and learning, all his deep prejudices and eagerness, could make to destroy it. But it is truly founded upon a rock, and will remain unshaken among us so long as we shall retain any just sense of the dignity of the nature of rational and moral man above that of the irrational and immoral brute, and are capable of any prosperity in this world, or happiness in that which is to come.

And now I might conclude, but that I think it first necessary to warn the Christian reader against being frightened from his religion, by the horrid picture which he will hereafter find to be drawn by Mr. Gibbon, and justly too, in his history of the next and the two following centuries, when the furious dissentions, animosities, persecutions, and cruelty of the Christians against each other, and when the luxury, pride, ambition, turbulence, of their great and powerful clergy, will present a horrid scene to his view; – very dishonourable, indeed, to the actors themselves, but not really hurtful to their religion; for, both by its most positive precepts, and by the whole tenor of its doctrines, it is the farthest removed from, it is the most adverse to, this abominable destructive spirit. But as long as men are men, and Satan is permitted to range abroad in the world, there will be such things in it; and especially concerning that which, of all others, deserves the greatest esteem, and is most worthy to be preserved and contended for, Christianity.

Phil. v. 12, "For we wrestle not against flesh and blood, but against principalities, against powers, against the rulers of the darkness of this world, against spiritual wickedness (margin, wicked spirits) in high places."

THE END.

AN EXAMINATION OF THE FIFTEENTH AND SIXTEENTH CHAPTERS OF MR. GIBBON'S HISTORY OF THE DECLINE AND FALL OF THE ROMAN EMPIRE
by Henry Edwards Davis

Introduction.
It has been judiciously observed, that it is not the business of the historian to profess himself a sceptic in matters of religion.

Machiavel, whose detestable principles, in his political works, are well known, found it necessary to assume a very different character, when he wrote the History of Florence. And even David Hume, in his History of England, is content with glancing at Sacred Truth by some oblique hints.

It is therefore to be wished, that Mr. Gibbon, satisfied with the applause due to him as an elegant historian, had not produced himself as an avowed champion for infidelity, in his fifteenth and sixteenth chapters, which have cast a blemish on the whole work.

It does not appear to have been essential to his history to touch at all on "*the Rise and Progress of Christianity*," much less to make so long a digression, which seems to have been wrought up with so much art, and care, and ingenuity, that we can easily trace the author's predilection for the subject. He treats it indeed *con amore*; which has induced many judicious persons to suspect, that the rest of the volume was written to introduce these two chapters with a better grace, and more decent appearance.

However, whether the conjecture be founded on truth, or not; had our author followed his design, as "*a candid enquiry*," which he professes to do[1], he would have had a better right to our approbation and esteem.

---

[1] Ch. xv. p. 449. 2d edition.

The artful insinuations of so agreeable a writer, imperceptibly seduce his readers, who, charmed with his style, and deluded with the vain pomp of words, may be apt to pay too much regard to the pernicious sentiments he means to convey. It is, therefore, absolutely necessary, that they should be reminded of the unfair proceedings of such an insidious friend[2], who offers the deadly draught in a golden cup, that they may be less sensible of their danger.

The remarkable mode of quotation, which Mr. Gibbon adopts, must immediately strike every one who turns to his notes. He sometimes only mentions the author, perhaps the book, and often leaves the reader the toil of finding out, or rather guessing at the passage.

The policy, however, is not without its design and use. By endeavouring to deprive us of the means of comparing him with the authorities he cites, he flattered himself, no doubt, that he might safely have recourse to misrepresentation; that his inaccuracies might escape the piercing eye of criticism; and that he might indulge his wit and spleen, in fathering the absurdest opinions on the most venerable writers of antiquity. For, often, on examining his references, when they are to be traced, we shall find him supporting his cause by manifest falsification, and perpetually assuming to himself the strange privilege of inserting in his text what the writers referred to give him no right to advance on their authority.

This breach of the common faith reposed in authors, is peculiarly indefensible, as it deceives all those who have not the leisure, the means, nor the abilities, of searching out the passages in the originals.

Our author often proposes second, or even third handed notions as new; and has gained a name among some, by retailing objections which have been long ago started, and as long since refuted and exploded.

In fact, sceptics and free-thinkers are of a date so old, and their objections were urged so early, and in such numbers, that our modern pretenders to this wisdom and philosophy can with difficulty invent any thing new, or discover, with all their

---

[2] We may, with *Virgil*, metaphorically compare the beauties of his language, to the fragrant flowers which conceal and shelter a snake;
"Qui legitis flores, et humi nascentia fraga,
Frigidus, ô pueri! fugite hinc, latet anguis in herbâ."
Bucolic. Eclog. iii. lin. 92, 93.

malevolent penetration, a fresh flaw. The same set of men have been alone distinguished by different names and appellations, from Porphyry, Celsus, or Julian, in the first ages of Christianity; down to Voltaire, Hume, or Gibbon in the present.

Such is the plan of our author. It must be mine to obviate and oppose it. In order to which, I have selected several of the more notorious instances of his misrepresentation and error, reducing them to their respective heads, and subjoining a long list of almost incredible inaccuracies, and such striking proofs of servile plagiarism, as the world will be surprised to meet with in an author who puts in so bold a claim to originality and extensive reading.

These offensive chapters of Mr. Gibbon's History have indeed met with some excellent remarks from a learned divine[3] of the university of Oxford. Nor has Cambridge neglected to send forth an able champion[4] in defence of our common faith[5]. But as both these gentlemen have confined themselves rather to confute the principles of Mr. G. than to expose the indefensible arts of supporting them, to which he has recourse, I flatter myself, the reader of the following pages will not accuse me of engaging in a controversy already exhausted.

An examination of the fifteenth and sixteenth chapters of Mr. Gibbon's History, &c. &c.

Mr. Gibbon's own words, in the advertisement prefixed to his history, will most aptly precede the instances I mean to produce, in confirmation of the heavy charge I have brought against him. "Diligence and accuracy (says he) are the only merits which an historical writer may ascribe to himself; if any merit, indeed, can be assumed from the performance of an indispensable duty. I may, therefore, be allowed to say, that *I have carefully examined all the original materials* that could illustrate the subject which I had undertaken to treat."

[3] Dr. Chelsum, the author of "The Remarks on Mr. Gibbon's History of the Roman Empire."

[4] Dr. Watson, author of "The Apology for Christianity."

[5] Oxford seems to be particularly pointed out by a sneering sarcastical observation of Mr. Gibbon's (Note 78. c. xv.) that its "University conferred degrees on the opponents of Dr. Middleton," his favourite author. But, we should imagine, it cannot appear otherwise than a commendation, that it then expressed a just indignation against the cavils of Dr. Middleton, as it does *now* against those of his follower, Mr. Gibbon.

Granting, then, for the present, that our author has performed what he boasts of as his merit, "That he has carefully examined all the original materials," this very circumstance will only serve to expose him to severer animadversion. For, I trust, I shall be able to lay before my readers, proofs as flagrant as they are numerous, that if he had consulted the authors, whose authority he had appeals to, only with a view to misrepresent them, he could scarcely have deviated more from plain truth, and fair interpretation of their meaning, than he now does.

Mr. Gibbon having, as a prelude to his attack on Christianity, first introduced the Jews, it may be proper that I should begin by pointing out some of the very extraordinary liberties he has taken, in his account of that people. We are told by him, that *"the Jews, who under the Assyrian and Persian monarchies had languished for many ages the most despised portion of their slaves, emerged from their obscurity under the successors of Alexander. And as they multiplied to a surprizing degree in the east, and afterwards in the west, they soon excited the curiosity and wonder of other nations."* In this short extract are to be found many instances of inaccuracy, if not ignorance. In the first place, the Jews were never under the Assyrian yoke; for the kingdom of Judea survived that monarchy, and was ruined by the Babylonians. And when they were carried into captivity, they were by no means held in low esteem; but, on the contrary, seem to have been greatly regarded. The chief officers of the courts where they resided, were often chosen from among them. They were admitted as statesmen; made cup-bearers to the princes; and appointed governors of provinces[6]. It is equally unjust to speak of them as slaves to the Persians: For the first king of that country gave them permission to go home; and this, in the very first year of his reign. The permit seems to have been general: so that those who stayed behind, must have been in a state of free service: Their not accepting of the leave, plainly shews it[7]. There is scarcely in history an instance of a conquered people being so respected; and nothing can be a greater proof of it, than their wonderful return. The Philistines, Edomites, Moabites,

---

[6] See Daniel, c. i. ver. 3. 17. – c. ii. v. 48. – c. iii. v. 30. – c. vi. v. 1. 3. Nehemiah, c. ii. v. 1. – Ezra, c. iv. v. 19.
  See also Josephus, lib. xxi. throughout, of the Antiquities of the Jews.

[7] Ezra, ch. i. ver. 3.

Hamathites, with many other ancient states in the vicinity of Judea, were about the same time subdued; and seem to have undergone a like captivity. But we do not read of any of them returning; much less of their being again constituted into a nation. And though they may not have been immediately extinct; yet their poor remains dwindled soon to nothing; while the Jews became a respectable people, and, as the author confesses, "*excited the curiosity and wonder of other nations.*"

It is to be observed, that Mr. G. not only speaks of their being held in great disrepute by their conquerors; but that they were despised *for many ages*. This is strange; for their captivity was but of seventy years duration; so that upon their return, some, who had seen the former temple, were present at the dedication of the second. But the author will perhaps say, that he includes the Israelites, the ten tribes, in the account here given. But they never returned, and he must speak with great inaccuracy to call the ten tribes Jews, and to talk of their "*emerging from obscurity:*" for they were never reinstated; and we have scarcely any history concerning them.

But the author proceeds, and assures us, that the Jews did *emerge*: and that it was "*under the successors of Alexander.*" He does not say, that it was in the time of those kings, but *under them*. By this we might be led to suppose, that this success was not owing to their own superiority and merit, nor to the divine assistance; but to the favour and indulgence of those princes. Now it is notorious, that the Jews never found any more bitter enemies, than some of these kings. Before the time of Alexander, the Jews had begun to recover themselves, and were increasing in affluence and splendour. But, upon his death, Ptolomy, the son of Lagus, his successor in Egypt, at one sweep carried off one hundred thousand of the inhabitants of Judea; of which thirty thousand were chosen persons, whom he forced to serve in his armies. The residue he gave up for slaves to his soldiers. He demolished the walls of Jerusalem, and transplanted many of the people to Egypt, and others were obliged to settle in the regions of Barca and Cyrene[8]. Nothing could be more critical to a growing state, than these misfortunes. But they were not to be compared to the cruelties of Antiochus, sirnamed Epiphanes, the tyrant of Syria. He

---

[8] See Josephus, Antiq. lib. xii. c. 1. - Contra Apion, lib. 1. Eusebii Chron. - Appiani Syriaca. - Aristeas de lxx Interp. Usher's Chronol. p. 221. - Prideaux's Connection, vol. ii.

defiled their temple, and persecuted them for their religion in a shocking manner; putting numbers of them, on that account, to death. In short, he was very *intolerant*: and the inveteracy of the Greeks in general was such, as that nothing but the divine protection could have saved the Jews from ruin; for their utter extirpation was aimed at[9]. Such was the mild influence under which Mr. G. supposes the Jews to have flourished; absurdly placing to their advantage, what tended to their ruin. Let us now turn our eyes back, and reconsider the account given by our author about the Jews being in *servitude* under the *Assyrians*, and under the *Persians*: and how they languished for *many ages*; and were the *most despised portion of all their slaves:* that they were of little consequence in former times; but *emerged* from their obscurity *under* the successors of Alexander: when they were dispersed to the *east*, and to the *west*; and *soon* become the wonder of the world. What a strange assemblage is here? It is like Milton's chaos, *"without bound, without dimension: where time and place are lost."* In short, what does this display afford us, but a deal of boyish colouring, to the prejudice of much good history.

The author will perhaps tell us, that he has the authority of Tacitus for all that he alleges. But the misfortune is, that Tacitus was very little acquainted with the ancient state of the Jews; and, setting this aside, there is nothing in the quotation, which comes up to the author's purpose. He totally mistakes the meaning of it, when he alludes to the Jewish captivity, and speaks of the people, as the most despicable of *Slaves*. I cannot find any thing of this purport in the Roman historian. He seems to have known nothing of the captivity; nor does he mention any state of slavery. There is, moreover, a mistake in Mr. G's quotation; for, according to him, the passage is – "despectissima pars *servitutis*;" (the most despised part of their *slavery*) but in the original we find it "despectissima pars *servientium*:" – of their foreign subjects.

This mistake, I am confident, was not designed; and must therefore be imputed to a slip in memory: but it is, however, of consequence; for the terms *serviens* and *servire* do not necessarily denote slavery. They may be applied to any people, who have been conquered, and rendered tributary and

---

[9] See Diodori Ecloga, lib. xl. p. 921. Joseph. Antiq. lib. xii. p. 611. Taciti Hist. lib. v. c. 8.

dependant[10]. Many nations have been reduced to a state of subservience and even vassalage: and yet have never been deemed slaves. The purport of the account given by the Roman historian, is this. He has been speaking of the chief city of the Jews, and of their sumptuous temple, and polity: and he supposes, that they began to make a figure soon after the time of Alexander the Great. He mentions their grandeur, the rise of which he dates from that æra; but, excepting some few vague traditions, he seems quite ignorant of every circumstance that has preceded. His words are as follow:

"[11]A great part of Judea is scattered in villages: they have also town or cities: Jerusalem is the metropolis. They have a temple there immensely rich, and the city is strongly fortified, as is also the palace. The temple is shut up within; the Jews have access only to the doors; none but the priests pass over the threshold. Whilst the East was under the dominion of the Assyrians, and the Medes and Persians, they were the most despised part of their subjects. After that the Macedonians gained the superiority, King Antiochus endeavouring to destroy their superstition, and to infuse into them the manners of Greece, in order to transform and amend a barbarous race, was impeded in his designs by the Parthian war."

In the account here given, the historian is not speaking of the Jews being carried into captivity, nor of any state of slavery; for, as I said before, he was totally unacquainted with it. He is

[10] Dion Cassius speaking of Phraates says, Ουτος δε Αραβιων μεν των νυν τοις Ρωμαιοις, ΔΟΥΛΕΥΟΝΤΩΝ μεχρι της ερυθρας θαλασσης εβασιλευς. Lib. xxxvii. p. 20. Edit. R. Steph. "He Phraates, *reigned over* the Arabians, who at that time *were subject* to the Romans, as far as the Red Sea."

 The Author does not mean, by the term ΔΟΥΛΕΥΟΝΤΩΝ "*they were subject, or subservient to*," that the Arabians were really slaves, but only that they were tributary.

[11] "Magna pars Judeæ vicis dispergitur: habent et oppida. Hierosolyma gentis caput. Iliic immensæ opulentiæ templum: et primis[12] munimentis urbs: dein regia. Templum intimis clausum: ad fores tantum Judæo aditus: limine præter sacerdotes arcebantur. Dum Assyrios penes Medosque et Persas oriens fuit, despectissima pars servientiam. Postquam Macedones præpotuere, rex Antiochus demere superstitionem & mores Græcorum dare annixus, quo minus teterrimam gentem in melius mutaret, Parthorum bello prohibitus est." Hist. lib. v. cap. 9.

[12] Would not the passage read better, if instead of *primis*, we read *firmis*?

speaking of Judea being a province to the eastern monarchs, and, he says, that the people were the meanest of all that were tributary. His reason for saying so was, because he had never heard of them antecedent to this æra; and he, therefore, makes his ignorance an argument for their obscurity.

It is to be observed, that Tacitus seems to have had as great a prejudice against the Jews, as Mr. Gibbon has; and it is therefore no wonder, that the latter so often applies to his authority. It should, however, have been considered by Mr. Gibbon, that whoever adopts another's evidence, at the same time makes himself accessary to his mistakes and absurdities. Of these, I think some traces may be found in the following quotation about the same people. Tacitus has been speaking of Antiochus being called off by the revolt of the Parthians under Arsaces; and then adds[13], "At that time the Macedonians being weak in power, the Parthians not yet arrived at their strength, and the Roman authority at a great distance, the Jews elected their own kings." It is well known, that Tacitus was fond of refinement, and would fain find out the spring of action in every great event. Hence, instead of being conducted by the sage and steady historian, we are often misled by the subtilty of the politician, till we are quite bewildered. Thus, in the extract above, having mentioned that the Jewish nation grew great, and erected themselves into a kingdom, he would likewise give us the reasons for this rise and alteration. But he founds it all upon negative principles; and, instead of shewing what was the cause, he tells us, what was not the impediment, which is surely a strange way of proceeding. It arose, we should imagine, from their being populous and powerful; and, at the same time, from the intrigues and ambition of particulars, who were desirous of a change in the government. No, says our historian; the reason of their admitting royalty was, because *the Macedonians were weak, the Parthians immature, and the Romans at a great distance.* He might have also inserted, because they were not ruined by a famine, nor destroyed by a pestilence, nor overwhelmed by a deluge. Their first king was Aristobulus (A.U.C. 649.) between whom and their return from captivity, was an interval of above 420 years. Hence they might have had a king, if they had chosen it,

---

[13] "Tum Judæi Macedonibus invalidis, Parthis nondum adultis, & Romani procul aberant, sibi ipsi rege reges imposuere."

An Examination of Mr. Gibbon's History 193

before the Macedonian, or the Parthian, was at all known; nay, before the name of the Roman had well reached to the foot of Italy.

It is remarkable, that not one of the authors referred to by Mr. Gibbon[14], in confirmation of his account of the Jews, mentions "their *emerging from obscurity*;" much less do they specify the particular period fixed on by our author, "*under the successors of Alexander.*" To what has been already shewn, I shall add the words of Diodorus Siculus.

"[15]Under the Persian and Macedonian government, from their intermixing with the Heathen World, many of the ancient laws and institutions of the Jews were *changed*," as having become obsolete.

This change seems to imply a prior establishment; and that *the Jews "did not emerge from obscurity"* under the Persian or Macedonian empire, but had long before enjoyed the free prerogatives of their laws and liberties. The words of the historian will admit of no other construction; for, what he had before said, absolutely contradicts Mr. Gibbon's assertion.

"After speaking of the Jews coming from Egypt under the guidance of Moses, and extolling his prudence as a legislator, and for training them up to labour and martial discipline:" he continues thus, "[16]He (Moses) waged war also with the neighbouring nations; and having gained large tracts of land, divided it among the people for an inheritance." And again he says, "[17]The Jewish nation was ever very populous."

It is not easy to say how this account can be made to coincide, even by the skilful Mr. G. with his representation, that "*they were the most despised portion of slaves*," and just "*emerged from obscurity.*" How could people in such a weak and despicable condition, invade the territories of their powerful neighbours, vanquish their forces, and take possession of their country?

---

[14] Note 2. chap. xv.

[15] Diodorus Siculus, lib. xl. p. 544. Wesseleng. Ed. Κατὰ δὲ τὰς ὕστερον γενομένας ἐπικρατείας ἐκ τῆς τῶν ἀλλοφύλων ἐπιμιξίας, ἐπὶ τετάρτης τῶν Περσῶν ἡγεμονίας, καὶ τῶν ταύτην καταλυσάντων Μακεδόνων, πολλὰ τῶν πατρίων τοῖς Ιουδαίοις νομίμων ἐκινήθη.

[16] ἐποίειτο δὲ καὶ στρατείας εἰς τὰ πλησιόχωρα τῶν ἐθνῶν· καὶ πολλὴν κατακτησάμενος χώραν, κατεκληρούχησε.

[17] ἀεί τὸ γένος τῶν Ιουδάιων ὑπῆρχε πολυάνθρωπον.

194 *Religious Scepticism*

Our author found, that Diodorus made mention of the Jews, and one would suppose, that he therefore deemed it necessary to *cite* such learned authority, without regarding how widely he differed from him in the relation of the facts, and of important points in their history.

Neither does *Justin*, another writer appealed to by Mr. Gibbon, authorise this his assertion. He says, that "[18]Xerxes first subdued the Jews: afterwards, with the Persian nation, they were subjected to the Macedonian empire under Alexander the Great, and were for a long time subservient to it. On revolting from Demetrius, and seeking an alliance with the Romans, they were restored to their liberty, the first of all the eastern nations."

This can hardly be said to agree with our author's sentiments. For, if Xerxes first made them tributary, they were previously free. Nor are they described as a despicable set of slaves; on the contrary, we find them the very first whom the Romans thought worthy to receive their liberties.

After all, were we even to admit, that Mr. Gibbon had asserted nothing concerning the Jews, but what he had really found in Justin, Diodorus, and Tacitus, would he not deservedly incur our censure, for calling in the testimony of witnesses whom he himself must know to be shamefully ignorant of the facts in question[19]?

Another part of Mr. Gibbon's account of the Jews, though given to us on the authority of Dion Cassius, is not really to be met with in that historian. Our author's words are these: "From the reign of Nero to that of Antoninus Pius, the Jews discovered a fierce impatience of the dominion of Rome, which

---

[18] Justinus, I. xxxvi. c. 2, 3. (8vo. edit. Lugd. Batav. 1650.)
 "Primum Xerxes rex Persarum, Judæos domuit: postea cum ipsis Persis in ditionem Alexandri Magni venere, diuque in potestatem Macedonici imperii subjecti Syriæ regno fuere. A Demetrio cum descivissent, amicitia Romanorum petita, primum omnium ex orientalibus libertatem recaperunt, facile tunc Romanis de alieno largientibus."

[19] For instance, Justin says, that "the Jews were exiled from Egypt as contagious – that Joseph used magic[20] arts – that it was the custom of the nation to consecrate the seventh day, called the Sabbath, by a *fast* – That, through veneration for their leader, Moses, they in all ages united the regal and sacerdotal offices in one person."

[20] "Cum magicas ibi artes sollerti ingenio percepisset septimum diem more gentis Sabbatum appellatum *jejunio* sacravit – semperque exinde hic mos apud Judæos fuit, in omne ævum, ut eosdem reges ac sacerdotes habuerunt." Diodorus Siculus adopts nearly the same erroneous opinions.

An Examination of Mr. Gibbon's History 195

repeatedly broke out in the most furious massacres and insurrections[21]."

To confirm this, he relates the dreadful accounts of those at Cyrene and Cyprus[22]; and appeals to Dion[23].

Now, although the reference to Dion in Reimarus's edition, leads us to the dismal relation of these horrid barbarities perpetrated under the reign of Trajan, which our author has circumstantially described, yet Dion gives no testimony to the preceding assertion, that "their fierce impatience of the dominion of Rome *repeatedly* broke out in the most furious massacres and insurrections," as these were which he had just related; *nor does he accuse them of being guilty of such*, during the long period of time which elapsed from "the reign of Nero to that of Antoninus Pius." But, on the contrary, there is no mention made by Dion of the Jews under Nero, Galba, or Otho. Under the reign of Vitellius, it is briefly said, that Vespasian "carried on a war against the Jews[24]." In that of Vespasian, Dion slightly speaks of Josephus[25], and of the taking of Jerusalem[26].

We read no further account of them under Titus, Domitian, nor Nerva. During the reign of Trajan, the massacres at Cyrene and Cyprus are mentioned by him; and he speaks of the emperor Hadrian's being engaged in a war with them on founding the colony of Ælia Capitolina.

We see that it does not appear from Dion, but that the Jews lived in quiet submission, *without impatiently breaking forth in repeated insurrections and furious massacres*; during the reigns of several emperors between Nero and Antoninus. If their impatience of the dominion of Rome had thus broken through every restraint, and gratified its rage with the blood of their enemies, the pen of the historian could not have passed it over in silence.

[21] Chap. xvi. p. 521.
[22] Chap. xvi. note 1.
[23] L. lxviii. p. 1145.
[24] Dion's words are, καὶ ὁ Υεσπασιανὸς Ιουδάιοις πολεμῶν. P. 1065. lib. lxv. Reimar. Ed.
[25] L. lxvi, p. 1077. Reim.
[26] ὁ δὲ Τίτος, τῷ, πρὸς Ἰουδαίους πολέμῳ ἐπιταχθεὶς, τὰ Ἱεροσόλυμα ειλε, καὶ τόν ναὸν ἐνέπρησε. Τοῖς δὲ Ἰουδαίοις οὐχ ὅτι ὄλεθρος, ἀλλά καὶ νίκη καὶ σωτηρια εὐδαιμονία τε εἶνα ἐδόκει, ὅτι τῷ ναῷ συναπώλοντο. P. 217. Steph. Ed. Xiphilin. Epitom.

So that, though Mr. G. could establish the truth of this part of his history from other authority; yet, as he has appealed to Dion alone, who does not give him reason for his assertion, he merits our censure.

Our author, in treating of the Jewish œconomy and ceremonies, has, in a particular passage, not only made use of a fallible argument, but misrepresented and manifestly perverted the authority he quotes. The sentence is this,

"If a strict obedience had been paid to the order, that every male, three times in the year, should present himself before the Lord Jehovah, it would have been impossible that the Jews could ever have spread themselves beyond the narrow limits of the promised land[27]."

The authority, to which Mr. G. directs[28] us, as corroborating the sentiment, is that of the Universal History[29]; – where we are to find "a sensible note[30]" on the subject. Such indeed it is; but it happens, somewhat unluckily, that this sensible note supports an hypothesis directly opposite to that of Mr. Gibbon. So far is it from *denying the possibility* "of paying a strict obedience to the order," or insinuating a *neglect* of it; that, on the contrary, it endeavours to remove the grand objections that have been raised against it[31].

[27] Page 453. c. xv.
[28] Note 11, c. xv.
[29] "Universal History, vol. i. p. 603." N.B. p. 603 is in vol. ii. fol. Lond. 1736.
[30] Note 11, c. xv.
[31] The two grand objections are, 1st. "If they assembled, from every part, at Jerusalem at once, how that city could contain such prodigious multitudes? and, 2dly. How they could leave their cities defenceless?" In answer to the first, the note (O) observes, that "the Talmud exempts from this obligation, 1. The women, who were to take care of their families. 2. Boys under twelve years of age. 3. All old men above sixty. 4. All the sick and impotent, lunatics, &c."
Though by these exceptions the numbers must be greatly diminished, yet the note adds also an exception which must crush Mr. G.'s objection. "And, lastly, all that either lived at such a distance from the tabernacle, and afterwards from the temple, that they could not perform the journey on foot." Besides this, "Calculation is here made of the capaciousness of Jerusalem; and the probability of their dwelling in tents round about it is urged." – It is noted also, "that they did not all appear together on the same day; but took it by turns, and stayed in the city but one night; and on the next morning, having performed their devotions, returned, and made way for others."
The latter objection is answered by shewing, that "half of the males

But what shall we say, if, indeed, no such *order* was ever given? Mr. G. in asserting that there was, may perhaps be thought more excuseable, as several men of learning agree with him here. But much may be urged to prove, that they are in a mistake. The matter stands thus. It is said in Exodus, *Thrice in the year shall all your men-children appear before the Lord God, the God of Israel*[32]. The like occurs in Deuteronomy. *Three times in the year shall all the males appear before the Lord thy God: in the place which he shall choose: – and they shall not appear before the Lord empty*[33]. The objection made to this is to shew the absurdity of such an ordinance; and the impracticability of its being carried into execution. It is particularly urged, that those, who lived at a great distance, could not go up so often to Jerusalem; and if they did go up, it was still impossible for the city to hold them. Besides, they must leave their lands for too long a time neglected; and their borders would be exposed to the inroads of any enemy, that would take advantage of their absence. To obviate these objections, many well-meaning persons have considered the extent of Jerusalem, and calculated how many it could hold. They have also made an estimate of the number of tents, which might be pitched without the walls; and of other accommodations, which might be procured. They mention, that all did not come up upon the same day; and their lands, therefore, need not be supposed to have been entirely neglected. The Authors of the Universal History, as we see in the foregoing note, have recourse to the Talmud, to shew, that children, sick persons, lunatics, and old men were excused. But these expedients are as unnecessary, as the objections are idle: These learned men have been labouring to find out a remedy, where there is no disorder; for the passage is totally misunderstood. What we find in our translation rendered *thrice*, and three

---

stayed at home to guard their houses, children, wives, lands, &c. whilst the other half went up:" and furthermore, that "some went one month, and the others the next."

Is it not strange that Mr. G. should corroborate his assertion, by appealing to an authority that contradicts it? What judgment must be formed of this proceeding? Shall we say he has not consulted the Universal History? Or that he has been guilty of gross misrepresentation, by producing this testimony to confirm his proposition, which it aims to refute?

[32] Chap. xxxiv. ver. 23.

[33] Chap. xvi. ver. 16, 17.

times; is, in the original, שלש פעמים בשנה, tribus vicibus anni – *at three of the changes, or seasons of the year*, every male was to present himself before the Lord. By this was not meant, that they should go up to Shiloh, or to the temple, all these three times; but only at one of the three. For three different seasons were appointed for the convenience of those who were to make their appearance. Instead of applying to the Talmud, and the Jewish rabbies, the best way to interpret the scriptures is by the scriptures; and that people went up only at one of these three times, may be seen from various passages. It is said of Elkanah, the father of Samuel, that he *went up out of his city* YEARLY *to worship, and to sacrifice to the Lord God of hosts in Shiloh*[34]. And it is repeated, that *the man Elkanah, and all his house, went up to offer unto the Lord the* YEARLY *sacrifice, and his vow*[35]. Concerning every firstling of the flock, and of the herd, it was thus enacted: – *Thou shalt eat it before the Lord thy God,* YEAR BY YEAR, *in the place which the Lord shall choose*[36]. We find, that once only in every year they were to make this offering. Hence it is said by the prophet Zechariah, *Every one that is left,* &c. &c. *shall go up from year to year to worship*[37]. In conformity to this we find, that the parents of our Saviour *went up to Jerusalem every year:* and we are told, that it was *at the feast of the passover*[38]: For this feast was more particularly observed. From these instances we may, I think, be assured, that it was once only in the year when this presentation was enjoined: at which time none *were to appear before the Lord empty*. At one of these seasons they brought all the offerings commanded by the law, and presented them before the Lord. *Three times in the year* (or at the three particular changes and divisions of the year) *shall all the males appear before the Lord thy God, in the place which he shall choose: in the feast of unleavened bread; and in the feast of weeks; and in the feast of tabernacles; and they shall not appear before the Lord empty. Every man shall give as he is able; according to the blessing of the Lord thy God, which he*

---

[34] Samuel, c. i. v. 3.
[35] C. ii. v. 21.
[36] Deut. c. xv. v. 20.
[37] Zech. c. xiv. v. 16.
[38] Luke, c. ii. v. 41.

hath given thee[39]. Among the presents then made were the first fruits, and the firstlings of their flocks and herds. *Thou shalt do no work with the firstlings of thy bullock, nor shear the firstling of the sheep. Thou shalt eat it before the Lord* YEAR BY YEAR *in the place, which the Lord shall choose, thou and thy houshold*[40]. But it may be said, that this is still a precept full of danger; for after all there must be a time, when one third of the people would necessarily be drafted away; and some of the provinces be bereft of their proper defence. It must likewise be inconvenient, and hardly practicable, for people at the extremities of the country to drive their cattle, and carry their other offerings to Jerusalem. And, lastly, there must have been many other impediments; such as arose from remoteness, sickness, badness of the roads, inclemency of the weather, which rendered the ordinance impolitic, as well as impracticable. These three objections are answered to our hands by the sacred writer. In respect to the injunction being injudicious, from the lands being left defenceless; it is observable that, when God appoints the yearly presentation to be made, he is pleased to promise the divine interposition and security. *For I will cast out the nations before thee, and enlarge thy borders: neither shall any man desire thy land, when thou shalt go up to* appear before the Lord thy God thrice (it is, in the original, *at the three changes*: in the seventy τρεις καιρους) *of the year*[41]. In respect to the second objection, about conveying their cattle and other offerings, we find, in the same place where the duty is enjoined, an occasional remedy provided. – *But if the way be too long for thee, or that thou art not able to carry it, or if the place be too far from thee, which the Lord thy God shall choose,* &c. *then shalt thou turn it into money, and bind up the money in thine hand, and shalt go up unto the place which the Lord thy God shalt choose*[42]. This, I think, affords a sufficient answer to the second cavil. As to the other difficulties, which might arise from poverty, or sickness, and distance from the capital; there was also an allowance made for such cases. Many of the people resided, according to their lot, beyond Jordan; some lived near Beersheba; and others as far as Dan, and the

---

[39] Deut. c. xvi. v. 16, 17.
[40] Deut. c. xv. v. 19.
[41] Exodus, c. xxxiv. v. 24.
[42] Deut. c. xii. v. 20.

entrance of Hamath. To many of these it must certainly have been very inconvenient, and, perhaps, impracticable, to take this annual journey. There must, likewise, among the children of Israel, as among all other nations, have been some persons in no degree of affluence. There were, undoubtedly, thousands in many of the tribes, who had their petty offerings to make, to whom, however, it would have been almost ruin to have taken such an expensive journey. All this is very true: and it was accordingly foreseen by the allwise and merciful framer of these laws. The same God who appointed the ordinance, admitted likewise of a dispensation. All reasonable excuse was allowed; and the affair seems to have been left to their own consciences. It is, therefore, farther said: – *When the Lord thy God shall enlarge thy border, as he hath promised thee,* &c. – *if the place, which the Lord thy God hath chosen, to put his name there, be too far for thee, then thou shalt kill of thy herd, and of thy flock, which the Lord hath given thee, as I have commanded thee: and thou shalt eat in thy gates, whatsoever thy soul lusteth after*[43]. That is, thou shalt eat it without offering it, or making any sacrifice; for all sacrifices, and all vows, were indispensably to be performed at Jerusalem. *Take heed that thou offer not thy burnt offerings in every place that thou seest; but in the place, which the Lord shall choose in one of thy tribes: There thou shalt offer thy burnt offerings; and there thou shalt do all that I command thee.* – *Thou mayest not eat within thy gates the tithe of thy corn, or of thy wine, or of thine oyl, or the firstlings of thy herds, or of thy flock,* &c. &c. *But thou must eat them before the Lord thy God, in the place, which the Lord thy God shall choose*[44]. Then comes the dispensation above-mentioned[45], that if *the place were too far from them*, they might remain at home; and without making any offering, enjoy the blessings bestowed upon them within their own precincts. *Thou shalt kill of thy herd and of thy flock,* – *as I have commanded thee: and thou shalt eat it within thy gates.* We see here an indemnity granted to those who could not, without great inconvenience, go up; and we may suppose, that thousands in every tribe availed themselves of it.

[43] Chap. xii. v. 21.
[44] Deut. c. xii. v. 13, 14, and 17, 18.
[45] Ver. 21.

We have not, as yet, done with our author's misrepresentations relative to the Jews. He tells us[46], "During the long period which elapsed between the Egyptian and Babylonian servitudes, the hopes as well as fears of the Jews appear to have been confined within the narrow compass of the present life."

In support of this he appeals to Le Clerc[47].

Now it is remarkable, that so far is this author from confirming the representation given by Mr. Gibbon, that he says not a word respecting the sentiments of the Jews on this subject, at the place to which our historian refers us. He tells us[48] indeed that the Pharisees really believed in a resurrection, and such a one as the gospel taught; but this relates to a much more distant period. This being the case, what opinion can the reader have of Mr. Gibbon's fidelity in appealing to this authority?

One more instance of our author's accuracy on the subject of the Jews appears in the following passage: "After Cyrus had permitted the exile nation to return into the promised land; and after Ezra had restored the ancient records of their religion, two celebrated sects, the Pharisees and Sadduces, insensibly arose at Jerusalem."

In confirmation of the above, Josephus[49] is the authority appealed to. But we may again observe, that our author builds without a foundation. For Josephus, as here referred to, says nothing of the *rise* of the Pharisees; but only speaks of their peculiar tenets.

On reading Mr. G.'s references to the testimony of *heathen* writers, cited by him in order to oppose and contradict the Jewish and scriptural history, I could not help reflecting on an admirable passage of bishop Warburton on this subject; which the reader will thank me for introducing here, as being equally applicable to Mr. G. as to his predecessors in infidelity, and serving to shew that he only treads over again the same beaten path.[50]

"This is ill enough", says the bishop, "but the perversity I speak of is infinitely worse: And that is, when the same

[46] Page 469.
[47] Note 57. c. xv. Prolegom. ad. Hist. Ecclesiast. c. i. § 8.
[48] C. ii. § 8.
[49] Joseph. Antiquit. Jud. lib. xiii. c. 10.
[50] See the dedication prefixed to the Divine Legation of Moses, p. 39. vol. 1. 8vo edit.

writer, on different occasions, assumes the dogmatist and sceptic on the very same question, and so abuses both characters, by the most perverse self-contradiction.

For instance, how common is it for one of your writers, when he brings *Pagan* antiquity to contradict and discredit the *Jewish*, to cry up a *Greek* historian as an evidence, to which nothing can be replied? An imperfect hint from *Herodotus*, or *Diodorus*, though one lived a thousand, and the other fifteen hundred years, after the point in question, picked up from any lying vagabond they met in their travels, shall now outweigh the circumstantial history of *Moses*; who wrote of his own people, and lived in the times he wrote of.

But now turn the tables, and apply the testimony of those writers, and of others of the best credit of the same nation, to the confirmation of *Jewish history*, and then nothing is more uncertain and fallacious, than ancient writings. All antiquity is darkness and confusion: Then we hear of

--Quicquid Græcia mendax
Audet in historia.

Then *Herodotus* is a lying traveller, and *Diodorus Siculus* a hasty collector.

Again, when the choice and separation of the *Israelites*, for God's peculiar people, is to be brought in doubt, and rendered ridiculous, then are they represented as the vilest, most profligate, and perverse race of men: Then every indiscreet passage of a *declamatory divine* is raked up with care to make them odious; and even the hard fate of the great historian *Josephus* pitied, that he had *no better a subject than such an illiterate, barbarous, and ridiculous people*[51].

But when the scripture account of the treatment, which the Holy *Jesus* met with from them, is thought fit to be disputed, these *Jews* are become an humane and wise nation; that interfered not with the teachings of sects, or the propagation of opinions, but where the public safety was thought to be in danger by seditious doctrines," &c. &c.

We have seen, at some length, how little foundation Mr. G. had for appealing to the several authors, whose names figure in his notes, in support of his gross misrepresentations concerning the Jews. Let us now pass on to a review of his treatment of the first defenders of Christianity.

---

[51] Discourse of Free-thinking, p. 157.

After attacking that revelation on which the gospel is founded, his next part was to encounter these champions of the gospel faith. The transition was easy, and natural enough.

The peculiar acrimony with which our author so frequently censures the fathers, having roused my indignation, led me to examine what reasons he had for such harsh language. And, upon examination, I found them to be either entirely groundless, or, where there was some ground for them, to be cruelly and unjustifiably exaggerated.

The views of Mr. G. are manifest; he wishes *per fas aut nefas* to lessen the authority of the fathers, and diminish the respect and reverence justly due to them; hoping, thereby, to aim an effectual blow at the religion, of which their testimony ever has been justly considered as a strong support. The vindication of them, therefore, is a cause in which I willingly engage; because it will appear to be equally the cause of truth, as it is that of Christianity. Still let it be remembered, that I do not undertake an *indiscriminate* defence of *all* the fathers; nor even of the *whole* works of any one of them. Whoever reads them must, amidst all his commendations, find something to blame. Nor shall Mr. G. go beyond me in expressing a disapprobation of their far-fetched allegories, and of their indefensible austerities.

I shall here beg leave to introduce the following passage from Dr. Gregory Sharpe[52], as expressive of my own sentiments.

"Some men had lifted up the authority of the fathers higher than could be justified: They were not content to make saints of them, but their opinions must be decisive in all matters of faith and religious controversy.

From one extreme are the fathers fallen to the other, from having been almost Gods, they are become lower than the children of men. The great reverence the Christian world once had for them, may have proceeded from the excellence of their characters, and a frequent reading of their productions; for it is hard to read them, and not to be prejudiced in their favour: And that this esteem is now gone, may be owing to a neglect of their writings: And perhaps they who have been most free in their censures of them, have been least conversant in their works. Men who knew nothing more of them, than that they were Christians, strangers to their very

---

[52] Sharpe's "Apology for some of the first Christians," added to his "Arguments in defence of Christianity." p. 88, 89. 8vo. edit.

names as well as to their real characters and writings, are most ready to pursue and join the cry against them, as if they had been the very worst, or the very weakest of men. – But for the sake of justice and honour, let us not condemn men without knowing what can be said for them; nor for the sake of common sense, as well as common honesty, condemn them without knowing what it is they have done.

From such voluminous writings, many strange things may and have been produced, but this is not peculiar to the Christian fathers; and if men, or books are to be judged of only by their faults, who shall be saved. It would be thought very partial, and very unjust, to glean from Diodorus, Herodotus, Livy, Pliny, Plutarch, and other good and antient pagan writers, the rubbish of all sorts that may be found in their writings, by a man who has the dirty disposition to look after such filth, and impose his medley of faults upon the world for a specimen of the veracity and approved abilities of those authors. But this has been done over and over again with the fathers; so that their latest enimies are not entitled so much as to the merit of discoverers; nor have they added much to the old heap, though they have much to clamour and abuse[53].

Tertullian, amongst the fathers, stands in a peculiar point of view. In his maturest compositions, warmth of temper betrayed him into indiscretions of sentiment and expression, perhaps not strictly defensible; and it is well known, that he at last adopted the most extravagant notions of childish enthusiasm. No wonder, therefore, that Mr. G. so frequently produces "the stern Tertullian" – "the zealous African," as an object of his sneering abuse. But I shall shew that the impartial historian has unfairly distorted his character.

* * *

53 The learned Cave has ingeniously pointed out the proper use of the Fathers.

"Veneramur patres non tanquam fidei *judices*, sed *testes* qui quid quovis sæculo gestum creditumvé sit nobis fideliter exponunt, sacrum fidei depositum ad nos transmittunt; quæ hereses, et quando ortæ, hunc vel illum fidei articulum oppugnârunt, perspicuè docent. Et quo vetustiores hi testes sunt, eò validius ferunt testimonium, et nos majori nitimur certitudine." See his "Epistola Apologetica" – p. 18, 19. – The reader may here also find an account of the ill-treatment which the Fathers have met with, and the probable causes of it assigned.

I might have noticed many other inaccurate references of this kind, but I really am afraid lest I should have already wearied out my reader's patience in such minute remarks: The whole, *collectively* considered, must give evident proofs that, had our author consulted the original materials, he could not have made so many mistakes. And though these several instances, considered in a *separate* view, appear trivial and minute, like the *scattered* beams of the sun, diffusing warmth with a benignant but *less sensible* influence; yet, when the many proofs are considered as composing *a great body*, like the same rays, *collected in a focus*; they make us instantly *sensible* of their *great power and effect*.

I should now proceed to my third charge of plagiarism; but as I have some other observations to make, which could not well be reduced under any distinct head, I beg leave to lay them before my reader at this place.

Though our historian descants upon "*the universal toleration of polytheism*," with the utmost exertion of his florid pen[54]; yet his assertions are frequently *inconsistent*.[55]

He tells us, that "the Jews, and *Christians* also, *justly* forfeited the rights of toleration by their inflexible zeal for their religions; and by refusing the accustomed tribute of indulgence to Polytheism[56]." Yet he himself speaks of "the *benevolent*, the *innocent*, the *inoffensive* mode of the Christian faith and worship, and extols them as the friends of human kind[57]."

In one place, our author speaks of "the *reverence* of the Roman princes and governors for the temple of Jerusalem, &c.[58]"

---

[54] These arguments of Mr. G. are opposed and confuted by D. Watson in his Apology (letter vi. p. 171, &c.) and by the Author of the Remarks (p. 47, &c.) who truly observes, that, "these pages of our author's disquisitions, (in c. xvi.) while they treat of the conduct of the Roman government towards the Christians, contain in reality *a laboured apology* for it, rather than a *disinterested relation* of mere facts," &c.

[55] See a particular instance noted by Dr. Watson, Apology, p. 188.

[56] The same author has refuted Mr. G.'s favourite reason, which he assigns for the cause of the persecutions, namely, that as "the rights of toleration were held by mutual indulgence: they were *justly* forfeited by a refusal of the accustomed tribute, which the Jews first, and the Christians afterwards, inflexibly refused."
This his argument teaches us what the *humane* toleration of Polytheism was; to *persecute* all those who were of a different persuasion.

[57] Page 519. 537.

[58] Page 521.

But what a *different* strain is this, from what we meet with at the beginning of the 15th chapter: "According to the maxims of universal toleration, the Romans protected a *superstition* (that is, the Jewish) which *they despised*[59]."

And though he adds, "the polite Augustus *condescended* to give orders, that sacrifices should be offered for his prosperity in the temple of Jerusalem:" Yet we find a contrast in his note on this very passage. "Augustus left a foundation for a perpetual sacrifice: Yet *he approved of the neglect* his grandson Caius expressed towards the temple of Jerusalem[60]."

In order to extricate himself from the difficulties with which he is embarrassed in endeavouring to give a specious pretext for the *polite* Romans having persecuted the Christians; Mr. Gibbon has made use of an argument, not only inconsistent with the avowed principles of *free-thinking*, but even with those of the *reformation*. "*It was incumbent on them*," says he, "*to persevere in the sacred institutions of their ancestors:* By embracing the faith of the Gospel, the Christians had incurred the *supposed guilt of an unnatural and unpardonable offence*. They dissolved the *sacred* ties of custom and education, *violated* the religious institutions of their country, and *presumptuously despised whatever their fathers had believed as true, or had reverenced as sacred*[61]." These are the weak arguments which popery so strenuously urged to maintain its establishment. The *validity* of which, had our forefathers acknowledged, we had still languished under its yoke; nor ever tasted the sweets of our glorious liberty in church and state. No wonder after this, that Mr. G. should speak of a possibility, that "circumstances could authorize religious persecutions by the most specious arguments of political justice and public safety[62]."

* * *

[59] Page 451.

[60] Note 6. c. xv.

[61] Page 523.

[62] As our author, with a view to prejudice Christianity, represents it as *necessarily* containing something *very criminal*, that it could compel the *polite* and *humane* people of Rome to persecute those who professed it, I shall obviate any such suspicion in the words of Mosheim,

"Qui hodie Christianæ religionis divinitatem oppugnant, uti avide captant omnia quæ suspicionis aliquid gignere in mentibus imperitorum possunt: ita etiam Romanorum erga Christianos odium adhibent ad invidiam religioni Christianæ creandam. Sapientissimus, aiunt, qui post

These proofs of our author's plagiarism which I have produced, as undeniable as they are numerous, I might still extend, by tracing him more closely. But I trust that I have sufficiently convinced every unbiassed person, within how narrow a compass the boasted extent of Mr. G.'s reading is contained. It might be very proper to present his readers with a body of notes, stuffed with a disgusting farrago of ancient learning; but he could employ his time better than by really examining the musty Fathers, whose writings he so frequently appeals to. *Middleton* could afford some topics of abuse; *Barbeyrac* had others ready prepared for his purpose; and *Dodwell*, in one dissertation, had collected erudition enough to furnish the far greater part of the materials for his sixteenth chapter. And I think I may boldly assert, that if I had added *Mosheim*'s Ecclesiastical History[63], and *Dupin*'s Bibliotheque, to my list of Mr. G.'s modern friends, I should hardly have left him a single sentence of his own to boast of in his two famous chapters, which were to give the death-wound to Christianity. In short, were I to restore to each of them the passages which Mr. G. has purloined, he would appear as naked as the proud and gaudy daw in the fable, when each bird had plucked away his own plume. The witty poet tells us what censure such proceedings merit,

--"Moveat cornicula risum
Furtivis nudata coloribus." --

I have now completed the task I proposed to execute; which was not to confute Mr. G.'s arguments against the divine original of Christianity; but to expose the indefensible arts to which he has recourse in supporting them; and to strip them of their boasted novelty, by restoring his pilfered erudition to their proper owners. Before I conclude, however, it may not be without its use to quiet the apprehensions of many a sincere, but, I must add, ill-instructed Christian, who, imposed upon

orbem conditum fuit, populus, idemque humanissimus, nullique mortalium religionis nomine molestos, Christianam tamen religionem unam saluti publicæ noxiam judicabat & ferre nolebat. Ex hoc rectissime effeceris, fuisse in primis Christianis vitia & maculas tranquillitati ac saluti civitatis magnum periculum & perniciem minantes. Qui tam inique suspicantur, suam ipsi produnt inscitiam, veterumque rerum Romanarum se ignaros ostendunt." Hist. Christ. sæc. i. § 27. p. 101.

63 Mosheim. de rebus Christianorum ante Constantin. M.

by our historian's parade of quotation and elegance of composition, have done him, what I must think, the unmerited honour of considering him as an adversary who had produced something of importance, unknown to his predecessors in the cause of infidelity, and which the friends of the Gospel would find it difficult to confute. – Be it observed, therefore, that Mr. G. does not give himself the trouble of starting any new objection against the truth of Christianity, but that his whole plan of *accounting for its progress from secondary causes* is a stale infidel topic, urged and confuted long before he was born[64]. As a proof of this, the reader will, I believe, thank me for the following extract from a sermon of bishop *Atterbury.*

"*Miraculous* it certainly was (to use the bishop's words), because the *natural* and visible causes which concurred to the production of this great effect, were not any ways equal to the effect produced; and therefore, some *supernatural* and invisible cause must needs have given birth to it.

But let us hear what causes, they say, conspired together to produce this wonderful effect." From the weakness and insufficiency of these the bishop thus deduces the proof of the miraculous propagation.

"In which truth (viz. the miraculous propagation of the Gospel) that we may be yet farther confirmed, let us consider what *shifts* the enemies of the gospel make use of, to evade the force of this pressing argument. And the utmost that any of them pretend to say, is as follows: It is true, they will own, Christians multiplied very fast, and the increase of them was, in some sense, *miraculous:* That is, it was *wonderful*; as every unusual thing is to those, who do not know, or consider the causes of it. But to a man, they say, who dares go out of the

[64] The following concise passages from *Mosheim*, (who is spoken of so highly on many occasions by our historian,) may with propriety be given to my readers, to shew that his sentiment on this subject is as widely different from Mr. G.'s, as it is more rational, more pious, and more grateful. They are thus translated by *Maclaine.*

"When we consider the rapid progress of Christianity among the Gentile nations, and the poor feeble instruments by which this great and amazing event was immediately effected, *we must naturally have recourse to an omnipotent and invisible hand, as its true and proper cause,*" &c.

"Such then were the *true* causes of that amazing rapidity with which the Christian religion spread itself upon the earth; and those *who pretend to assign other reasons* of this surprizing event, *indulge themselves in idle fictions*, which must disgust every attentive observer of men and things." Sect. 8. 10.

common road, and to think for himself, it will appear, that there was at that time a set of *natural* causes on foot, sufficient to account for this effect, without any recourse to a *divine* and *supernatural* agent. The apostles indeed were twelve plain illiterate men, who had not, of themselves, force or skill enough, to bring about such an event: But their natural inability was supplied by a favourable juncture, by a happy coincidence of such conspiring causes, and accidental advantages, as mightily helped on the work.

For example–

The *purity of the Christian morals* was a mighty argument to bring the men of probity and virtue into the interests of the Gospel.

The *distribution* of *goods*, which the first Christians made, and their living together in common, was a good reason for many men's embracing that faith, which, they were sure, would maintain them. – In the mean while, the *rulers* of the world *overlooked*, and *neglected* to *crush*, a doctrine, which was so harmless in itself, and so unlikely to succeed on the account of its abettors; till, through their connivance, it was at last universally received among the vulgar sort, and the number of its votaries was grown so formidable, that even princes themselves were forced, for their own ease and interest, to come into it, and profess it.

And thus, say they, several extraordinary and unheeded advantages concurring to favour the growth of Christianity, it *grew* indeed *mightily*, and *prevailed*; as a little river will swell high, and spread itself wide, and run far, when swoln by casual rains, and by many other streams, which have emptied themselves at once into it. Such is the account they pretend to give of the rise and progress of our faith, from *second causes*, without calling a *first*, to solve the appearance.

The *purity of the Christian morals*, and the answerable lives of Christian converts, did indeed very naturally lead men to admire and value the doctrine of Christ, but by no means to come under the yoke of it: for though most men have an esteem for strict rules, and strict lives; yet few care to practice the one, or to imitate the other. And nothing, I think, could be contrived so effectual (next to the former wise motive from the sufferings of the martyrs) to *deter* men from Christianity, as to tell them, that, when they took it upon them, they must renounce their dearest appetites and passions, and deny their very selves. And I desire the men, who raise these objections against the divine original of the Gospel, to tell us fairly, whether, if they had lived at that time, they would have come in upon *this* principle? I am sure they would not; because it is *this* principle alone (that they must part with their unlawful satisfactions and pleasures, if they do) which keeps them out of it now. Therefore neither can this be any sufficient reason for the sudden and wide growth of Christianity.

Again, neither can any probable account be given of this matter, from the *charitable distribution of their goods, which the first Christians made*. For, supposing that some of the poorer sort might be tempted by this motive; yet, surely, those who had wherewithal to sustain themselves, and were easy in their circumstances, did not come in upon it: It will not be said, I hope, that such as *made* this distribution of their goods (which will be found to have been an inconsiderable number) came in themselves to *partake* of it. Nor could these hopes have any great influence, even on the meaner sort; since there was something in the Christian religion, of far more force to frighten them, than this was to allure them; the strict rules of honesty and temperance, according to which they were bound to live, and the great calamities and persecutions which they were sure to undergo.

Lastly, No weight can be laid in this case, on that *contempt*, which the *heathen princes* are said to have had of the *Christian religion*, and the little care they, therefore, took to restrain it: for it is not true, that they stood by unconcerned at it's growth; on the contrary, it is certain, that they looked upon it with a jealous eye, from its first rise; and the early persecutions of *Nero* (not to mention those of *Domitian*, which were after the destruction of *Jerusalem*) shew that he took great notice of it, and endeavoured to extirpate it. However, let the Roman emperors have been never so regardless of its increase; yet it is certain, that they did no ways countenance it; and that every one, who turned Christian, was sure by that means to forfeit the favour of his prince, and to be looked upon as an apostate from the religion of his country. And how, even under such a pressure as this, could Christianity have made so rapid and astonishing a progress, if He, who is mightier than the mightiest, had not bid it *go forth and prosper* against all human discouragements? Had *this counsel, or this work been of Men*, it would, even without any direct opposition from the temporal power, have certainly *come to nought*, as *Gamaliel* argued; *but being of God, nothing could overthrow it.*

I do not deny after all, but that every one of these particulars might in a natural way contribute somewhat, either to the planting, or spreading of the Gospel. But I think it is evident, from the short hints I have suggested to you, that all of them together were not able to do the thousandth part of that work, which is allotted to them. And, therefore, to resolve this great event into a *conspiracy of second causes*, as it is called, without any regard to the *first*, is *an absurd and senseless attempt*; and only shews us, how very strong an inclination and bias there is in some minds towards *infidelity*, which they can be brought to espouse upon so very slight grounds.

A man, who should see an acorn put into the earth, and perceive in a few weeks, or months, an oak shooting up from it to a prodigious height, and spreading its branches to an amazing extent, so as to overtop the loftiest mountains, and even to cover the whole field where it grew; might as well say, that there was a strange *conspiracy of natural causes*, an extraordinary degree of warmth, moisture, and so forth, which concurred to produce this effect; as affirm, that the vast success of the Gospel was owing to those *petty principles*, from whence some men pretend to derive it[65].

And now, upon a review of the charges which I have urged against Mr. G., I think I cannot better address him than in the words of bishop Pearce, on a similar occasion, to Dr. Middleton.

"By this time, Sir, the reader I believe has fully seen how little credit your writings deserve in their appeals to the authors which you cite[66] – You have hardly made one *original* quotation of an author in his true sense, very often in the sense most opposite to his true one; and *have represented not only passages, but facts too, in so wrong a light,* that, whatever you searched for, it is plain you missed of truth[67]. – But in God's name, Sir, is any cause worth such a proceeding? can a good one want falsehoods? or does a bad one deserve them? Let facts, of whatever kind, be sifted thoroughly, and examined freely; but let impartiality always go along with the search, and

---

[65] Bp. Atterbury, serm. iii. vol. i.
[66] Reply to the Defence of a Letter to Dr. Waterland, p. 46.
[67] Reply to a Letter to Dr. W. p. 7.

let it always be thought one ingredient in free-thinking, to follow truth in every inquiry: He that suffers himself to be imposed upon, or tries to impose upon others, has no right to the title of a free-thinker[68].

With what justice I have applied these words to our author, I leave those to determine who have perused my Examination. One would think that Mr. G. had deemed his studied elegance of stile alone sufficient to compensate for unfair quotation and false assertion. But surely it is not the lengthened period, the flow of polished words, the harmonious diction, which can of themselves constitute the character of a good historian. These indeed serve to amuse the fancy, and delight the ear: Yet they conduce little to our information or instruction; but, rather, beguile the judgment of the unwary. It is *the indispensable duty* of an historian, to give a fair and impartial relation of facts, and to support this relation by citing the testimony of credible authors. I might add to this, that accuracy and impartiality are peculiarly requisite in a writer whose subject leads him to enter upon an investigation of the truth of religion, which is so intimately connected with the most important interests of mankind.

"The historian," says the ingenious and elegant author of the History of America, "who delineates the transactions of a remote period, has *no title to claim assent*, unless he produces evidence in proof of his assertions. Without this, he may write *an amusing tale*, but cannot be said to have composed an authentic history." Excellent and just reflection! how unhappily applied to Mr. Gibbon!

"In these sentiments," continues Dr. Robertson, "I have been confirmed by the opinion of an author, (Mr. Gibbon) whom his industry, erudition, and discernment, have deservedly placed in a high rank among the most eminent historians of the age[69]."

Will the reader of the foregoing sheets agree with the Doctor in his compliment? What *industry* can Mr. G. lay claim to, whose researches, we see, notwithstanding all his pretences, have been lazily confined within so narrow a circle? What *erudition* can he boast of, whom we have convicted of inaccuracies so striking as to be scarcely pardonable in any one

---

[68] Ibid. p. 40.

[69] See the preface to Dr. Robertson's History of America.

who would pass for a scholar? And what *discernment* can he be said to possess, who, not satisfied with "being placed in a high rank among the most eminent historians of the age," chose to relinquish that superiority of fame, and to be handed down to posterity, as a very insidious, but a very superficial advocate of infidelity, the retailer of obsolete sneers against sacred truths, the misrepresenter of venerable antiquity, and the plagiary of modern compilers?

Mr. G. has indeed written "*a tale amusing*" enough to Unbelievers and Free thinkers, but "*he cannot be said to have composed an authentic history: he has no title to claim assent, unless he produces evidence in proof of his assertions.*" What pity is it then that the *reverend* and *courtly* historian, through politeness, should have made a needless digression, to bestow *applause*, before he had examined whether *censure* was not rather due?

I mean not to represent *Dr. Robertson* as singular in this high tone of compliment to *Mr. Gibbon*. He has only spoken the language of others who have professedly answered him.

May I be permitted, before I conclude, to hazard it as my opinion, that this civility has been carried beyond all due bounds; and that our historian is entirely indebted for his supposed eminence among the enemies of the gospel, to the over candid encomiums of some of its friends? When men of learning, and good Christians, tell us, that he is "respectable for his *great merits, - of real eminence in learning* as well as composition[70] - and *applaud the erudition with which the materials* (of his history) *are compiled*[71];" it consequently elevates his fame, and bestows upon him an unmerited consequence, which may puzzle the ignorant, and seduce the unwary believer. It is thus that the credulous superstition of former ages, arising from their ignorance of philosophy, attributed to the glaring comets a malignant influence, and caused them to be viewed with a groundless horror as tokens of impending danger.

---

[70] When we reflect on the great credit, which has been given to Mr. G. chiefly, for his elegance of style, we may justly apply to him the words of Bp. Jewell. "Ut cum *eleganter et copiose* ageretur, homines imperiti possent in eâ aliquid esse suspicari." Juell. Apolog. pro Eccles. Anglican.

[71] The same author, who pays Mr. G. these compliments, tells us, that "he has adopted an entertaining but *superficial* manner of writing history," and agrees with me, that he "gives himself the privilege of *mutilating*, and selecting, and arranging *at discretion*, the records of past ages."

I shall now only add, that nothing but the evident goodness of my cause, and the undeniable weakness of Mr. Gibbon's assertions, could have encouraged me to undertake this examination. But as my plan required nothing more than to have recourse to the authors he cites (with which the copious stores of learning treasured up at *Oxford*, and the kindness of some private friends, amply furnished me), and merely to transcribe their words; *diligence and accuracy* were the principal qualifications for engaging in such a task; nor was the judgment of riper years so necessary to enable me to execute it successfully.

Let me now take my leave of *Mr. Gibbon* by assuring him, that if, in the warmth of composition, I have made use of any expressions too harsh and severe, it is entirely owing to the indignation I could not but feel, to see him perpetually vilifying the most venerable and sacred truths with contemptuous irony. I could wish to advise him (would he accept of such humble counsel), when he favours us with his next volume, to keep close to his department as an historian, and to drop the character of a champion of infidelity, which, he may now find, has not added to his literary fame. In the prosecution of his plan, it will fall naturally in his way to treat of the *corruptions* of Christianity; and as his *diligence* and *accuracy* will find ample materials for accounting for the rise and progress of *popery* from *natural causes*, we trust that he will not continue to attack genuine Christianity; at least, that he will, for the future, beware of such arts as have been sufficiently exposed in the foregoing sheets.

FINIS.

GIBBON'S ACCOUNT OF CHRISTIANITY CONSIDERED
by Joseph Milner

PART I. *Facts and Characters*
SECTION I. *The Jews.*

Mr. Gibbon speaking of the Jews observes, "The contemporaries of Moses and Joshua had beheld with careless indifference the most amazing miracles. Under the pressure of every calamity the belief of those miracles has preserved the Jews of a later period from the universal contagion of idolatry; and, in contradiction to every known principle of the human mind, that singular people seems to have yielded a stronger and more ready assent to the traditions of their remote ancestors, than to the evidence of their own senses."[1]

Let the reader weigh the tendency of the passage before us:

– – Crimine ab uno
Disce omnes. – – VIRG.

For there is a remarkable uniformity of insinuation, which runs through every thing that affects Christianity in his history. It is incredible that the Jews should act in contradiction to every known principle of the human mind, more so; would he not insinuate? than that all the accounts we have of the miracles of Moses and Joshua should be false. A lover of the human species, who valued their immortal interests, and saw in any degree that *these* depended, or even might depend, on a cordial regard for the oracles of the Old and New Testament, would be extremely careful of saying any thing that might have so much as a remote tendency to lessen that regard. Nothing but the most confirmed and the most decisive proof of the falsehood of the Bible, which no Deist ever did or can, in the nature of things, attain, can surely warrant this egregious, and I will add, inhuman trifling with a book, which, for any thing the trifler knows to the contrary, may require the most serious and

[1] Page 482. Second Edition.

respectful treatment, on pain of eternal ruin. Either Mr. Gibbon believes the Bible to be God's word, or he does not; or, if he pleases to have it so, he is in doubt. Under none of these suppositions can his conduct be justified. As to the first case, words are superfluous: The second would ask a more manly and a more open way of opposition; even the impious honesty of Lord Bolingbroke, horrible as it is, is less offensive to a lover of plain dealing than the sly, insinuating, artful mode of Mr. Gibbon. As a Gentleman, he must scorn it in common life: and the thing itself is so reprehensible, that I do not see any way but to deny the charge itself, is left for him, in order to attempt a vindication of his character in this point. And here I can only appeal to every unprejudiced reader, whether in his two last chapters he does not constantly practice the very contrary of that with which he charges Eusebius, suppress what would tend to the honour of the Gospel, and enlarge on whatever would disgrace it. You see not in his account of the primitive Christians the sincerity, the charity, the good qualities of all sorts, with which the universal voice of all ancient writers, who knew what they were, adorns them. But their faults, their imprudence, their inhumanity is enlarged on. And if you look at their persecutors, the lion is turned into a lamb; their ferocity is evaporated through the emollient power of his smooth diction, and he has a world of excuses for whatever he cannot still defend in them; yet he talks at times with a sort of respect for Revelation and for Saints: But, surely, here is a flagrant abuse of the gift of speech. Men of honest minds would be content with less elegance, if they were favoured with more frankness of language. In a word, if he disbelieves the Bible altogether, he ought never to have spoken of it at all, as a Divine Revelation. And in the third case, a state of doubt would have restrained a mind seasoned with any devout regard to the Almighty, from writing any thing to the discredit of the Gospel. For one thing is clear, amidst all the mazes of his pen, that he cordially hates Christianity. It is not so easy a thing, even for Mr. Gibbon, to disguise his heart. Who suspects, when he is praising Antoninus, or Tacitus, his real esteem of the men? who can help suspecting his sincerity, even when he does bestow some encomiums on Christian persons and subjects? If then his guarded manner of speaking would not allow one to call him a Deist, this at least must be said, the whole of what he writes on religion has a Deistical tendency. But –

We are called on to account for this phænomenon, the remarkable propensity of the Jews to idolatry before the Babylonish captivity, during the ages of miracles, and their exemption from it in after-ages to this day, so long after miracles have ceased. I own the case is remarkable; it has cost me serious thought, before I saw Mr. Gibbon's remark upon it, which whether it was copied from Lord Bolingbroke I must not presume to say. But he has observed the same thing, and glories in the inefficacy of all the Mosaic miracles. We may justly observe, with Dr. Watson, that the Jews did not behold these miracles with careless indifference; with Dr. Warburton, that in all their idolatries they never avowedly gave up the God of their Fathers; with the common stream of Christian Divines, that the seventy years captivity of Babylon had a great effect in curing their idolatrous propensities. But though all this may alleviate, it does not seem entirely to remove the difficulty. Even if we could not do it, I see no reason to argue from thence against the truth of the Scriptures. The rational belief of their truth, surely, does not oblige us to be able to account for all the ways of Providence. It is a satisfaction, however, to gain an insight into an affair of this nature, where we can. The following train of thought has satisfied my own mind on the point, whether it may that of the reader, he must determine for himself.

We first find the Jews as a nation in Egypt. They there so deeply imbibed the spirit of idolatry, as not easily to part with it; and that the impression of miracles was transient, while that of old habits was permanent, will give no surprise to those who know human nature in general, and the excessive idolatry of Egypt in particular. Their mixture with heathen nations after their conquest of the land of Canaan, and the constant view of idolatrous objects all around, so similar to those which had overcome them in Egypt, and so apt to revive the force of old temptations, these things, joined to the common principles of human depravity, will account for the continuance of their idolatry, from age to age, though frequently favoured with miracles, and scarce ever totally deprived of them till the Babylonish captivity. When we come to Ezra's age, we find a generation of a stamp almost entirely different from any preceding one[2]. I say almost entirely, because I am aware of the distinguished godliness of Joshua's generation. Perhaps, however, an attentive observation of the character given of them in Ezekiel xx. 21, may lessen, if not destroy, the idea of their excellent qualities. Be that as it may, a religious education with which Ezra's pious age (so pious universally as to break the most endearing connections for the honour of Jehovah[3]) would favour posterity, must have had large and lasting influence, as it always has, unless impeded by untoward adventitious circumstances, such as great prosperity, and a bad neighbourhood, both of which would unite their malignant influence to prevent any similar good effect from religious education in the days of Joshua. But in Ezra's days the people are poor, despised, persecuted, oppressed. They are no more the haughty victors of Canaan, but the humble vassals of a Persian despot; and though, by his favour, restored to their own land after a seventy-years exile, yet burdened with taxes, and depressed with servitude. Add to this, their exemption from the objects of idolatrous temptation, which, in the early days of their Theocracy, before the Canaanites and Canaanitish abominations were destroyed, must have been very common in the land. The state of the Puritans in Charles the Second's time was in some respects not much unlike their own; and the effects of education, we may well conceive, would be much the same. We know the effects of the latter case, a tenacious aversion to Popery, or to whatever they please to call so. This aversion has not ceased; it has continued, and is likely still to continue, though it has not kept many of them from evils to the full as opposite to the spirit of their religious ancestors. Socinianism much abounds at this day among the descendants of the Puritans. But their education had not so strong a guard against that, nor did the circumstances of the times require it, as against Popery. Perhaps it will not now be wondered at, if the salutary effect of religious education, of humbling adversity, and other favourable circumstances conjoined, be placed in review, that the Jews after Ezra's time should be far less addicted to idolatry than in any former period of their history.

2 Should I be asked to account for this, I must desire the reader to consult Jerem. xxiv. 7. There the piety of Ezra's age is foretold, and also the influence by which it was effected.

3 Ezra, the end.

Yet we find them verging to idolatry again in the time of Antiochus Epiphanes. The particular wickedness of some venal priests, and the influence of Greek connections account for it. Antiochus, however, took an effectual method to cure them, the *argumentum baculinum* of persecution. It succeeded, and scarce a vestige of Jewish idolatry can since be found. This was the first instance of national persecution for religion they ever underwent[4]. For Nebuchadnezzar and other conquerors disturbed them not on account of religious principles. This had the same effect as Mary's argument of the same nature had in England. The sanguinary proceedings of two or three years have prevailed in both cases to this day, to impress a most cordial hatred against the persecuting religion. If idolaters persecute, the Jew, though still deplorably enslaved to every other vice, will give up his idolatrous propensity; and in consequence of Mary's persecution, Popery will ever be hated by Englishmen, even by those who are void of principle or conscience; and our Legislators are, perhaps, now more sensibly convinced, by the ferment which their late indulgences to Papists occasioned, that the effect of aversion, once rouzed by persecution, bids fair to endure till time shall be no more. Thus, from the joint influence of adverse circumstances, of religious education, and, above all, the aversion to persecution, principles each of steady influence on the human mind, the matter of fact of this section is, I think, accounted for, and in this view there is not any contradiction, but rather a conformity to every known principle of the human mind in the conduct of the Jews.

SECTION VIII.
Miracles.

Our author acquaints us with the difficulty he is under of defining the miraculous period. "Every age, says he, bears testimony to the wonderful events by which it was distinguished, and its testimony appears no less weighty and respectable than that of the preceding generation, till we are insensibly led on to accuse our own inconsistency, if in the eighth or in the twelfth century we deny to the venerable Bede,

---

[4] For some individuals had been persecuted, as appears from the book of Daniel.

or to the holy Bernard, the same degree of confidence which, in the second century, we had so liberally granted to Justin or to Irenæus[5]."

He does not say, totidem verbis, that the testimony of every age appears no less weighty and respectable than that of the apostolic age. But it is evident that he wishes his readers so to understand him, because his manner of representing the affair is as much calculated to lead them into that idea, as if he had expressed it. Let any unprejudiced person examine then the evidence of Lazarus's resurrection, as recorded with inimitable simplicity of pathos by the Apostle John. Let him weigh the evidence of the miraculous subterraneous fire and earthquake, which attended Julian's attempt to rebuild the temple of Jerusalem, as it has been solidly and triumphantly stated by the late learned and laborious Bishop of Gloucester. I am far from meaning to weigh them in the same scale, or to place them in the same important light. But surely the just evidences of a miraculous interposition, though not in an equal degree, are conspicuous in both. The outward testimony of witnesses competent in number, ability, and veracity, and all the just measures of probability, and the inward testimony of the importance and nature of the event itself, abound with an exuberance of proof in the first case, but are by no means wanting in the second.

Let the unprejudiced examiner now turn his eyes to the opprobrious scene of those lying wonders, which Antichrist so liberally exhibited during the middle ages, yet not without a distinct forewarning from God by his prophecies. Let him apply the allowed rules of inward and outward evidence to all or any of the supposed miraculous events. In the middle of the tenth century behold the haughty, the inhuman Dunstan seizing the Devil by the nose with a pair of red-hot pincers, as he put his head into his cell, being one day more earnest than usual in his temptations[6]. Those who are conversant in Roman Legends know that this story, however ludicrous and absurd, is no improper sample of them all. Horace's rule,

Nec Deus intersit, nisi dignus vindice nodus
Inciderit ———

---

[5] Page 477.
[6] Hume's History, vol. i, p. 112.

is as proper in Divinity, as it is in Poetry. This, with every other mark of evidence, external or internal, is so palpably wanting in such stories, that it would be an egregious insult on my readers' understanding to attempt in form to evince it.

It would ask a long train of reasoning to adjust the evidences of a really miraculous interposition, that are sufficient to produce conviction, and to distinguish them from those that are not so. Mr. Locke's grounds of probability, in the latter part of his essay on the human understanding, throw a sufficient light on the subject; and all the scripture-miracles, as well as many of the more early times, that especially which has been hinted at, and which, perhaps, was the last, with which the Church of God has been favoured, might easily be shewn to tally with Mr. Locke's measures of probability. Mr. Hume tells us, indeed, that no evidence can be sufficient to confirm the evidence of miracles, though surely the least careful attention to the natural motions of the human mind, not yet sophisticated by artful reasonings, or clouded by prejudice, in many cases that might be conceived to happen, must invalidate such assertions. It is enough that we have shewn the extreme weakness of our author's artifice in attempting to confound all cases of miracles together. If he meant to do any thing to the purpose in justifying the cause of infidelity, he ought to have demonstrated, that all the miracles, believed by real Christians, were on a par in point of evidence with those of the Roman Hierarchy. Till this be done, the page on which we are animadverting will stand a monument of a jaundiced mind, but will do no honour to the solidity of his judgment. Dr. Watson has shewn him that it is quite natural to suppose, that genuine miracles would be succeeded by spurious ones: So natural indeed is it, that one is no more surprised at it, than that adulterated money should be made in imitation of genuine; and the existence of false miracles, had there been no true ones, is almost as difficult to be accounted for as the corruption of the coin would be, if genuine money had not been first produced. That which our author calls "a cold and passive acquiescence," may be easily conceived to be the utmost which men will attain, whose hearts are no way interested in Christianity. The merchant does not, however, reject all money, because much is adulterated. The scales are applied; and why? because there is something in money that arrests his attention and engages his affection. And thus will our author act with respect to miracles, whenever the religion, they are meant to support, shall appear in any degree worthy his attention, as a sinner seeking the favour of his Maker.

Certain, however, it is that miracles have long since ceased; and there seems a plain hint given us that they should do so after a time, in the 13th chapter of St. Paul to the Corinthians, though faith, hope, and charity, the soul of the true Church, should always abide in it. The well-attested evidence of past miracles, joined to the constant and even increasing evidence of prophecy, have satisfied the minds of thousands, that Christianity is true; and that there is no just reason to apprehend that the continuance of them would have any other effect than to aggravate the guilt of those who persist in unbelief. The gradual cessation, together with the difficulty of determining in some cases no way essential to the Being of Christianity, and the easiness of belief in these things which the minds of the most pious and the most judicious in the early ages would naturally contract, may sufficiently explain the cause, why the earliest Christians expressed not more surprise, when the supernatural operations ceased. Good men needed them not: The power of the Gospel on their own hearts and lives has ever been with them a most satisfying witness. *Tongues are for a sign, not to them that believe, but to them which believe not*[7].

CONCLUSION.

To recapitulate what has been attempted in this tract, may at once refresh the reader's memory, and pave the way to a free address, in conclusion, to the different sorts of characters interested in the subject.

The union between Infidelity and Infallibility was never more practically, though it is by no means speculatively, believed than at the present day. The Pope of Rome has lost his throne in the eyes of all men of sense; and Voltaire, Rousseau, Hume, and Gibbon may seem to contend for the vacant seat, or rather reign in conjunction. Their decretals in religion are swallowed without examination; they argue, or they assert; and historical objects must be seen only through the medium which they give to the publick. The censure of Infidelity is theirs; but the prompt belief of their assertions,

---

[7] I. Cor. xiv. 22.

and the affected mimicry of their contempt of Christianity, are to be ascribed to the sceptical propensity of the age, joined to its indolence and inconsideration. Thus one learned and laborious enemy of the gospel furnishes assertions, if not arguments, for thousands; they are prepared to answer whatever may have been suggested by the most judicious Divines, with this "Mr. Gibbon has shewn the matter in another light."

Of these four men, the two first, though men of genius, are allowed to have possessed no true judgment. To the two last, every candid person will attribute the praise of a sound and vigorous understanding. That the abilities of the last, eminently respectable in other subjects, have failed him in theology, was the design of the first part to shew; and I shall think the labour not to have been in vain, if the discovery of his mistakes and misrepresentations may strip him of his infallibility in the eye of the publick, and dispose them to listen with attention to the far more important matter which follows.

With this view it was shown in several miscellaneous articles, some of more, others of less importance, that he has misrepresented Christianity. None of his mistakes are ascribed to want of capacity; but all of them purely to the power of prejudice, of which there is this strong presumption, that none of his errors are in favour of Christianity, but are all of an opposite tendency.

As he has shewn a particular dislike to the character of Cyprian of Carthage, one Section is appropriated to wipe off the aspersions cast on the name of that excellent Prelate.

The conduct of the Roman Emperors, with reference to Christianity, has been examined; the character of the suffering Christians has been vindicated; it has been evinced that they were an innocent people, and that their persecutors exercised rigorous cruelties to a degree far beyond what Mr. Gibbon assigns.

But what is Christianity itself? A view of its real nature may more directly lead to a just discovery of the truth on these subjects, and open the way to the most important speculations which can influence the mind of man.

This the second part has briefly attempted. The third part, in a variety of considerations, deduces the natural consequences, and attempts to prove, that, in the ideas of faith, of holiness, of a future state, of humanity, of chastity, of glory, of rationality, and of the Church of Christ, a real Christian is essentially distinct not only from avowed Infidels, but also from thousands of those who profess Christianity, but really believe it not; and whom I beg leave to call by the name of FORMALISTS.

This review not only obviates many charges of Mr. Gibbon, because it shews that those whom he accuses were no more real Christians than professed Pagans were; but, it is hoped, may lead the serious person to an earnest investigation of the Scriptures themselves, that he may educe his creed from thence, and not implicitly take up with the prevailing fashions of the times.

Hence also the grand design of Mr. Gibbon, in his two last chapters, or, if he pleases, the tendency of those two chapters, is refuted. If one may be allowed to guess the design of a writer so void of frankness, it seems to have been this, to shew that such a religion as Christianity might have had an origin merely human; and that there is no occasion to have recourse to miracles, or indeed any supernatural agency, to account for its establishment in the world. Mr. Gibbon has too much good sense not to perceive that this is the evident tendency of the former of the two chapters in question, and that every reader who agrees with his reasonings, will naturally form this conclusion. And if this be allowed, it is not necessary that I should have a positive proof of this design, in order to justify the severity with which I have treated him. I have endeavoured then to point out the necessity and the reality of a supernatural influence, even that of divine grace, resulting from the peculiar nature of Christianity itself, in order to account for the successful propagation of this religion. It has amply appeared, I hope, that *such* a religion must have been from God, is *peculiarly his*, and could neither have been invented nor propagated by *man*.

The true cause of the enmity against the Christians is laid open, the insufficiency of that assigned by Mr. Gibbon is exposed, and it is shewn that the spirit by which Galerius *persecuted*, and that by which Mr. Gibbon has *written*, was, in reality, the same.

Thus one great argument for the truth of Christianity is illustrated, drawn from its peculiar nature and successful propagation in conjunction; which, independently of all others, it is apprehended, forms a complete demonstration of its DIVINITY.

It seemed not amiss, however, to retouch the more common standing arguments in its favour, and to evince their solidity. And as, at the very threshold of Divine Truth, a stubborn antagonist presented himself, an attempt was made to overturn the subtil reasonings of Mr. Hume in favour of universal scepticism. This was done by shewing that the proofs of religion remain in all their strength, notwithstanding the ignorance of man; and that the objections are justly overthrown because of the same ignorance.

What we are competent to decide, and what not, and the application of this distinction to the point in question, has been shewn. The same mode of reasoning is applied in a more obvious and easy way to the proofs of revealed religion.

There are three sorts of persons evidently interested in this whole subject.

1. SCEPTICS or INFIDELS, who professedly doubt of or disbelieve Christianity.

2. FORMALISTS, who fancy they believe it, when they do not, and who do not even understand what it is.

3. REAL BELIEVERS in the proper sense of the words.

A few serious words to each at parting may not be amiss: They surely cannot be unseasonable.

1. The favourite notion of Sceptics is, that all religious opinions are much alike with respect to practical influence; and thus, in religion, the most important concern of any to mankind, if it be of any importance at all, they dissolve that connection between the understanding and the will, which is allowed to subsist in every other concernment. No wonder, with these views, that they exclaim against the injustice and bigotry of condemning men for mistakes of the understanding. But it is hoped that the connection between Divine Truth and Holiness of life has been evinced in the course of these sheets. Christianity condemns no man for mistakes of the head *as such*, but always for baseness of heart. And the thing which it behoves every Infidel to disprove, in order to justify his contempt of revelation, is, that he is not guilty of any insincerity of mind toward God in his unbelief. It affords, at first sight, a strong suspicion that he is, because he turns a deaf ear to all arguments in favour of the Gospel, while similar arguments, and far weaker, gain his ready assent on other

subjects. Such men must allow the evidences of Christianity to be very considerable, and yet they reject them as of no weight at all. The worst part of this business is, that they take it for granted, that their hearts are honest, impartial, sincere; though the whole process of human affairs might shew them, that nothing is more common than for men to deceive themselves here through the blindness of self-love. The formal nature of unbelief, in the scriptural sense of the word, comprehends in it a baleful assemblage of all wickedness. The authority of God, his attributes and perfections, and even his Being, so far as any thing practical is concerned, is denied by it. O, Sirs! if ever your consciences operate with any thing of their native force, they will convince you, that such a pure religion as that of Jesus deserved not to be dismissed without being seriously heard. It is easy for you, in health and prosperity, to despise such plain reflections as these; but a near prospect of eternity, attended with the least sensation of the value of your souls, must awaken you into very just and rational fears of the most alarming nature. If you fancy moral honesty and humanity will save you, consider that this is not the language of conscience. Is duty owing to man only? Is none owing to the God who made you? And if he has presented you with a religion the most beneficial and the most holy that can be conceived, becomes it you to reject the present with scornful indifference? "But how do we know that the religion is his?" In this address I only intreat you to be serious, candid, and fair enquirers. There is no medium in the case. If Christianity be true, this sentence of it must be true also, *He that believeth not shall be damned*[8]. I am under no pain for the consequence, if once, in the spirit of prayer and serious enquiry, levity and bantring apart, you begin to examine. *If any man will do his will, he shall know*[9]. Your unbelief is represented in Scripture as the result of pride, perverseness, rebellion. *You hate the light, lest your deeds should be reproved*[10]. You ought to be certain that this is not the case, before you exclaim against the unreasonableness of condemning men for mere opinions. Yours is an unfair state of the case. The Scripture is as uniform in representing all virtue to be involved in faith, as it is in representing all wickedness to

---

[8] Mark xvi. 16.
[9] John vii. 17.
[10] John iii. 20.

be involved in unbelief. Mr. Gibbon, in the case of Paul of Samosata[11], supposes, that the Christians were unreasonable in condemning him for nice and subtil errors in doctrine, rather than for the immorality of his life. But his errors were not so unimportant as he imagines. His views seem on the whole to have much resembled those of the modern Socinians[12]. No wonder that his life was wicked. Men may talk of virtue, but provision for the effectual practice of it is only attained in the school of Christ, from which, in reality, Socinianism is as abhorrent as any Deism whatever. The atonement and intercession of God the Son, and the influence of God the Holy Ghost, being excluded or explained away, nothing remains of the Gospel, in effect, but what it has in common with the religion of nature.

And if experience prove, that as we have advanced in infidel principles, we have advanced in wickedness, the connection, I would earnestly put you in mind of, has the strong support of matter of fact. The times are awful, Sirs! and call for serious thought. Christianity has been scorned without examination, and in a levity of spirit extremely unbecoming the dignity of the subject. And as if the tide of unbelief were not strong enough already in the land, an author of the first estimation for learning and talents has aided the cause. Could a person of my obscurity hope to attract the attention of the Great, I would say, Be serious for your souls; search the Scriptures; examine closely the evidences of its truth; and pray for that Spirit which the Scriptures promise to those who petition the Almighty.

2. It must have appeared to the most superficial reader, that the Gospel, in my view of it, is quite a different thing from that which it is apprehended to be by the major part of those who call themselves Christians. This, it ought not to be dissembled, is really the case. The doctrines of Scripture were very early perverted; and though a pure Church, in some individuals, has ever been successively preserved, yet, on the whole, a darkness, not radically better than that of Paganism itself, seems to have prevailed, after the perversion once took place, even till the æra of the Reformation. I am sensible how obnoxious to the charge of supercilious arrogance I am rendered by this view of

---

[11] Page 562.

[12] Mosheim's Eccl. Hist. p. 188. Quarto Edition.

things. But, in truth, he who confesses himself to be as vile and as ignorant as others by nature, and to be indebted to a very peculiar Divine light and grace, if indeed he be now different from them, has of all men the least right to be proud. And even the suspicion of arrogance he would gladly avoid, if the interest of truth and duty, and compassion to souls would admit it. The candid reader will then bear with the appearance of a dogmatical spirit; I hope it is not the reality.

The Reformation was one of the brightest periods of evangelical truth, and its happy religious and moral effects were extremely palpable in Protestant countries. But let us mark the *dire crisis* of its decline in England.

Beyond all doubt much hypocrisy and much real enthusiasm prevailed during the civil confusions of the last century, though much real piety prevailed also at the same time. After the Restoration, some leading men in the Established Church endeavoured to correct these evils. The method they took can scarce be better explained than by one, who so deeply entered into their scheme, that he owns he learned the best part of what he knew from some of them[13]. Speaking of one of them, Whichcot, he says, "Being disgusted with the dry systematical way of those times, he studied to raise those who conversed with him to a nobler set of thoughts, and to consider religion as a seed of a *deiform* nature. In order to this, he set young students much on reading the antient philosophers, chiefly Plato, Tully, Plotin; and on considering the Christian religion as a doctrine sent from God, both to elevate and sweeten human nature." So this set of men at Cambridge studied to assert and examine the principles of religion and morality on clear grounds, and in a philosophical method – the making out the reasons of things being a main part of their studies. – But let the reader see the whole account in Burnet himself, who enters with evident pleasure into every part of their scheme.

Had these men, in attempting to correct certain abuses and errors, made use only of the Scriptures, which are certainly sufficient to *perfect the man of God*, and completely *furnish him for every good work*[14], they doubtless might have found ample matter of rebuke for mere Enthusiasts, and of correction for really good men, who should have needed it: But, alas! in

---

[13] Burnet's History of his Own Times, vol. i. p. 319.
[14] 2 Tim. iii. 17.

attempting to cure the *patient*, they destroyed him. For is it so indeed, that Scripture-truth needs to be retouched and polished by Pagan philosophers?

Were the Platonists the great enemies of Christianity while living, and could the works they left behind them be serviceable to it? Might not these *rational* Divines have learned from the knowledge they had, or might have had, from history of the deadly opposition of Platonism to the Gospel, that it was impossible they should ever incorporate? and was no more respect due to the inspired writings of St. Paul, who expressly guards us against the poisonous effects of philosophy?[15]

But they administered the poison, and posterity feel the malignant effect to this hour. It has pleased God, in his infinite mercy, in various local instances, to revive among us the doctrines of the Reformation at this day. But in general the Church of England has drooped, as to every holy purpose, ever since this proud attempt of employing reason to correct the Gospel. It surely is its own guard; it disdains any other; and if every part of it be impartially studied, one part will check and balance another. But these men, by introducing heterogeneous matter, adulterated its very nature. It was no peccadillo; it was an error of the first magnitude, and the consequences have shewn it to be so. With difficulty, a barren orthodoxy of sentiment, with reference to the Trinity and the Atonement, was for a while preserved: But the influence of the Holy Ghost in regeneration and sanctification, together with justification by faith in Christ alone, and the Scripture-views of the true character of God and of fallen man, were soon destroyed or debilitated among us. All idea of feeling in religion, or of what St. John calls *fellowship with the Father and the Son*[16], was ridiculed as Enthusiasm. The indolent part of the Clergy contented themselves with a servile imitation of these admired models; the laborious and more enterprizing have made bolder advances into the province of haughty reason. Many Dissenters have caught the infection, and, being less restrained by subscriptions, have openly avowed principles directly opposite to the real Gospel. The science of Ethics alone is left in repute; Christian mysteries are excluded as occult, or frivolous, or

---

[15] Colos. ii. 8. 1 Tim. vi. 20, 21.
[16] 1 John i.

false; and the leaven of reason[17] has spread itself through all Christianity, and threatens to leave neither root nor branch.

What the precious truths of the Gospel are, which have been by this means corrupted among us, has appeared for the most part in the foregoing sheets, in which, if not the whole of Gospel-truth, yet its leading features have been described. In a word, Philosophy and Christianity will not, cannot be united.

The advantage hence given to Infidels is evident. Scepticism has prevailed abundantly: How was it possible that it should be otherwise? The defenders of Christianity understood it not themselves; and while they ably defended the outworks, I mean its external evidences, they betrayed its citadel to the enemy. And the inward and best proof of its truth deduced from its peculiar nature, they could not see, they could not defend, while they rejected, with a scorn nothing less than Deistical, its distinguishing peculiarities.

Practice has grown as corrupt as principle. This must be the case. The preaching of morality is not God's appointed way of making men holy in their lives. It has a place, an extremely necessary place in doctrine to sustain, but not a prominent one. Christ and him crucified is the chief Gospel-theme. Who does not see what an increase of wickedness has prevailed among us! Look at the Clergy. I would be tender in speaking of my brethen; but is there not a loud call for it in charity? That sermons should be sold to them by a person advertising in the news-papers[18], is a flaming proof of the low state of their religious views and studies.

With regard to the Universities I would be tender also; but truth calls for a charitable animadversion. The neglect of true theological knowledge among the students is palpable; and a general insensibility to divine things, is, I fear, too sadly prevalent in the Colleges, the servants of the Colleges, and the country around them.

But to dwell on particular corruptions of the times is needless; nor does Satire make any part of my design; that we are a selfish, profane, licentious people is evident. *The whole*

---

[17] The candid reader will easily see, that I mean by the word *reason*, a spirit of religious investigation, which exerts itself independantly of revealed truth.

[18] Dr. Trusler.

head is sick, and the whole heart faint. I shall be happy, if any real light has been thrown on the true cause of it. Let me desire those who may find themselves concerned in these animadversions, particularly my brethren the Clergy, to weigh in charity what has been in charity advanced. And if they are at all convinced of its truth, to apply themselves, by prayer and scriptural investigation, to the attainment of the knowledge of the real Gospel, the true and only cure of infidelity and immorality, however strong, however inveterate.

3. Though this tract is not peculiarly designed for the use of real believers, yet as it is hoped the subjects handled in it may not be altogether unserviceable to them, let a cordial word in the close engage their attention. You are fallen on evil days and evil tongues; your principles are to the last degree unfashionable. On that account hold them fast, and maintain and confess them before the world as freely and as tenaciously, as the world adhere to their maxims and customs. I do not mean that you should be noisy, ostentatious disputants; it is worth no man's while to contend vehemently for opinions merely as such: But, oh! *contend earnestly for the faith which was once delivered to the Saints*, by an hearty exercise of it in all your conduct. Give no way to any conciliatory schemes, which vainly attempt to unite the interests of God and Mammon. The self-knowledge which you have, bears witness to the concurrent testimony of Scripture, that reason, the more decent and plausible part of man, is as much alienated from God as the passions. Cherish, by constant prayer and inward communion with God, the Divine Life which you have received, and support it by faith, notwithstanding all the noise which men, ignorant of Divine Truth, may make concerning enthusiasm and licentiousness, and all the wise caution of lukewarm professors. The peculiar truths of the Gospel are not merely matters of expedience and of preference to other sorts of religious views; they are your very LIFE, and that holiness, *without which no man shall see the Lord*, and which is the ultimate end of all your religion, can have neither subsistence nor growth without them. And be not seduced from the *truth as it is in Jesus*, by the falls of many false professors: Be assured, that though many who profess the Gospel disgrace it altogether by their practice, yet that there is, however, no other way than that of the genuine Gospel, which leads to real virtue. Men may deceive themselves with a false faith, and the

fruits may awfully prove it; but still the true faith is absolutely necessary for the production of the least degree of real holiness. A life of faith in the Son of God is as necessary for holiness here, as it is for glory hereafter. We have seen what dismal consequences flowed from the vain attempts of those who, in the last century, endeavoured to correct religious abuses by the light of nature, reason, and common sense. These should be taught to know their proper sphere, the affairs of human life, and to move cautiously within it; it is not at all their province to amend what is wrong in the religious world. Errors and abuses will in this imperfect state of things be arising from time to time; the *puritanical* age was not singular in this respect; and even good men may, in a certain degree, be infected with these evils. The temptation is very strong in such cases to have recourse to *rational* expedients of correction; and the mind, before it is aware, contracts a secret, but powerful contempt of the simplicity of Gospel-faith, as if that had either brought on the evils, or was too weak to counteract them: But remember, that not the excess, but the defect of faith is ever the cause of a religious decline of all sorts and degrees. Apply yourselves to Jesus for the promised Spirit, do every thing in unreserved dependance on him; and if that course do not effectually sanctify your souls, then say *Christ is dead in vain, and your faith is also vain.* But it is not a merely systematical faith, to the efficacy of which such great things are to be ascribed; but to a cordial dependance on your Divine Saviour, cherished by constant prayer, and close walking with God in the way of his commandments.

Nor do I mean to discountenance the cultivation of the rational faculties. God forbid; they are his gift; and if the improvements of them be sanctified by grace, they answer many valuable purposes, which need not be here recounted: I only mean to exclude them from the province of dictating in religion. Christianity is from heaven, and is not understood, exercised, and practiced, but by a *spiritual understanding*[19], far superior to that which is merely *rational.* Nor would I be understood to discountenance the study of the antient Classics and Philosophers by any thing I have said: I only mean to exclude them wholly from the office of teaching religion. The study of them answers many important purposes; while manly

---

[19] Coloss. i. 9.

sense and good taste shall be at all respected among men, they will be esteemed as excellent models of both. But this is an age of dissipation and sloth; and it surely adds not to our virtue, that the antients are held in such sovereign contempt. I wish the knowledge of them was more deep and more general among real Ministers of the Gospel than it is. St. Paul seems, by some Scripture-hints, to have made a profitable use of his human learning, as Moses before him no doubt converted the wisdom of Egypt, which he had studiously learned, to the service of the Church. The Reformers made a glorious use of their secular knowledge in the same way as St. Austin had done before them. And the really learned and excellent Dr. Owen in later times did the same.

It will be well if the fashionable, and even affected contempt of antient learning, which has infected even godly men, arise not in them more from sloth than from spirituality. Man was not made to be idle. Ministers of the Gospel should least of all be so. A lively and close attendance to every branch of duty, in connection with that best jewel of life, *inward communion with Jesus*, is not incompatible with some degree of secular study. Sure I am, that prayer and human learning are better companions than prayer and that sauntering, gossiping spirit, which so much disgraces the practice, devours the time, and vitiates the imagination of many, of some even good men, who have not from youth been habituated to close thinking. The Bible, and books written in the spirit of the Bible, must ever claim by far the principal part of the attention of studious men, who mean to glorify God by all their studies. Perhaps the learned antients deserve the next place; I am confident the *light reading* of modern pamphlets does not. We seem to embrace the maxim as true, *a great book is a great evil*. But notwithstanding the contrary current of the times, I am free to say, that if those who love reading employed themselves more in severer, more voluminous, and of course more antient authors, they would find their time and trouble to be better repaid. Were the antient Philosophers in particular more known among Ministers, they would be far better enabled to defend the truths of God against learned Infidelity, and to evince the importance of revelation than at present they are.

But a Christian owes various duties to society. To pray for our nation; to sigh before God for its abominations; to study to do all possible good to the souls and bodies of men; to demean himself as a loyal subject, and as a peaceable citizen, and even to return good for evil, these are his ornaments; thus it is that his light should shine before men. If he is ill treated on account of his faith and piety, patience and meekness are his arms. "God himself," as St. Cyprian sublimely observes in his excellent Treatise on Patience, "is not yet avenged for all the insults he has received from his creatures." His creatures should wait with him for the retribution of the last day. That, O Christian, is thy day of triumph, reserve thyself for this, by *patient continuance in well-doing*; always maintaining thy interest in Jesus by faith, till the mystery of God shall be finished; then thy eternal day of rest shall commence, and *God shall wipe away all tears from thy eyes.*

FINIS.

AN HISTORY OF THE CORRUPTIONS OF CHRISTIANITY
by Joseph Priestley

THE GENERAL CONCLUSION.
PART I. CONTAINING,
*Considerations addressed to unbelievers,
and especially to* MR. GIBBON.

To consider the system (if it may be called a *system*) of christianity *a priori*, one would think it very little liable to corruption, or abuse. The great outline of it is, that the universal parent of mankind commissioned Jesus Christ, to invite men to the practice of virtue, by the assurance of his mercy to the penitent, and of his purpose to raise to immortal life and happiness all the virtuous and the good, but to inflict an adequate punishment on the wicked. In proof of this he wrought many miracles, and after a public execution he rose again from the dead. He also directed that proselytes to his religion should be admitted by *baptism*, and that his disciples should eat bread and drink wine in commemoration of his death.

Here is nothing that any person could imagine would lead to much subtle speculation, at least such as could excite much animosity. The doctrine itself is so plain, that one would think the learned and the unlearned were upon a level with respect to it. And a person unacquainted with the state of things at the time of its promulgation would look in vain for any probable source of the monstrous corruptions and abuses which crept into the system afterwards. Our Lord, however, and his apostles, foretold that there would be a great departure from the truth, and that something would arise in the church altogether unlike the doctrine which they taught, and even subversive of it.

In reality, however, the causes of the succeeding corruptions did then exist; and accordingly, without any thing more than their natural operation, all the abuses rose to their full height; and what is more wonderful still, by the operation of natural causes also, without any miraculous interposition of providence, we see the abuses gradually corrected, and christianity recovering its primitive beauty and glory.

The causes of the corruptions were almost wholly contained in the established opinions of the heathen world, and especially the philosophical part of it; so that when those heathens embraced christianity they mixed their former tenets and prejudices with it. Also, both Jews and heathens were so much scandalized at the idea of being the disciples of a man who had been crucified as a common malefactor, that christians in general were sufficiently disposed to adopt any opinion that would most effectually wipe away this reproach.

The opinion of the mental faculties of man belonging to a substance distinct from his body or brain, and of this invisible spiritual part, or *soul*, being capable of subsisting before and after its union to the body, which had taken the deepest root in all the schools of philosophy, was wonderfully calculated to answer this purpose. For by this means christians were enabled to give to the soul of Christ what rank they pleased in the heavenly regions before his incarnation. On this principle went the Gnostics, deriving their doctrine from the received oriental philosophy. Afterwards the philosophizing christians went upon another principle, personifying the wisdom, or λογος of God the Father. But this was mere Platonism, and therefore cannot be said to have been unnatural in their circumstances, though at length they came, in the natural progress of things, to believe that Christ was, in power and glory, equal to God the Father himself.

From the same opinion of a soul distinct from the body came the practice of praying, first *for* the dead, and then *to* them, with a long train of other absurd opinions, and superstitious practices.

The abuses of the *positive institutions* of christianity, monstrous as they were, naturally arose from the opinion of the purifying and sanctifying virtue of rites and ceremonies, which was the very basis of all the worship of the heathens; and they were also similar to the abuses of the Jewish religion. We likewise see the rudiments of all the *monkish austerities* in the opinions and practices of the heathens, who thought to purify and exalt the soul by macerating and mortifying the body.

As to the abuses in the *government of the church*, they are as easily accounted for as abuses in civil government; worldly minded men being always ready to lay hold of every opportunity of increasing their power; and in the dark ages too many circumstances concurred to give the christian clergy peculiar advantages over the laity in this respect.

Upon the whole, I flatter myself that, to an attentive reader of this work, it will appear, that the corruption of christianity, in every article of faith or practice, was the natural consequence of the circumstances in which it was promulgated; and also that its recovery from these corruptions is the natural consequence of different circumstances. LET UNBELIEVERS, IF THEY CAN, ACCOUNT AS WELL FOR THE FIRST RISE AND ESTABLISHMENT OF CHRISTIANITY ITSELF. This is a problem, which, historians and philosophers (bound to believe that no effect is produced without an adequate cause) will find to be of more difficult solution the more closely it is attended to.

The circumstances that Mr. Gibbon enumerates as the immediate *causes* of the spread of christianity were themselves *effects*, and necessarily required such causes as, I imagine, he would be unwilling to allow. The revolution produced by christianity in the opinions and conduct of men, as he himself describes it, was truly astonishing; and this, he cannot deny, was produced without the concurrence, nay notwithstanding the opposition, of all the civil powers of the world; and what is perhaps more, it was opposed by all the learning, genius, and wit of the age too. For christianity was assailed as much by ridicule and reproach as it was by open persecution; and, be the spread of it what Mr. Gibbon pleases, he cannot deny that it kept uniformly gaining ground, taking in all descriptions of men without distinction, before it had any foreign aid; and what then remained of the old religions was not sufficient to occasion any sensible obstruction to the full establishment of it. The Jewish religion alone was an exception; and this circumstance, together with the rise of christianity among the Jews, are facts that deserve Mr. Gibbon's particular attention.

Of all mankind, the Jews were the most unlikely to set up any religion, so different from their own; and as unlikely was it that other nations, and especially the polite and learned among them, should receive a religion from Jews, and those some of the most ignorant of that despised nation.

Let Mr. Gibbon recollect his own idea of the Jews, which seems to be much the same with that of Voltaire, and think whether it be at all probable, that they should have originally invented a religion so essentially different from any other in the world, as that which is described in the books of Moses; that the whole nation should then have adopted without objection, what they were afterwards so prone to abandon for the rites of any of their neighbours; or that when, by severe discipline, they had acquired the attachment to it which they are afterwards known to have done, and which continues to this day, it be probable they would have invented, or have adopted another, which they conceived to be so different from, and subversive of their own. If they had been so fertile of invention, it might have been expected that they would have struck out some other since the time of Christ, a period of near two thousand years.

On this subject Mr. Gibbon says[1], that "in contradiction to every known principle of the human mind, that singular people seem to have yielded a stronger and more ready assent to the traditions of their remote ancestors, than to the evidence of their own senses." A singular people, indeed, if this was the case; for then they must not have been *men*, but beings in the shape of men only, though internally constituted in some very different manner. But what facts in history may not be represented as probable or improbable, on such loose suppositions as these? Such liberties as these I shall neither take, nor grant. Jews are *men*, and men are beings, whose affections and actions are subject to as strict rules as those of the animate or inanimate parts of nature. Their conduct, therefore, must be accounted for on such principles as always have influenced the conduct of men, and such as we observe still to influence men.

I wish Mr. Gibbon would consider whether he does not, in the passage above quoted, use the word *tradition* in an improper manner. By tradition we generally mean something for which we have not the evidence of histories written at the time of the events. We never talk of the tradition of the wars of Julius Cæsar, or of his death in the senate house, nor even of the tradition of the conquests of Alexander the Great; because there were histories of those events written at the time, or so near to the time, as to be fully within the memory of those who were witnesses of them.

Now Moses, and the other writers of the Old Testament, were as much present at the time of the transactions they relate, as the historians of Julius Cæsar or Alexander. An incautious reader

[1] History, vol. 1. p. 539.

(and there are too many such) would be apt to imagine from Mr. Gibbon's manner of expressing himself, that the Jews did not even pretend to have *written histories* of the same age with the origin of their religion, but that it was in the same predicament with what he calls "the elegant mythology of Greece and Rome;" whereas, the fact is, that every tittle of it was committed to writing at the time. It is generally in such an *indirect* manner as this, and not by a fair and candid representation of facts, that unbelievers endeavour to discredit the system of revelation.

Let Mr. Gibbon, as an historian, compare the rise and progress of Mahometanism, with that of Judaism, or of christianity, and attend to the difference. Besides the influence of the *sword*, which christianity certainly had not, Mahometanism stood on the basis of the Jewish and christian revelations. If these had not been firmly believed in the time of Mahomet, what credit would his religion have gained? In these circumstances he must have invented some other system, which would have required *visible miracles* of its own, which he might have found some difficulty in passing upon his followers; though they were in circumstances far more easy to be imposed upon than the Jews or the heathens, in the time of our Saviour. This was an age of light, and of suspicion; the other, if any, of darkness and credulity. That christianity *grew up in silence and obscurity*, as Mr. Gibbon says[2], is the very reverse of the truth. He could not himself imagine circumstances in which the principal facts on which christianity is founded should be subject to a more rigid scrutiny. *These things*, as Paul said to king Agrippa, *were not done in a corner.* Acts xxvi. 26.

It appears to me, that, admitting all the miraculous events which the evangelical history asserts, it was not probable that christianity should have been received with less difficulty than it was; but without that assistance, absolutely impossible for it to have been received at all.

Mr. Gibbon represents the discredit into which the old religions were fallen, as having made way for the new one. "So urgent," says he[3], "on the vulgar is the necessity of believing, that the fall of any system of mythology will most probably be succeeded by the introduction of some other mode of superstition."

[2] Vol. 1, p. 535.
[3] Ib. p. 602.

But are not the vulgar, *men*, as well as the learned, their understandings being naturally as good and as various, and certainly subject to the same laws; and *necessity of believing*, or *proneness to belief* is not greater in the one than in the other; but the expression is loose and inaccurate, and calculated to impose on superficial readers. Besides, if any set of men had this property of *proneness to believe*, they must, to be all of a piece, have a proportionable unwillingness to quit their belief, at least without very sufficient evidence; and yet those *vulgar* of all nations, are supposed by Mr. Gibbon to have abandoned the belief of their own mythology some time before christianity came, to supply the vacancy. Such *vulgar* as those I should think intitled to the more respectable appellation of *free thinkers*, which with many is synonymous to *philosophers*. And, in fact, it was not with the vulgar, but with the philosophers, that the religions of Greece and Rome were fallen into discredit. We ought, therefore, to judge of their case by that of the philosophical part of the world at present.

With many of *them* christianity is now rejected; but do they, on that account, seem disposed to adopt any other mode of religion, or any other system of mythology in its place? And would not such men as Mr. Hume or Helvetius among the dead, and Mr. Gibbon himself among the living, examine with scrupulous exactness the pretensions of any system of divine revelation, especially before he would regulate his life by it, and go to the stake for it. And yet philosophers of antiquity, men of as good understanding as Mr. Gibbon, and who, no doubt, loved life, and the pleasures and advantages of it, as much as he does, embraced christianity, and died for it.

But besides the *urgency of this necessity of believing*, another cause of the rapid spread of christianity, was that it held out to mankind something worth believing. "When the promise of eternal happiness," he says[4], "was proposed to mankind, on condition of adopting the faith, and observing the precepts of the gospel, it is no wonder that so advantageous an offer should be accepted by great numbers of every religion, of every rank, and of every province in the Roman empire."

Now it is certainly no discredit to christianity, that the views it exhibits of a future state appeared more rational, and more inviting, than the accounts of *Tartarus* and the *Elysian shades*.

[4] History, vol. 1. p. 561.

But besides appearing more *inviting*, they must also have appeared more *credible*, from the general external evidence of the truth of christianity. And here also Mr. Gibbon seems to have been inattentive to the principles of human nature.

In general, the more *extraordinary* any event appears to be, the more evidence we require of it. It is this consideration that makes more definite evidence necessary for a miracle, than for an ordinary fact; though it is acknowledged that the *desirableness* of any particular event, by interesting our *wishes*, will tend to make us admit it on somewhat less evidence. The great advantages, therefore, proposed to men from any scheme, especially one in which they were to run some risque, and in which they were to make great sacrifices, would not dispose them to receive it without evidence. *It is too good news to be true*, is a remark perpetually made by the very *vulgar* of whom Mr. Gibbon is speaking. When the disciples of our Lord saw him for the first time after his resurrection, it is said (Luke xxiv. 41.) that *they believed not through joy*; and when, before this, they were told by three or four women of character, and for whom they had the highest respect, that they had themselves seen him alive, and had a message from him to them, *Their words seemed to them as idle tales, and they believed them not*. Ib. ver. 11. This was perfectly natural; and such circumstances as these are strong internal evidence of the historians describing real facts, and real feelings of the human heart corresponding to those facts.

Besides, how can any man, to use Mr. Gibbon's own language, *adopt the faith* of the gospel, whatever promises might be made to him for so doing, unless its tenets appeared to him to be *reasonable*? What would Mr. Gibbon take to believe the doctrine of the Trinity, or what would he sacrifice in this life for the most magnificent promise in a future one, made by a person whose ability to make good that promise he at all suspected. Plato's doctrine of the *immortality of the soul* was sufficiently flattering; but whom was it ever known to influence, like the christian doctrine of a *resurrection*? The plain reason was, that the latter was proposed with sufficient *evidence*, whereas the former was altogether destitute of it.

It is amusing enough to observe how very differently Mr. Gibbon represents the state of the heathen world with respect to christianity, when he would insinuate an apology for the persecution of the christians. "It might be expected," he says[5], "that they would unite with indignation against any sect or people, which would separate itself from the communion of mankind, and, claiming the exclusive privilege of divine knowledge, should disclaim every form of worship except its own, as impious and idolatrous."

Mr. Gibbon, I suppose, never asked himself whether it was natural for the same kind of people to be so very differently affected towards the same thing. But, unfortunately, his purpose required that to account for the ready reception of christianity upon insufficient evidence, some of those heathens must be furnished with an *urgent necessity of believing* any new religion that was proposed to them, especially one that promised such great and glorious things as christianity did; while, on the other hand, to account also for the very ill reception that the preachers of christianity met with (which he cannot deny) others of them must be furnished with a disposition to hate and detest those who pretended to so much.

I do not know any thing that can help Mr. Gibbon in this case better than the known principles of his favourite *mythology*. As the present race of mankind are derived from the stones which Deucalion and Pyrrha threw over their heads (when perhaps they were in too much haste to repeople the vacant world) they might not be sufficiently attentive to the nature of those materials of the future race of mortals, but take stones of different degrees of hardness. In consequence of this, some of them may have been of a softer disposition, and more easy of belief than others. Being, therefore, so differently constituted, the descendants of some of them might be instinctive believers, and others instinctive persecutors of those believers. They would then be, of course, as hostile to each other as those men who sprung out of the earth, from the sowing of the serpents teeth, in the elegant mythology of Greece, as the story is most elegantly related by Ovid[6].

---

[5] History, vol. 1. p. 622.

[6] I have heard of a young gentleman of a sceptical and jocular turn, taking off his hat to a statue of Jupiter (who makes the most respectable figure in this system of mythology) and saying, "If ever you come into power again, please to remember that I shewed you respect when nobody else did." Mr. Gibbon, I hope, has no serious views in complimenting the religion of Greece and Rome, meaning to pay his court to the *powers that may be*, as others do to those that *are*.

Besides these considerations, Mr. Gibbon mentions the *zeal* of the primitive christians, and the strictness of their *discipline*, as causes of the spread of the new religion. But he should have told us whence came that zeal, and that strictness of discipline. If no sufficient *cause* of it had appeared, their zeal would have exposed them to contempt; and their discipline would have discouraged rather than have invited proselytes.

Any person may hold himself excused from investigating the causes that gave birth to the opinions of *individuals* of mankind, on account of the difficulty and uncertainty of such an investigation. The same may, in some degree, be said of particular classes of men. But christianity recommended itself to every description of men then existing, and influenced them not for a short time only, which might be accounted for from temporary and local circumstances, but *permanently*; so as to leave no reasonable doubt, but that it would have gone on to establish itself in the world, and to extirpate idolatry, if the civil powers had continued to oppose its progress three thousand, as they did three hundred years; and what is more, notwithstanding the gross corruptions and abuses which soon crept into it.

A fact of this kind requires to be accounted for from the most obvious principles of human nature, principles common to all men, and all classes of men; and therefore none but the plainest and most cogent *causes of assent*, deserve to be attended to. This assent to the truth of christianity could only be produced by such evidence as always will, and always ought to determine the assent of the human mind.

It is acknowledged that to be a christian a man must believe some facts that are of an extraordinary nature, such as we have no opportunity of observing at present. But those facts were so circumstanced, that persons who cannot be denied to have had the best opportunity of examining the evidence of them, and who, if they had not been true, had no motive to pay any regard to them, could not refuse their assent to them; that is, it was such evidence as we ourselves must have been determined by, if we had been in their place; and therefore, if not fully equivalent to the evidence of our own senses at present, is, at least, all the evidence that, at this distance of time, we *can* have in the case. It goes upon the principle that human nature was the same thing then that it is now; and certainly in all other respects it appears to be so.

That miracles are things in themselves *possible*, must be allowed, so long as it is evident that there is in nature a power equal to the working of them. And certainly the *power, principle*, or *being*, by whatever name it be denominated, which produced the universe, and established the laws of it, is fully equal to any occasional departures from them. The *object* and *use* of those miracles on which the christian religion is founded, is also maintained to be consonant to the object and use of the general system of nature, viz. the production of happiness. We have nothing, therefore, to do, but to examine, by the known rules of estimating the value of *testimony*, whether there be reason to think that such miracles have been wrought, or whether the evidence of christianity, or of the christian history, does not stand upon as good ground as that of any other history whatever.

Now, though I am far from holding myself out as the champion of christianity, against all the world, I own I shall have no objection to discuss this subject with Mr. Gibbon, as an historian, and a philosopher. We are only two individuals, and no other persons can be bound by the result of our discussion. But those who have given less attention to the subject than we have done, may be instructed by it, and be assisted in forming their own judgment, according to the evidence that shall be laid before them. At least, it may be a means of drawing some degree of attention to a subject, which cannot be denied to be, in the highest degree, interesting.

Indeed, if any man can say that it is not an interesting question, whether his existence terminate at death, or is to be resumed at a future period, and then to continue for ever, he must be of a low and abject mind. To a rational being, capable of contemplating the wonders of nature, and of investigating the laws of it, and to a being of a social disposition, his existence, and the continuance of his rational faculties, must be an object of unspeakable value to him; and consequently he must ardently wish that christianity (which alone *brings life and immortality to light*) may be true. For to a philosopher, who forms his judgment by what he actually observes, the doctrine of a *soul*, capable of subsisting and acting when the body is in the grave, will never give any satisfaction. To every person, therefore, who is capable of enjoying his existence, the christian doctrine of a *resurrection*, opens a glorious and transporting prospect.

Voluntarily to shut one's eyes on such a prospect, and really to wish to see no more of the wonders of nature, and of the progress of being, and especially of the human race, towards perfection, but to hide one's head in everlasting obscurity, must be to have a disposition as groveling, base, and abject, as that of the lowest of the brute creation. A man of the least elevation of mind, and of a cultivated and improved understanding must, surely, lament such a catastrophe.

The fear might be, that every truly sensible and virtuous man would be too strongly biassed in favour of christianity and (if Mr. Gibbon's observation above-mentioned be true) give his assent long before he had waited to weigh the evidence as he ought to do. I do not, however, wish Mr. Gibbon to shew this disposition. On the contrary, I wish to examine every thing with the greatest rigour, and I will not contend with him for trifles. With respect to some points which he has laboured, though I am satisfied his representations are partial and unfair, I have no objection to concede almost all that he contends for; because, though he has taken very liberally, he has left me enough.

When the circumstances of the Jews and heathens, at the time of the promulgation of christianity, shall be sufficiently considered (but to which it is evident Mr. Gibbon has given but a slight attention) the reception that this new religion met with among them, and the total subversion of the several systems of paganism by it, will be found to be a more extraordinary thing, on the supposition of the gospel history not being true, more contrary to the present course of nature, and consequently more improbable, than the history of Christ and the apostles as contained in the New Testament, which makes the whole of the subsequent history perfectly easy and natural. In short, the question is, whether Mr. Gibbon, or myself, believe in more numerous, more extraordinary, or more useless miracles. On this fair, unexceptionable ground I am willing to meet him.

I also shall not contend with him for quite so much as his late antagonists, members of the church of England, must include in the system of christianity. But by abandoning their outworks, I may perhaps be better able to make an effectual defence.

My religion does not suppose, with bishop Hurd, "that the offices in which the godhead is employed are either degrading, or imply an immoderate and inconceivable condescension[7]," I shall not urge Mr. Gibbon to admit, that "a divine person, divine in the highest sense of the word, descended from heaven, and suffered death[8], that the *divine nature* condescended to leave the mansions of glory, was made man, dwelled among us, and died for us[9]."

I shall not pretend, with the same learned bishop, that *a third divine person* gave this second divine person "power to cast out devils, and raised him from the dead[10]." Neither shall I urge him with "a purpose to save and sanctify men by means that he himself can think fanciful or delusive[11]," and maintain that Christ, "in virtue of his all atoning death, has opened the gates of eternal life to the whole race of mortal men[12]," which the bishop enumerates among "the great things of which Christ spake, and the amazing topics with which he filled his discourses[13]."

I am sensible that it would be in vain to urge any external historical evidence of a revelation, of which such doctrines as these should make a part. They are things that no miracles can

---

[7] See Bishop Hurd's Sermons, vol. 3. p. 33.

[8] Ib. p. 63.

[9] That the *divine nature* of Christ should *die*, is, surely, more than Dr. Hurd's christian creed obliges him to assert, unless he may think that without this, his doctrine of *atonement* could not be completed.

[10] Bishop Hurd's Sermons, vol. 2. p. 337.

[11] Ib. vol. 3, p. 33.

[12] Ib. vol. 3, p. 64.

[13] A common reader might peruse our Lord's discourses many times, before he found any such *topics* as these, with which they are here said to be *filled*. But I the less wonder at this when I find this writer attempting to prove at large, that by *washing the disciples feet* our Lord meant to teach the great doctrine of *atonement by his blood*, and wondering that Grotius and other commentators should not see it in the same light. Sermons, vol. 1. p. 177, &c.

But I own I am surprised that he should maintain, vol. 3. p. 67, that "Christ spake by virtue of his own essential right, from himself, and in his own name, as well as by especial appointment of God his Father," when he himself, in the most unequivocal language repeatedly asserts the contrary; as John 5. 30. *I can of my own self do nothing*, ch. 7. 6. *My doctrine is not mine, but his that sent me*. ch. 14. 10. *The words that I speak to you, I speak not of myself, but the Father, who dwelleth in me, he doth the works*. It must be strong bias in favour of a system that can make a person overlook such texts as these. But even the greatest and best of men have been misled in the same way.

prove. As soon should I propose to him the belief of Mahomet's journey to the third heavens, and all his conversations with God while a pitcher of water was falling, or the doctrine of transubstantiation, neither of which are more absurd, and both of them are much more innocent.

I am sorry, however, to have occasion to admonish Mr. Gibbon, that he should have distinguished better than he has done between christianity itself, and the corruptions of it. A serious christian, strongly attached to some particular tenets, may be excused if, in reading ecclesiastical history, he should not make the proper distinctions; but this allowance cannot be made for so cool and philosophical a spectator as Mr. Gibbon.

He should not have taken it for granted, that the doctrine of three persons in one God, or the doctrine of *atonement* for the sins of all mankind, by the death of one man, were any parts of the christian system; when, if he had read the New Testament for himself, he must have seen the doctrine of the proper *unity of God*, and also that of his *free mercy* to the penitent, in almost every page of it. As he does speak of the *corruptions of christianity*, he should have examined farther, both as an historian, and as a man. For as an individual, he is as much interested in the inquiry as any other person; and no inquiry whatever is so interesting to any man as this is.

As to what Mr. Gibbon, with a sneer of triumph, says[14], of "Plato having 360 years before the christian æra, anticipated one of the most surprising discoveries of the Christian revelation," and of "the theology of Plato having been confirmed with the celestial pen of the last and most sublime of the evangelists, 97 years after that æra;" like all his other sarcasms against christianity, it is founded on ignorance. But he is more excusable in this than in other cases, as too many christians have been chargeable with the same; confounding the *Logos* of Plato with that of John, and making of it a second person in the trinity, than which no two things can be more different, as has been clearly explained by my excellent and judicious friend Mr. Lindsay, especially in his *Catechist*, in the preface to which he has very properly animadverted upon this passage of Mr. Gibbon.

Mr. Gibbon has much to learn concerning the gospel before he can be properly qualified to write against it. Hitherto he

14   Vol. 2. p. 240. 242.

seems to have been acquainted with nothing but the corrupt establishments of what is very improperly called christianity; whereas it is incumbent upon him to read and study the New Testament for himself. There he will find nothing like Platonism, but doctrines in every respect the reverse of that system of philosophy, which weak and undistinguishing christians afterwards incorporated with it.

Had Mr. Gibbon lived in France, Spain, or Italy, he might, with the same reason, have ranked the doctrine of transubstantiation, and the worship of saints and angels among the essentials of christianity, as the doctrines of the trinity and of atonement.

The friends of genuine, and I will add of rational christianity, have not, however, on the whole, much reason to regret that their enemies have not made these distinctions; since, by this means, we have been taught to make them ourselves; so that christianity is perhaps as much indebted to its enemies, as to its friends, for this important service. In their indiscriminate attacks, whatever has been found to be untenable has been gradually abandoned, and I hope the attack will be continued till nothing of the wretched outworks be left; and then, I doubt not, a safe and impregnable fortress will be found in the center, a fortress built upon a rock, against which *the gates of death will not prevail.*

When the present crisis is over (and I think we may see that the period is not far distant) that by means of the objections of unbelievers, and the attention which, in consequence of it, will be given to the subject by believers, christianity shall be restored to its primitive purity, the cool and truly sensible part of mankind will, in this very circumstance, perceive an argument for its truth; and thus even the corruptions of christianity will have answered a very valuable purpose; as having been the means of supplying such an evidence of its truth, as could not have been derived from any other circumstance. Let any other religion be named that ever was so much corrupted, and that recovered itself from such corruption, and continued to be professed with unquestionable zeal by men of reflection and understanding, and I shall look upon it with respect, and not reject it without a very particular examination. The revival of a zeal for the religion of Greece and Rome under Julian is not to be compared with the attachment to christianity by inquisitive and learned men in the present age. Let literature and science flourish but one century in Asia, and what would be the state of Mahometanism, the religion of the Hindoos, or that of the Tartars, subject to the Grand Lama? I should rejoice to hear of such a challenge as I give Mr. Gibbon, being sent from a mahometan Mufti to the christian world.

Should what I call pure christianity (the most essential articles of which I consider to be the proper *unity of God*, and the proper *humanity of Christ*) continue to spread as it now does, and as, from the operation of the same causes, I have no doubt but that, in spite of all opposition, it will do, and literature revive among the Jews and Mahometans (who, it is remarkable, were never learned and inquisitive, but in an age in which all the christianity they could see must have struck them with horror, as a system of abominable and gross idolatry, to which their own systems are totally repugnant). Should learning and inquiry, I say, once more revive among the Jews and Mahometans, at the same time that a great part of the christian world should be free from that idolatry which has given them such just offence, they would be much more favourably impressed with the idea of christianity than they were in former times.

It, also, can hardly be supposed, but that the general conversion of the Jews, after a state of such long and violent opposition (which will in all future time exclude the idea of their having acted in concert with the christians) will be followed by the conversion of all the thinking part of the world. And if, before or after this time, the Jews should return to their own country, the whole will be such a manifest fulfilment of the prophecies of scripture, as will leave no reasonable colour for infidelity.

In the prospect of this great and glorious event I rejoice; and I wish to contribute a little towards hastening its approach, both by unfolding the history of christianity, with all the corruptions of it, and submitting to the most rigid examination whatever I think to be really a part of it. To this, all the friends of genuine christianity will chearfully say, AMEN.

BAMPTON LECTURES
SERMON III
by Joseph White

In vain therefore has the insidious ingenuity of the infidel and sceptic been employed in the preposterous endeavour of accounting for the miraculous success of Christianity from causes merely human. The true philosopher, who will rest satisfied with no cause but what is fully adequate to the effects produced, readily acknowledges the assistance of God, in the witness he bare to the preaching of the Apostles, by many signs, and wonders, and mighty deeds.

The rational advocate for Christianity scorns to shelter himself in sceptical and disingenuous misrepresentation. He knows the force of secondary causes; he with well-founded exultation employs them as additional arguments for the soundness of his faith; he derives the strongest support from their admirable and striking consistence with the pretensions of a religion, which disclaimed the use of those engines by which imposture is usually maintained, the intrigues, I mean, of policy, and the violence of arms. But he, at the same time, contends, that while the interests of the gospel were promoted by those circumstances which must have been fatal to every false religion, they were chiefly and primarily promoted by other and more efficacious methods; by the power of God which enabled the founder of Christianity to perform what unaided man never performed; and by the wisdom of God, which assisted him in speaking as man never spake.

A living writer, the elegance of whose style seems to have conferred a very alarming popularity on the licentiousness of his opinions, has assigned the reception of Christianity to FIVE CAUSES: each of which he has represented, as in reality unconnected with any divine interposition.

---

[1] Gibbon's Hist. of the decline and fall of the Roman Empire, p. 536. Edit. 4to. 1777.

First, "¹the inflexible and intolerant zeal of the first Christians, derived from the Jews, but purified from the unsocial spirit, which had deterred the Gentiles from embracing the law of Moses."

Now, zeal which is at once intolerant, and purified from any unsocial spirit, is a quality, which we leave it to the singularity of this writer to conceive, and to his eloquence to describe.

But we deny the fact, that any kind or any degree of intolerance existed among the primitive Christians: and as to their zeal, we maintain that it did not bear the slightest similitude to the fierceness and bigotry of the Jews. It was derived from very different causes, and aimed at far nobler ends. It was not the narrow and temporal interests of one nation, but the general reformation, and the spiritual happiness of the whole world, which the teachers of Christianity were anxious to promote. That firmness, which may be misconstrued into intolerance, and that activity, which we are content to call by the name of zeal, had in the usual course of human affairs, a tendency to retard, rather than to facilitate the propagation of the gospel. The Christian, instead of falling into the fashionable and popular intercommunity of worship, disdained, amidst the terrors of impending death, to throw incense on the altar of Jupiter: he boldly pronounced the whole system of Pagan mythology imposture; and charged the whole ritual of its external devotions, with groveling superstition, and profane idolatry.

A second Cause he finds "in the doctrine of a future life." Such a doctrine, doubtless, is congenial to the nature of man as an accountable and moral agent; it is repeatedly insisted upon in the gospel; and must ultimately, and in a favourable state of things, have increased its efficacy. But the future life taught by the Apostles had few recommendations in the sight of the Heathen world. It was offensive to the Epicureans by the punishments it threatened: it was not attractive to the vulgar by the very rewards which it proposed. The pride of the philosopher was shocked by the doctrine of a resurrection, the mode of which he was unable to comprehend: the imaginations of other men were feebly impressed by the representation of a future state, which did not hold out the serene sky, the verdant garden, and the luxurious enjoyments of an Elysium.

A third Cause he finds in "the miraculous powers ascribed to the primitive church;" and then proceeds, in a style of the most contemptuous and bitter derision to insinuate that these powers were never possessed.

Now, the hardiest adversaries of the gospel, a Porphyry, a Celsus and a Julian, do not deny the existence of those miracles: and Christianity has little to fear from the improbable causes to which these writers impute them.

It is, however, worthy of remark, that when Christianity was published, a general prejudice in the people, and a very severe spirit of suspicion in the government, prevailed against the belief of Miracles. They were stigmatized by the opprobrious appellation of *Magic:* and Augustus, it is well known, had published very rigorous edicts against the whole race of Præstigiators.

The peculiar difficulties, which obstructed the reception of Christian miracles have been explained with great acuteness of reasoning, and great depth of erudition, by a modern writer, whose remarks defeat indeed the fallacies, but seem to have escaped the notice of our ingenious and indefatigable historian.

The sum of his arguments I will give in his own words.

"[2]The multitude of popular gods admitted amongst the Heathens did by necessary consequence occasion such a multitude of pretended miracles, that they insensibly *lost* their force, and *sunk* in their esteem. Though the philosophers in general, and men of reading and contemplation could not but discover the grossness and absurdity of the Civil Religion; yet this could have little effect on the *Vulgar*, or *themselves:* not on the *Vulgar*, because it was the business of the wisest and most politic heads zealously to support and encourage them in their practices; not on *themselves*, because if they despised their Gods, they must despise their Miracles too."

Now, under these circumstances, miracles *ascribed* to the first propagators of Christianity, must have created an immediate and stubborn prejudice against their cause: and nothing could have subdued that prejudice, but miracles really and visibly performed.

A fourth Cause is "the virtues of the first Christians:" which are themselves reduced to a mean and timid repentance for

---

[2] Weston on the rejection of Christian Miracles by the Heathen, p. 348.

former sins, and to an impetuous zeal in supporting the reputation of the sect newly embraced.

But surely in the eyes of the haughty and jealous Romans, such repentance and such zeal must have equally excited opposition to Christianity. The first would have provoked contempt among persons of their daring self-sufficiency; and the other would have awakened the jealousy of the magistrate. True it is, that the Christians had virtues of a nobler kind. It is also true, that those virtues did ultimately triumph over the scorn and malice of their foes: and it is true, that a religion producing such effects on its followers, and deriving success from such means, carries with it a presumptive proof, of which imposture never could boast.

The last secondary Cause mentioned by this writer, "is the union and discipline of the Christian church."

We acknowledge the force of union in securing the order, and enlarging the interests of every society; and we heartily wish, that such union could be found in the earlier ages of the gospel. But the distractions, and internal divisions of the Christians present a very different prospect. And if the gospel succeeded, not only amidst the furious assaults of its enemies, but the no less violent contentions of its friends, we must look for its success in some other cause, than those which our historian has assigned.

Observations similar to these have been most properly produced, and most ably enforced by various writers, who have repelled the base and disingenuous assaults of this most dangerous enemy. But in reviewing the circumstances which attended the propagation of the gospel, I could not, consistently with the spirit of this Institution, avoid taking some notice of his treacherous and insidious endeavours to undermine this important argument for the truth of our faith: nor could I neglect so favourable an opportunity as the present, of cautioning the younger part of my audience, against being unwarily seduced into an approbation of his sentiments, by the insinuating arts of his sophistry and the captivating graces of his language.

We are by no means insensible to the merits of our historian; but at the same time we know and lament his eagerness to throw a veil over the deformities of the Heathen theology, to decorate with all the splendor of panegyric the tolerant spirit of its votaries, to degrade by disingenuous insinuation, or by sarcastic satire, the importance of revelation, to exhibit in the most offensive features of distortion the weakness and the follies of its friends, and to varnish over the cruelties, and exalt the wisdom of its merciless and unrelenting enemies.

P. 395. l. 7. *Yet Christianity far surpasses every other religion in its visible tendency to make us better men, and in its real effects upon the sentiments and the manners of mankind*] Even from the testimony of Mr. GIBBON, if we attend to his facts, without assenting implicitly to his opinions, it appears, that Christianity had in some degree contributed to the moral improvement of that empire, which under the inauspicious influence of Paganism had been plunged in the foulest immoralities. Frailties, absurdities, and crimes are to be found in those who wielded the sceptre after the establishment of Christianity; but the catalogue is not so numerous, or so black and portentous, as that which presents itself, to the dispassionate enquirer, in the preceding ages. We are not shocked with the cold and deliberate inhumanity of a Tiberius, with the outrageous debaucheries, and frantic cruelties of a Nero, with the gross sensualities of a Vitellius, with the disgusting puerilities and odious barbarities of a Domitian.

But we may be told, that after the introduction of the Gospel, this stupendous empire fell into ruin. Be it so. But was not the superstructure itself much defaced, and were not the very foundations loosened, long before, under the dissolute manners of the people, the turbulent spirit of the Prætorian bands, the profligate servility of the Pagan senate, and the enormous oppressions of Pagan emperors?

Is extensive empire, we may ask the objectors, a blessing to the general interests of society? Did the Roman empire, founded as it was upon the violence of conquest, and supported by all the arts of corruption, and all the rigours of despotism, give rise to such a political or a moral condition of the world, that any mind enlightened by philosophy and softened by benevolence, could seriously wish for its continuance?

To arm the hands of conquerors, or to glut the ambition of kings, made no part of that Teacher's design, whose kingdom was not of this world. It is therefore no solid objection to his religion, that it did not promote those secular interests, with which both the founder, and the immediate supporters of its pretensions disclaimed even the slightest connection. But the

Gospel, be it remembered, even amidst the convulsions and distractions of the Roman empire, gradually infused juster notions of virtue and piety into the bosoms of individuals. It tamed the savage spirits, and enlightened the understandings, of the barbarians who reduced the scattered provinces to subjection, and at last pushed their arms to the enfeebled and unresisting Capital. And let it not be forgotten, that from the subversion of this empire arose all the improvements in arts, in science, in civilization, and in government, which are now established in Christian countries, and to which Christianity itself was indirectly instrumental. The Gospel, before the fall of this empire, first spread its influence in private life, and then it put a partial check on the crimes of those who acted on the great theatre of public life. If the fall of the Roman empire was, upon the whole, an evil, Christianity was not the sole, or the obvious cause of that evil. If it was eventually a good, we are indebted for a share of that good to the just notions of their duty, which the Gospel had implanted in the minds of its professors, and to the powerful motives by which it encouraged them in the prosecution of their true happiness.

ALSO IN THE SERIES

LIBERTY
Contemporary Responses to John Stuart Mill
Edited and Introduced by **Andrew Pyle**

ISBN 1 85506 244 5 : Hb : 466pp : **£45.00**
ISBN 1 85506 245 3 : Pb : 466pp : **£14.95**
Key Issues No. 1

POPULATION
Contemporary Responses to Thomas Malthus
Edited and Introduced by **Andrew Pyle**

ISBN 1 85506 344 1 : Hb : 320pp : **£40.00**
ISBN 1 85506 345 X : Pb : 320pp : **£13.95**
Key Issues No. 2

GROUP RIGHTS
Perspectives since 1900
Edited and Introduced by **Julia Stapleton**

ISBN 1 85506 403 0 : Hb : 320pp : **£45.00**
ISBN 1 85506 402 2 : Pb : 320pp : **£14.95**
Key Issues No. 3

AGNOSTICISM
Contemporary Responses to Spencer and Huxley
Edited and Introduced by **Andrew Pyle**

ISBN 1 85506 405 7 : Hb : 310pp : **£45.00**
ISBN 1 85506 404 9 : Pb : 310pp : **£14.95**
Key Issues No. 4

LEVIATHAN
Contemporary Responses to the Political Theory of Thomas Hobbes
Edited and Introduced by **G. A. J. Rogers**

ISBN 1 85506 407 3 : Hb : 318pp : **£45.00**
ISBN 1 85506 406 5 : Pb : 318pp : **£14.95**
Key Issues No. 5

THE SUBJECTION OF WOMEN
Contemporary Responses to John Stuart Mill
Edited and Introduced by **Andrew Pyle**

ISBN 1 85506 409 X : Hb : 338p : **£45.00**
ISBN 1 85506 408 1 : Pb : 338pp : **£14.95**
Key Issues No. 6

THE ORIGIN OF LANGUAGE
Edited and Introduced by **Roy Harris**

ISBN 1 85506 438 3 : Hb : 344pp : **£45.00**
ISBN 1 85506 437 5 : Pb : 344pp : **£14.75**
Key Issues No. 7

PURE EXPERIENCE
The Response to William James
Edited and Introduced by **Eugene Taylor** and **Robert H. Wozniak**

ISBN 1 85506 413 8 : Hb : 294pp : **£45.00**
ISBN 1 85506 412 X : Pb : 294pp : **£14.75**
Key Issues No. 8

GENDER AND SCIENCE
Late Nineteenth-Century Debates on the Female Mind and Body
Edited and Introduced by **Katharina Rowold**

ISBN 1 85506 411 1 : Hb : 344pp : **£45.00**
ISBN 1 85506 410 3 : Pb : 344pp : **£14.95**
Key Issues No. 9

FREE TRADE
The Repeal of the Corn Laws
Edited and Introduced by
Cheryl Schonhardt-Bailey

ISBN 1 85506 446 4 : Hb : 372p : **£45.00**
ISBN 1 85506 445 6 : Pb : 372pp : **£14.95**
Key Issues No. 10

HUME ON MIRACLES
Edited and Introduced by **Stanley Tweyman**

ISBN 1 85506 444 8 : Hb : 180pp : **£45.00**
ISBN 1 85506 443 X : Pb : 180pp : **£14.95**
Key Issues No. 11

HUME ON NATURAL RELIGION
Edited and Introduced by **Stanley Tweyman**

ISBN 1 85506 451 0 : Hb : 350pp : **£45.00**
ISBN 1 85506 450 2 : Pb : 350pp : **£14.95**
Key Issues No. 12

Key Issues
ALSO IN THE SERIES

HERBERT SPENCER AND THE LIMITS OF THE STATE
The Late Nineteenth-Century Debate between Individualism and Collectivism
Edited and Introduced by **Michael Taylor**

ISBN 1 85506 453 7 : Hb : 280pp : **£45.00**
ISBN 1 85506 452 9 : Pb : 280pp : **£14.95**
Key Issues No. 13

RELIGIOUS SCEPTICISM
Contemporary Responses to Gibbon
Edited and Introduced by **David Womersley**

ISBN 1 85506 509 6 : Hb : 282pp : **£45.00**
ISBN 1 85506 510 X : Pb : 282pp : **£14.75**
Key Issues No. 15

RACE
The Origins of an Idea, 1760–1850
Edited and Introduced by **Hannah Augstein**

ISBN 1 85506 455 3 : Hb : 298pp : **£40.00**
ISBN 1 85506 454 5 : Pb : 298pp : **£13.95**
Key Issues No. 14